Writing
Voyage

Writing Voyage

A Process Approach to Basic Writing

EIGHTH EDITION

Thomas E. Tyner
Reedley College

THOMSON

WADSWORTH

Australia • Brazil • Canada • Mexico • Singapore • Spain • United Kingdom • United States

Writing Voyage: A Process Approach to Basic Writing
Eighth Edition
Thomas E. Tyner

Publisher: *Lyn Uhl*
Acquisitions Editor: *Annie Todd*
Editorial Assistant: *Daniel DeBonis*
Marketing Manager: *Kate Edwards*
Marketing Associate: *Kathleen Remsberg*
Advertising Project Manager: *Darlene Amidon-Brent*
Content Project Manager: *Karen Stocz*
Senior Art Director: *Cate Rickard Barr*

Print Buyer: *Betsy Donaghey*
Cover Designer: *Susan Shapiro*
Photo Manager: *Sheri Blaney*
Production Service: *Hearthside Publishing Services*
Compositor: *International Typesetting and Composition*
Printer: *Edwards Brothers*
Cover Photo: © *Royalty-Free/Corbis*

Library of Congress Control Number: 2006940138

10-Digit ISBN 1-4130-2949-3
13-Digit ISBN 978-1-4130-2949-9

Thomson Higher Education
25 Thomson Place
Boston, MA 02210-1202
USA

For more information about our products,
contact us at:
Thomson Learning Academic Resource Center
1-800-423-0563
For permission to use material from this text or product, submit a request online at
http://www.thomsonrights.com
Any additional questions about permissions can be submitted by email to
thomsonrights@thomson.com

Contents

Unit 6   Writing About Issues 185

Preface

The purpose of this text is to provide an integrated writing experience for students. Textbooks often isolate basic elements of writing from the developmental process. Students are left with a fragmented approach to writing, in which it is difficult to make connections between textbook instruction and their writing.

Writing Voyage: A Process Approach to Basic Writing, Eighth Edition, incorporates these writing elements within the process so that students write papers and work concurrently on specific writing skills to apply at different stages of the drafting process. Students learn which elements of writing are most important at each stage of the process, and they develop a variety of skills to help them communicate their ideas most effectively.

NEW TO THIS EDITION

This eighth edition of *Writing Voyage* contains a number of new features:

- All new professional readings
- New student writing samples throughout the text
- New online activities in each unit
- New writing-related activities in each unit
- New section on writing critiques in unit on "Writing About Opinions"
- New sentence-combining activities in the Appendix.

The following features continue to make *Writing Voyage* a highly effective writing text.

FOCUS ON PROCESS

In each unit, students are taken through the process of prewriting, drafting, revising, and proofreading their papers. The text emphasizes that writing is a process that develops in general stages that most writers go through. As students progress through the book, they tailor the process to their needs and preferences. By the book's end they are well-versed in the basic elements of effective writing and in command of a process that works for them.

CONTENT ORIENTATION

Throughout the text, the primary emphasis is on writing content: what the writer wants to communicate to his or her readers. All other elements of effective writing—organization of ideas, paragraphing, wording, correctness—are addressed as a *means* to communicate a writer's ideas most effectively. Substance is always emphasized before structure, and structure is evaluated by how it contributes to the reader's appreciation of the substance.

ROTATING FORMAT

Writing texts frequently introduce a subject in one unit and then virtually abandon it. From my teaching experience, students who have been taught parallel construction in the first unit may have forgotten what they learned by the third or fourth unit unless the topic has been regularly reinforced. Therefore, this text is designed so the basic elements of writing—prewriting, audience/purpose consideration, paragraphing, sentence structure, organization—are covered in every unit. Many students in basic writing courses have problems that cannot be solved with the traditional block-coverage textbook approach. *Writing Voyage* provides reinforcement of basic writing skills throughout the book.

EMPHASIS ON WRITING

On the assumption that students cannot learn to write well without writing often, the text provides constant writing opportunities: free writing, drafting essays, paragraph writing, sentence combining exercises, and a variety of sentence writing activities. In addition to the major assignments that students take through the writing process in each unit, there are numerous shorter writing assignments, each emphasizing a particular aspect of the process.

STUDENT WRITING SAMPLES

Throughout the text, students will find student writing samples that relate to the kinds of writing they are doing. The writing samples are interesting to read, provide realistic models for students, and supply material to be analyzed from a number of angles: thesis development, purpose, audience consideration, organization, paragraphing, style, originality, and overall effectiveness. Each unit also contains first-draft writing samples through which students can sharpen their revising skills. Throughout the text, students will analyze and learn from the essays of other student writers.

PEER EDITING

Often students share their writing with no one but their instructor. This text is designed for students to share their writing with classmates at each step in the process. They use their classmates as an audience, and they develop their critiquing and revising skills by helping other writers. Students learn to view writing as a shared communication, and they see the effects that their ideas have on readers.

SELECTED READINGS

A selection of essays by professional writers, including a number of new readings, appears in each unit. The readings and questions for discussion reflect the writing emphasis for that unit. These essays serve as models for structural and content analysis, provide a link between the related skills of writing and reading, and offer additional reading experiences that will benefit students.

FINAL EDITING

Grammar, punctuation, and spelling receive thorough treatment in each unit of the text, as well as in the Appendix, where students can work on particular problems they may have. All of the major problem areas—run-ons and fragments, comma usage, subject-verb agreement, pronoun-antecedent agreement, irregular verbs—are covered in detail. Each section, as well as the Appendix, contains a number of exercises for students to work through. Ideally, students will refer to the editing sections as they proofread and edit their papers throughout the text. Grammar and punctuation study should be linked to the editing process students go through with each writing assignment.

WRITER'S JOURNAL

A new feature in the sixth edition was the "Writer's Journal." Students will keep a journal of their writing experiences throughout the semester by making regular entries reflecting on different aspects of their writing process. The journals will have students writing regularly, thinking about how they write, and providing their instructor with insights into individual writing processes.

ONLINE ACTIVITIES

The online activities send students to the website writing labs of different universities. Once there, they find help and suggestions on specific aspects of writing, such as prewriting tips, eliminating wordiness in first draft sentences, using descriptive language, writing introductions and conclusions for a paper, and providing appropriate evidence to support ideas. The online activities accompany and supplement the text's coverage of a specific writing topic, and give students a glimpse into the growing online assistance available to writers.

ACKNOWLEDGMENTS

Thank you to the reviewers whose valuable insight guided this eighth edition: Jon Brammer, *Three Rivers Community College*, and Donald Moore, *University of Southern Indiana*.

Readings

Writing from Experience

Writing is a voyage of discovery. As a writer, you discover more about yourself, others, the world you live in, and how you think and feel about different things. You learn what it is like to be a writer and how your writing experiences are both personal and unique but also similar to those of other writers. While the thoughts you express on paper may be distinctly yours, the process by which you develop ideas and craft your wording may be similar to that of others.

Already a writer of some experience, you bring to this course considerable skills and knowledge from previous writing experience. The purpose of this text is to build on those skills and knowledge and to help you progress as a developing writer. Most writers continue to develop their skills as long as they write, and as you write for this course, read and analyze your own writing and that of your classmates, and work through the text, your writing skills will undoubtedly continue to develop and improve.

Some of the most valuable writing experiences are those that lead to self-discovery, helping you to understand better the different influences that have helped to shape your thoughts and feelings, and that have contributed to the person you are. These insights may come from reflecting on events in your life, relationships with different people, choices that you've made, or changes in your life circumstances.

Your writing for this unit focuses on personal experiences that remain vivid in your mind. You will recall these experiences for yourself, as well as for your classmates and instructor, and analyze them to understand better the impact they had or may continue to have on your life.

Sharing life experiences through your writing is interesting and valuable for both the writer and readers. You learn to re-create experiences to make them real and vivid for your readers, and by reflecting on such experiences, you pass on to readers what you have learned, and connect with your readers through common experiences.

WRITING PROCESS

From your previous writing experiences, you have probably learned that writing is a process rather than a one-step task. For many years, writing researchers have studied how people write to discover characteristics shared by effective writers. What they discovered was that most writers do similar things as they write, and that they go through different steps in their writing process, commonly identified as prewriting, drafting, rewriting (or revising), and editing.

During these steps, however, different writers do different things, and the steps often tend to overlap and intermix rather than being separate and distinct. The writing process, then, is not a step-by-step formula for producing good writing, but rather a general framework for thinking and writing that you may find useful.

In defining the writing process, the following characteristics, discovered by researchers and reconfirmed by writers like yourself, are generally included:

1. Writing is not easy for anyone. All writers, novice and experienced, struggle at times with what to write about, what they want to say, and how best to put their thoughts into words. All writers experience "writer's block" at times, where they struggle with how to begin or how to continue their writing.

2. Most writers don't just sit down and begin writing. They spend time deciding what to write about and what they want to say. They may start with a rough outline, jot down a list of ideas, talk to other people, or plan in their minds. Whatever writers do to help themselves get started is called *prewriting*, and most writers do some form of it.

3. Writing is a *recursive* process, meaning that writers regularly go back over what they have written, rereading a previous paragraph, sentence, or part of the sentence they are working on. They do this to help decide what to write next, to keep a stream of thought going, to reword sentences or passages that don't sound right, and to build momentum to continue their writing.

4. Writing is a process of discovery. Writers seldom know everything they are going to write before they begin. The writing act itself helps writers to discover things they want to say, and to find new ideas and connections they hadn't thought of. The process of writing helps writers discover meaning that they may have never consciously considered. This occurs because the act of writing encourages writers to focus on and think more deeply about their writing subject.

5. Rewriting is an important part of writing. Seldom can any writer word his or her thoughts most effectively the first time. Initially, it is a challenge to get a thought on paper in a comprehensible manner. Often thoughts are just partially developed in the writer's mind before he or she tries them out on paper. Getting an idea on paper gives writers something to work with. Once that occurs, they may revise a sentence several times before they are satisfied with what it says and how it sounds.

6. Writers generally write drafts of their work, which culminate in a final paper. For most writers, writing is too complex a task to accomplish successfully in one sitting. Writers will often write a first draft of a paper to get their thoughts down, then in subsequent drafts, reword, reorganize, and further develop those thoughts until they have a final draft that is ready to share with readers.

   The use of computers for writing has changed the drafting process for many writers. Since it is easier to revise on a computer than on a handwritten draft, writers may do substantial revision as they write rather than waiting until they have completed a draft. While this may result in fewer drafts, it doesn't result in less revision. In fact, some studies have shown that writers revise even more on computers because of the ease of deleting and replacing words or phrases, or moving sentences or paragraphs around.

7. Before completing their final drafts, writers usually *proofread* their papers to find and correct any errors in spelling, punctuation, or grammar. While writers sometimes correct errors as they discover them during drafting, error correction is generally the last phase of the writing process after all other changes have been made.

PREWRITING

In the "Prewriting" section of each unit, you lay the groundwork for writing the first draft of your paper. Thinking about what you want to write, generating some ideas for a paper, talking to others, and doing some organizational planning are common prewriting steps for many writers.

However, writers seldom have an entire paper "laid out" in their minds before they begin. Some of the best ideas and insights that you have on a topic may reveal themselves as you write. Writing is a process of discovery and creation where one sentence or word may trigger a new idea, example, or perspective. Papers that are too "scripted" in advance may lack the creative spark that often produces the most insightful and interesting writing. Any prewriting plan should be flexible enough to allow for the process of discovery and creation that is an essential part of good writing.

TOPIC SELECTION

For your writing assignment in this unit, you will choose a memorable experience from your childhood or early teens to write about. Take some time to think about different experiences that you can recall. The following questions may help you remember particular experiences.

What is one of the most frightening experiences that comes to mind from your childhood?

What is one of the happiest times in your life that you can remember, when life seemed particularly good?

What is something that occurred in your school life that made you feel particularly proud?

What is something that occurred in your school life that made you feel terrible?

What particular event do you recall from your youth when you made an adult very mad?

What is one of the biggest changes in your life situation that you had to deal with when you were young (moving, divorce, loss of a friend or relative, etc.)?

What was one of the most painful (physical or emotional) experiences from your childhood?

In selecting a topic for your paper, consider the following:

1. What particular experience stands out most strongly in your mind?

2. What particular experience do you have the most vivid memory of or feelings about?

3. What particular experience do you want to explore and analyze its impact on you?

4. What particular experience would you like to share with readers, and why?

STUDENT SAMPLE IDEAS   There's the incident in first grade when the dad of a girl I liked died and I got in trouble for making noise at her house a few days later. The memory is pretty fuzzy though. Then there was my first "fight" when I was in second grade. It really wasn't much of a fight, just a little wrestling match, but I remember I didn't enjoy it. Not sure I'd have much to write about. I don't even remember how it started.

Then there was the problem I had with a long-time friend in eighth grade, but I'd rather go back further in my childhood. There was the time in kindergarten when I buried a neighbor kid's gun in a field and we never found it again. I remember that pretty well, including how mad the kid got and how scared I was. There were other neighbor kids around to see what was going on, and I remember my mom getting involved. Then I moved to another town and, of all things, this kid moves in right behind me. I may write about the gun experience because I remember it well, I remember the kid well, and I remember how I felt about my mom helping me. The experience bothered me for some time, and I still remember it.

TOPIC SELECTION ACTIVITY 1.1

Based on the suggestions presented for topic selection, come up with two or three experiences from childhood that you may want to write about. Think of things that happened to you at home, at school, with friends, with relatives, and at different times and places in your childhood.

SMALL GROUP ACTIVITIES

Throughout the course you will be doing various activities in small groups with your classmates. The small group activities will accomplish a number of things: help you get to know your classmates better, help you discover possible topics for writing, allow you to read and react to other students' writing, allow other students to read and react to your writing, and improve your writing as you learn to analyze more closely your own writing and that of your classmates.

Working in small groups may be new to you, and initially it may feel uncomfortable talking and working with people you may not know well. You may also feel reluctant to express your thoughts or share your writing, fearing how others might react. Such concerns are certainly natural, and the more you work in small groups, the easier it will become.

Other students have the same concerns as you, and by working together, you will help one another overcome them and enjoy the process.

GROUP ACTIVITY 1.2

In small groups, share experiences that you recall from childhood. Give everyone an opportunity to talk about an experience or two, but no one should feel forced to talk. Feel free to ask questions about classmates' experiences. The purpose of this activity is to try out some of your topic ideas on your classmates, to find out what may interest them about your topics, and to get other ideas from listening to their experiences.

When you finish, reconsider the experiences that you have been thinking about, and decide on one specific experience to write about.

PREWRITING REFLECTION

To continue your prewriting work, once you have chosen a topic for your paper, you can reflect on the experience by thinking about the following questions:

1. What actually happened? Try to visualize the experience as accurately as you can remember it: where it took place, who was involved, what occurred, what was said. Run the experience visually through your mind.

2. What did you think and how did you feel? Try to recall your thoughts and feelings at the time of the experience. What different things went through your mind as the experience unfolded? How did you feel at different times?

3. What were the results of the experience? How did it turn out for you and for others involved? How did it affect your life?

4. Why is the experience so memorable or important? What significance might it have? Did you learn anything about yourself, other people, or life in general? Did you gain or lose anything from the experience? What might you be able to pass on to readers based on this experience?

STUDENT SAMPLE RESPONSE   I remember I was just in kindergarten. There was the big dirt lot with the eucalyptus trees and the old rabbit hutches near the front. It was hot—summer vacation time—and the gang had gathered at the lot. Then I remember Brian coming with this big beautiful gun and everything that happened afterward—my burying it, trying to find it later, going home to Mom, Brian coming over, Mom digging in the lot. I can see everything.

I felt envious when I saw that gun, and I didn't like Brian much anyway. Then I felt scared when I couldn't find the gun, and when Brian yelled at me in front of the others. Then I felt ashamed when I was home with Mom, and when she was digging in the lot trying to find the gun. Then I was relieved when Mom bought Brian another gun. Then when we moved and Brian moved to the house behind us, I was shocked and unhappy, like it was meant for me to suffer for what I did.

Everything turned out all right in the end for everyone, except that the experience stayed with me and made me feel ashamed and cowardly. I wasn't so sure of myself after that, and I knew what it was like to have an enemy. I think I learned I don't like people mad at me or making me look bad, and that has stayed with me my whole life. I also think maybe I was more of a momma's boy than I thought.

REFLECTION ACTIVITY 1.3

Write your reflections on the experience you have selected by briefly answering the questions just presented. The purpose of the activity is to help you recall the experience more clearly, to think about it more deeply, and to generate some ideas for your first draft.

AUDIENCE AND PURPOSE

Two important things to consider when writing are your audience—the people you are writing for, and your purpose—why you are writing to them. Your audience and your writing purpose will help to determine what you write about a particular topic and how you choose to write it.

For example, let's say you are a writer on the student newspaper, and the college administration has decided to discontinue the newspaper the next school year for budgeting reasons. Assuming you want the newspaper to continue, you may be moved to write two letters on the topic: one to the school administration, and the other to the students of the college. Your purpose for the letter to the administration may be to persuade them to keep the newspaper going. Your purpose for the letter to students may be to get them upset over the possible loss of their newspaper and to move them to action. Because of the two very different audiences and your purpose for each audience, your letters would be very different although your topic would be the same.

When you are thinking about your audience and your purpose for writing on a particular topic, consider the following:

1. What does my reading audience know about the topic? Are they knowledgeable about it, or will I have to explain some things to them? (For example, if you were writing about an experience in a ballet class where you were doing different steps, you might have to explain to readers exactly what a pirouette is.)

2. What is my audience's attitude toward the topic? Do they care about it one way or another, are they basically neutral, or do they know enough about it to have an opinion?

3. How should the characteristics of my audience—age, gender, education level—affect the way I write to them? (For example, you may not write the same way to young children on the dangers of smoking as you would to high school students.)

4. Why am I writing to this particular audience about this topic? What is my purpose in writing to them? (For example, your purpose in writing to a young audience about the dangers of smoking may be to keep them from ever starting, while your purpose in writing to high school students may be to get them to stop.)

5. How do I want my audience to respond? How do I want them to feel or think, or what do I want them to do after reading my paper? (For example, you may want to leave your young readers frightened about what cigarette smoking can do to their bodies.)

PREWRITING ACTIVITY 1.4

Your audience for your personal experience paper is your classmates. Apply the five points on audience and purpose to your classmates, and think about how those considerations may affect what you write about your topic.

For example, are you writing about an experience that many of your classmates may have also gone through, or are you writing about a unique experience? Second, think about your purpose for writing to your classmates about this particular experience. Do you mainly want them to enjoy reading about the experience, to learn something from it that you learned, to understand you better based on the experience, or to feel the fear, joy, pain, excitement, or embarrassment that you may have felt?

STUDENT SAMPLE IDEAS What I'm writing about is a pretty common experience, so I think my classmates will understand it without any problem. Some of them may have had similar experiences, or felt similar things when they were young—especially the guys in class, who may relate more than the girls. I want my classmates to enjoy reading about the experience. The part where the kid moves into my new neighborhood was a huge coincidence, and might be interesting to read. They'll also learn something about me, because I'm going to be pretty honest about being scared and relying on my mom. Maybe some classmates will understand that.

GROUP ACTIVITY 1.5

Throughout this text are essays written by professional writers, such as the upcoming "Foul Shots" by Rogelio R. Gomez. While you may notice that the professionally written essays seem more polished, you will also notice similarities between the writings of professionals, the student writings in the text, your own writings, and those of your classmates.

Read the following essay, "Foul Shots." In small groups, discuss the following audience and purpose considerations:

1. Although we don't know for sure, what particular audience may "Foul Shots" have been written for, and why?

2. What do you think Gomez's purpose may have been for writing "Foul Shots"? What did he learn from the experience, and what is he passing on to his readers?

Foul Shots
Rogelio R. Gomez

Now and then I can still see their faces, snickering and laughing, their eyes mocking me. And it bothers me that I should remember. Time and maturity should have diminished the pain, because the incident happened more than 20 years ago. Occasionally, however, a smug smile triggers the memory, and I think, "I should have done something." Some act of defiance could have killed and buried the memory of the incident. Now it's too late.

In 1969, I was a senior on the Luther Burbank High School basketball team. The school is on the south side of San Antonio, in one of the city's many barrios. After practice one day our coach announced that we were going to spend the following Saturday scrimmaging with the ball club from Winston Churchill High, located in the city's rich, white north side. After the basketball game, we were to select someone from the opposing team and "buddy up"—talk with him, have lunch with him and generally spend the day attempting friendship. By telling us that this experience would do both teams some good, I suspect our well-intentioned coach was thinking about the possible benefits of integration and of learning to appreciate the differences of other people. By integrating us with this more prosperous group, I think he was also trying to inspire us.

But my teammates and I smiled sardonically at one another, and our sneakers squeaked as we nervously rubbed them against the waxed hardwood floor of our gym. The prospect of a full day of unfavorable comparisons drew from us a collective groan. As "barrio boys," we were already acutely aware of the differences between us and them. Churchill meant "white" to us: It meant shiny new cars, two-story homes with fireplaces, pedigreed dogs, and manicured hedges. In other words, everything we did not have. Worse, traveling north meant putting up a front, to ourselves as well as to the Churchill team. We felt we had to pretend that we were cavalier about it all, tough guys who didn't care about "nothin'."

It's clear now that we entered the contest with negative images of ourselves. From childhood, we must have suspected something was inherently wrong with us. The evidence wrapped itself around our collective psyche like a noose. In elementary school, we were not allowed to speak Spanish. The bladed edge of a wooden ruler once came crashing down on my knuckles for violating this dictum. By high school, however, policies had changed, and we could speak Spanish without fear of physical reprisal. Still, speaking our language before whites brought on spasms of shame—for the supposed inferiority of our language and culture—and guilt at feeling shame. That mixture of emotions fueled our burning sense of inferiority.

After all, our mothers in no way resembled the glamorized models of American TV mothers—Donna Reed baking cookies in high heels. My mother's hands were rough and chafed, her wardrobe drab and worn. And my father was preoccupied with making ends meet. His silence starkly contrasted with the glib counsel Jim Anderson offered in "Father Knows Best." And where the Beaver worried about trying to understand some difficult homework assignment, for me it was an altogether different horror, when I was told by my elementary school principal that I did not have the ability to learn.

After I failed to pass the first grade, my report card read that I had a "learning disability." What shame and disillusion it brought my parents! To have carried their dream of a better life from Mexico to America, only to have their hopes quashed by having their only son branded inadequate. And so somewhere during my schooling I assumed that saying I had a "learning disability" was just another way of saying that I was "retarded." School administrators didn't care that I could not speak English.

As teenagers, of course, my Mexican-American friends and I did not consciously understand why we felt inferior. But we might have understood if we had fathomed our desperate need to trounce Churchill. We viewed the prospect of beating a white, north-side squad as a particularly fine coup. The match was clearly racial, our need to succeed born of a defiance against prejudice. I see now that we used the basketball court to prove our "blood." And who better to confirm us, if not those whom we considered better? In retrospect, I realize the only thing confirmed that day was that we saw ourselves as negatively as they did.

After we won the morning scrimmage, both teams were led from the gym into an empty room where everyone sat on a shiny linoleum floor. We were supposed to mingle—rub the colors together. But the teams sat separately, our backs against concrete walls. We faced one another like enemies, the empty floor between us a no-man's-land. As the coaches walked away, one reminded us to share lunch. God! The mere thought of offering them a taco from our brown bags when they had refrigerated deli lunches horrified us.

Then one of their players tossed a bag of Fritos at us. It slid across the slippery floor and stopped in the center of the room. With hearts beating anxiously, we Chicanos stared at the bag as the boy said with a sneer, "Y'all probably like 'em"—the "Frito Bandito" commercial being popular then. And we could see them, smiling at each other, giggling, jabbing their elbows into one another's ribs at the joke. The bag seemed to grow before our eyes like a monstrous symbol of inferiority.

We won the afternoon basketball game as well. But winning had accomplished nothing. Though we had wanted to, we couldn't change their perception of us. It seems, in fact, that defeating them made them meaner. Looking back, I feel these young men needed to put us "in our place," to reaffirm the power they felt we had threatened. I think, moreover, that they felt justified, not only because of their inherent sense of superiority, but because our failure to respond to their insult underscored our worthlessness in their eyes.

Two decades later, the memory of their gloating lives on in me. When a white person is discourteous, I find myself wondering what I should do, and afterward, if I've done the right thing. Sometimes I argue when a deft comment would suffice. Then I reprimand myself, for I am no longer a boy. But my impulse to argue bears witness to my ghosts. For, invariably, whenever I feel insulted I'm reminded of that day at Churchill High. And whenever the past encroaches upon the present, I see myself rising boldly, stepping proudly across the years and crushing, underfoot, a silly bag of Fritos.

WRITER'S JOURNAL

During the course, you will keep a Writer's Journal in which you will respond to different activities that you do in the text. The purposes of the journal writing are to give you writing practice, to get you thinking more about how you write and what you write, to provide your instructor with some understanding of your writing process, to give your instructor feedback on the benefits of different writing activities, and to improve your writing.

JOURNAL ENTRY ONE

Under Journal Entry One in your notebook, relate how useful the prewriting activities have been in preparing you to write the first draft of your personal experience paper. What, if any, activities have been particularly useful? How have the activities prepared you to write your first draft?

STUDENT SAMPLE JOURNAL ENTRY The group discussion of personal experiences gave me some idea of what interested other students about my experience. Recalling my thoughts and feelings helped me rethink the incident in detail and made me aware to include how I felt as I write about the experience. The emphasis on audience will help me keep my classmates in mind as I write. I've been ready to start writing for awhile, so I'm getting tired of the activities.

FIRST DRAFTS

Now that you have selected a topic, reflected on your experience, and considered your audience and purpose for the paper, you are ready to write the first draft. When you write the draft, you are relating a true story. Keep in mind the following *narrative*—or story telling—elements as you write.

NARRATIVE ELEMENTS

1. *Setting:* When and where does the experience take place? What can you include to help your readers visualize the setting?

2. *People:* What people were involved in the experience? What do readers need to know about these people to understand their involvement? What do they need to know about you?

3. *Story:* When is the best place to begin the story so that readers can best understand what happened? What are the most important parts of the story to include?

4. *Resolution:* How did this particular situation turn out for you? For others? What, if anything, did you learn, or what do you understand better? What thoughts do you want to leave your readers with?

Before writing your first draft, read the following student draft and notice how the writer handles the narrative elements.

The Lost Gun

On Saturdays, the neighborhood gang of five- and six-year-olds gathered at the vacant lot to play cowboys. The open space was great for range wars, and the eucalyptus trees were used for hideouts. There were even some old rabbit hutches for locking up prisoners. As we gathered with our assortment of guns and holsters, Brian swaggered in with the biggest, shiniest gun I'd ever seen. It had a ten-inch barrel and an ivory handle. It made my gun look like a peashooter. It wasn't fair that the youngest, brattiest kid in the gang had the best gun.

Before we started, I asked Brian, a fat-faced kid with a smirk on his face, to let me see the gun. He reluctantly handed it over, and I told him I wanted to borrow it for a while. Since I was the big leader of the gang, he couldn't refuse. As soon as we broke up for cowboys and Brian was out of view behind the trees, I ran to a far corner of the lot and buried the gun in the soft dirt. I wanted to give Brian a scare.

Before long, the bad guys were rounded up, and Brian was demanding his gun back. I let him squirm awhile, then laughed and said I'd hidden it. He didn't laugh and demanded I find it. We all trudged across the lot to the corner, and I dug where I thought I'd buried it. No gun. I dug some more, and then I dug deeper and faster. Still no gun. Brian started yelling, "Find my gun!" and I started getting sick. I knew it was there somewhere, but the whole corner was looking the same to me. Everyone stood around and watched as I desperately dug at the ground. No one helped. Brian finally screamed, "My dad's gonna get you, you bastard!" My eyes started burning, and I knew I was going to cry. I took off running across the lot with Brian yelling, "You bastard! My dad will get you!"

That afternoon, I lay down with my mom for a nap, but I couldn't sleep. I felt terrible about what I had done, and I was frightened about what would happen to me. I hadn't told Mom a thing, but when I heard Brian calling outside the window, I told her everything. She calmly listened to me, then went out to the garage and got the shovel. We met Brian outside and the three of us returned to the lot.

By now it was very hot outside, and my mom dug in the heat for an hour. She turned up most of the dirt in that corner, but the gun was never found. I stood and watched helplessly, and I felt worse and worse as she worked and sweated because of me.

My parents bought Brian a new gun, so he was satisfied. But I wasn't the big shot of the gang any more. Little Brian had pushed me around that day, and the gang didn't forget. I was just one of the boys. I wasn't really that brave, and I still needed Mom to bail me out of trouble. Now I realize how lucky I was to have someone who stood up for me and loved me. I guess I realize I was more of a momma's boy than I like to admit.

We moved to another town forty miles away the next year, and of all coincidences, a year later Brian moved into the house behind the alley. His moving there was a constant reminder of what had happened. That one incident with the gun kept us from ever becoming friends although we were neighbors for five years. I could never get it out of my mind that he was still the little punk who had embarrassed me in front of my buddies. And I've carried that trait since then: having trouble letting go of grudges or forgiving people. I know I've worried a lot more about Brian than he ever did about me, and that's my problem. I need to learn to let go and move on.

GROUP ACTIVITY 1.6

In small groups, analyze "The Lost Gun" by applying the four narrative elements to the story. What are the details of setting? What do we learn about other people involved in the experience? Where does the writer express his thoughts and feelings? What features stand out in the way the writer tells his story? How is the experience resolved in the end? What did the writer learn?

DRAFTING ACTIVITY 1.7

Write the first draft of your paper, keeping in mind the elements of narration, your reading audience—your classmates—and your purpose for writing. As a general guideline, change paragraphs as you move to something new in your experience: a different time, place, or situation. (Paragraphing will be covered in some detail during the "revision" stage of the writing process.)

REVISIONS

Now that you have written the first draft of a paper, you have taken a major step toward your final draft, but there is usually more work to be done. As you reread your paper, you will probably find things that you want to change to make it more interesting, more complete, or clearer. It often helps to set the draft aside for awhile—a few hours or a day—so you can read it more objectively.

First drafts of personal experiences often require similar revisions. The following suggestions will help you evaluate your draft and make effective revisions.

REVISION GUIDELINES

1. *Read your draft to make sure that readers can visualize where the experience took place and when it occurred.* (See the upcoming section on "Descriptive Language.")

2. *Evaluate your draft to see if you have told the experience in a way that emphasizes the most important parts.* (Sometimes writers spend too much time leading up to the experience and too little time showing readers what happened.) Also make sure that readers know what you were *thinking* or *feeling* at critical times.

3. *Evaluate your conclusion to make sure your readers understand why this experience was significant enough for you to write about, and what your purpose was for writing about it.*

4. *Reread each sentence to make sure it clearly says what you want.*

5. *Review your paragraphing to see if you have changed paragraphs as you move to different parts of the experience.* (See the upcoming section on "Paragraphing.")

REVISION ACTIVITY 1.8

In small groups, evaluate the following draft by applying the suggestions for revision. Make note of what the writer does well, and provide suggestions for possible revisions to improve the draft. Your instructor may also have you share or exchange your draft with a classmate or two to get some ideas for revision.

The Accident

When I was a child at home with my brother and sister, I decided to wash the clothes in the washer, but it was not a normal washer like the ones we have now. It was an old washer, one that has the two rollers, you know the one that you put the clothes in the middle of the rollers to squeeze out the water before hanging up the clothes. When I put in the clothes, my arm got caught in between the rollers.

I started crying and screaming at the same time, and my sister came out of the house and she couldn't get my arm out. She ran to get Mr. Tatai, who was the owner of the apartments in which we were living. He got my arm out after it had been in there about thirty minutes. My arm was cut wide open and there was a lot of blood. It was hurting badly.

The ambulance arrived to take me to the hospital in Orosi. My mother was not there. She was in Texas at my grandpa's funeral, so they called my dad at work, so he went to the hospital with my grandmother.

At that time I was in the surgery room. The nurse called my dad to go in with me, but the nurse did not know that my dad gets very nervous when it comes to blood. So they started cleaning and disinfecting the area. Then the doctor performed the surgery.

After two long hours, the surgery was done. I was in so much pain that I told the nurse to give me some pain medication. So after two days, I got to go home with my family, and everyone came to visit and also brought flowers and balloons, and some sympathy cards. So I gave thanks to everyone for being there with me when I most needed it.

That was the most painful experience in my life, and my mother not being there for me made it worse. The only good thing was we got rid of the old washing machine with the rollers. But to this day, I have a long scar on my arm that reminds me of what happened. It was a horrible experience.

REVISION ACTIVITY 1.9

Write the next draft of your paper, including any improvements you want to make based on the revision guidelines.

JOURNAL ENTRY TWO

In your journal under Journal Entry Two, relate the kinds of changes you made from your first draft to your second draft. How do you feel the revisions improved the paper? How did the group evaluation activity help you in revising your draft?

STUDENT SAMPLE JOURNAL ENTRY

I reworded some sentences that didn't sound too good. I also included my feelings in a couple places where something important happened. I redid my paragraphing because I had changed paragraphs every two or three sentences in the first draft and it chopped up the paper.

PARAGRAPHING

Effective paragraphing is based on common sense. Most readers don't prefer reading extremely long paragraphs or strings of very short paragraphs. Neither helps them to get the most out of what they are reading.

Readers also can become confused by a paragraph that jumps randomly from idea to idea, or by papers that change paragraphs for no particular reason.

The following points will help you paragraph your papers so that readers can follow your ideas easily:

1. *Don't run paragraphs on too long.* When you reread an overly long paragraph—one that goes on for a half page or more—you will usually find a natural break where you can begin a second or third paragraph.

2. *Don't string several short paragraphs—two or three sentences each—together.* If you are writing in very short paragraphs, you can usually combine paragraphs containing related information, or sometimes you need to develop a paragraph further by adding more information.

3. *Make sure the sentences in a paragraph are related.* In most writing, each paragraph contains a different aspect of the paper's topic: a different point, example, time, event, or idea. When a paragraph tries to combine two or three different points, incidents, or changes in time, readers can become confused.

4. *As a general rule, change paragraphs as you move to something new or different in your paper: a different point, example, incident, time, or idea.*

PARAGRAPHING ACTIVITY 1.10

Read the following essay, "The Struggle to Be an All American Girl" by Elizabeth Wong, and analyze its paragraphing. When does the author change paragraphs? How do the paragraph changes help the reader?

In addition, discuss how the last sentence in the essay, "Sadly, I still am," surprisingly changes the writer's—and the readers'—viewpoint of her experiences. What did Wong learn that she is sharing with readers?

The Struggle to Be an All-American Girl
Elizabeth Wong

It's still there, the Chinese school on Yale Street where my brother and I used to go. Despite the new coat of paint and the high wire fence, the school I knew ten years ago remains remarkably, stoically the same.

Every day at 5 p.m., instead of playing with our fourth- and fifth-grade friends or sneaking out to the empty lot to hunt ghosts and animal bones, my brother and I had to go to Chinese school. No amount of kicking, screaming, or pleading could dissuade my mother, who was solidly determined to have us learn the language of our heritage.

Forcibly, she walked us the seven long, hilly blocks from our home to school, depositing our defiant tearful faces before the stern principal. My only memory of him is that he swayed on his heels like a palm tree, and he always clasped his impatient twitching hands behind his back. I recognized him as a repressed maniacal child killer, and knew that if we ever saw his hands we'd be in big trouble.

We all sat in little chairs in an empty auditorium. The room smelled like Chinese medicine, an imported faraway mustiness. Like ancient moth-balls or dirty closets. I hated that smell. I favored crisp new scents. Like the soft French perfume that my American teacher wore in public school.

There was a stage far to the right, flanked by an American flag and the flag of the Nationalist Republic of China, which was also red, white and blue, but not as pretty.

Although the emphasis at the school was mainly language—speaking, reading, and writing—the lessons always began with an exercise in polite-ness. With the entrance of the teacher, the best student would tap a bell and everyone would get up, kowtow, and chant, "Sing san ho," the pho-netic for "How are you, teacher?"

Being 10 years old, I had better things to learn than ideographs copied painstakingly in lines that ran right to left from the tip of a *moc but,* a real ink pen that had to be held in an awkward way if blotches were to be avoided. After all, I could do the multiplication tables, name the satellites of Mars, and write reports on *Little Women* and *Black Beauty.* Nancy Drew, my favorite book heroine, never spoke Chinese.

The language was a source of embarrassment. More times than not, I had tried to disassociate myself from the nagging loud voice that followed me wherever I wandered in the nearby American supermarket outside Chinatown. The voice belonged to my grandmother, a fragile woman in her seventies who could outshout the best of the street vendors. Her humor was raunchy, her Chinese rhythmless, patternless. It was quick, it was loud, it was unbeautiful. It was not like the quiet, lilting romance of French or the gentle refinement of the American South. Chinese sounded pedestrian. Public.

In Chinatown, the comings and goings of hundreds of Chinese on their daily tasks sounded chaotic and frenzied. I did not want to be thought of as mad, as talking gibberish. When I spoke English, people nodded at me, smiled sweetly, said encouraging words. Even the people in my culture would cluck and say that I'd do well in life. "My, doesn't she move her lips fast," they would say, meaning that I'd be able to keep up with the world outside Chinatown.

My brother was even more fanatical than I about speaking English. He was especially hard on my mother, criticizing her, often cruelly, for her pidgin speech—smatterings of Chinese scattered like chop suey in her conversation. "It's not 'What it is,' Mom," he'd say in exasperation. "It's 'What *is* it, what *is* it, what *is* it!'" Sometimes Mom might leave out an occasional "the" or "a," or perhaps a verb of being. He would stop her in mid-sentence: "Say it again, Mom. Say it right." When he tripped over his own tongue, he'd blame it on her: "See, Mom, it's all your fault. You set a bad example."

What infuriated my mother most was when my brother cornered her on her consonants, especially "r." My father had played a cruel joke on Mom by assigning her an American name that her tongue wouldn't allow to say. No matter how hard she tried, "Ruth" always ended up "Luth" or "Roof."

After two years of writing with a *moc but* and reciting words with multiples of meanings, I finally was granted a cultural divorce. I was permitted to stop Chinese school.

I thought of myself as multicultural. I preferred tacos to egg rolls; I enjoyed Cinco de Mayo more than Chinese New Year.

At last, I was one of you; I wasn't one of them.

Sadly, I still am.

PARAGRAPHING ACTIVITY 1.11

Following the four paragraphing suggestions, mark the beginning of each new paragraph in the following personal experience papers. Change paragraphs as the writer moves to something new within the experience, and avoid overly long paragraphs or strings of very short paragraphs.

When you finish, review the paragraphing of your latest draft, and if necessary, make changes to improve it.

Humiliation

I remember first grade was going along well. I was having fun in school. I liked my teacher, I got to play the wood block in the percussion band, and I even had a girlfriend. Then a string of events happened that ruined the year for me. My girlfriend's name was Karen, a quiet, dark-haired girl with a shy smile. After school, we'd go over to her house and sit on top of the slanted shingle roof, enjoying the sun, the view, and just being together. We'd sit there day after day, sometimes holding hands, and I was very happy. Then Karen was absent from school for a while, and the teacher, Mrs. Bray, told us Karen's father had been killed in an electrical accident. I remember being shocked by the news. I'd never heard of anyone's father being killed; it wasn't something that happened. I wondered how Karen was doing, but I was afraid to go and see her. Then one day the entire class walked together to Karen's garage to pick up some old hobbyhorses and props Karen's mother was lending our class for a play. We were all in the dusty old garage collecting the wooden stick horses and everyone was pretty quiet. Then I blurted out something loudly, I don't remember why. I liked to be the center of attention, but why I picked that time to say something stupid is beyond me. When I did, Mrs. Bray really jumped on me. "Shut up, Ben!" she hissed angrily. And I didn't open my mouth the rest of the day. Walking back to school, I felt awful. Mrs. Bray had never scolded me before, and I now had done something so terrible that she told me to shut up. On top of that, I had been acting stupid at Karen's house only a week after her father died. That made me a doubly evil person, and even though Karen hadn't been in the garage with us, I knew she'd find out. I felt miserable. I never saw Karen again. She stayed home from school for a long time, and then apparently she and her mother moved away. I walked by her house a couple of times before she moved, but I never had the courage to stop. I really never recovered that year from the incident. Things weren't right again between me and Mrs. Bray; I always felt I'd failed her. We moved that summer, and since I never saw Karen again, I assumed she thought the worst of me, and I'd never believe otherwise. Thinking back on that year, I still feel sad some fifteen years later. It's an awful feeling to do something you feel is terrible and never be able to make amends. I just wish I could have seen Karen one last time and said, "I'm sorry."

Seeing Grandpa

A week after my grandfather died, my mother told me she saw him standing in our backyard. She said he had returned to speak to her and that he would be back again. Mother believed in dead relatives returning to visit loved ones before they finally rested, and she said he might visit me too. It scared me to think about it. Three nights later I awoke and saw Grandpa standing at the foot of my bed. There was no doubt that it was Grandpa: the tall, thin body, the tousled white hair, the big, watery eyes. He stood there and stared at me with those big, sad eyes, but he never spoke. It somehow seemed natural for him to be standing there, and he was such a kind, gentle man that I wasn't the least frightened. We just looked at each other for the longest time, and then he turned slowly and walked out my bedroom door. I crawled out of bed and followed him. He walked out the back door, and by the time I peeked out the back window, he was gone. It was the last time I ever saw my grandfather. I slept with my mother the rest of the night, and the next morning I told her about Grandpa. She wasn't at all surprised or concerned. She said he was probably contented now and wouldn't return. We talked about the incident as though it was the most natural thing in the world. No matter how absurd it sounds, it seems like the right thing for my grandfather to have come back one last time. It made me feel good, and it must have helped him. Since the incident, I have had more respect for some of my mother's beliefs that I once thought were nonsense. There are some things that happen that logic can't explain. Grandfather's return was one of them.

Caught in the Act

When I was in fourth grade, I got caught cheating on a test, the first and last time I ever got caught. It was an incident that stands out from my elementary school years, probably because I was so embarrassed. Our class was taking one of those standardized state tests that you take twice a year. Each section is timed, and you have to stop when the teacher tells you. We were sitting in rows of desks, and the smartest girl in the room sat just to the right of me. She was smarter than me, but I always tried to compete against her. On one section of the test, I don't remember which one, I couldn't get this one answer and time was running out. Many students had already finished the section, which we finished right before noon, and had gone outside for lunch break. I was still sitting there and sweating it out over that question and getting desperate. I just had to get that answer. The smart girl was still sitting beside me, and a glance over made me realize that she had filled in the bubble on that answer on her answer sheet. Before I even knew what I was doing, I couldn't have given it much thought, I leaned over to see what letter she had bubbled in, and I saw it. So I filled in the same answer on my answer sheet, and as I was doing it, I felt the teacher standing by my desk. I don't remember exactly what she said, but I do remember she was pretty stern and made me erase the answer and took my booklet away from me and told me to go outside. Here I was, supposed to be a good kid and a good student, and the teacher had caught me cheating. Luckily, a lot of kids weren't around to see it, but the smart girl I cheated off of saw the whole thing. I remember I was really embarrassed and ashamed, and I felt bad that the teacher was mad at me and seemed shocked that I had cheated. It's just that I always wanted to do good, actually I wanted to be on top because I was so competitive, and I went too far, but getting that one answer seemed at the time like the most important thing in the world. Fourth grade went on, and the cheating was eventually forgotten, but it's something I'll never forget. As for the smart girl, I don't remember how she reacted; she probably didn't care one way or the other. She knew she was smarter than me anyway, and maybe felt good that I'd tried to cop an answer from her. I can't say that I never cheated again in school, because I did copy someone's homework assignment a couple times, nothing really bad, but I never got caught again. It was the getting caught more than the cheating that bothered me I guess. It was like I'd been exposed for who I really was. I've always had this other side to me that most people don't see because I hide it pretty good and it's not really that terrible, but when I get caught doing something, it's like my real self is being exposed or something.

SENTENCE REVISION

All writers share the task of revising first-draft sentences to make them smoother, clearer, and more interesting. In this section, you learn to use descriptive wording to bring your sentences to life.

DESCRIPTIVE LANGUAGE

Descriptive language helps readers to see, hear, and feel most clearly what a writer is experiencing. For example, compare these two descriptions of the pain felt by the writer:

> My finger hurt a lot and I started to cry.

> My mangled finger throbbed with pain and hot tears streamed down my face.

Clearly, the second sentence provides a more vivid and interesting description of the writer's experience.

Here are some suggestions for using descriptive language in your writing.

1. Use the most specific word to refer to a particular thing. For example, you might use *German shepherd* instead of *dog*, *TWA 747* instead of *airplane*, *six-lane freeway* instead of *road*, *Buddhist temple* instead of *church*, and *lemon chiffon pie* instead of *dessert*.

2. Use vivid, descriptive verbs to make your sentences lively and interesting. For example, the sentence "Breanna *glowered* at her laughing brother and *peeled* the leaves off her jacket" is more interesting than "Breanna was mad at her laughing brother and removed the leaves from her jacket."

3. Make your writing as visual as possible. Use language that helps readers see and feel what you did. For example, the sentence "The huge man careened down the slope, crashed into a startled skier, and knocked her head-long into a snow bank" provides a better picture than "The man went fast down the slope, hit another skier, and knocked her to the ground."

Here are some examples of vaguely worded first-draft sentences followed by more descriptive versions.

Vague	The tree in my yard is very colorful.
Improved	The pear tree behind the house is covered with pink blossoms.
Vague	Slobber comes out of my dog's mouth sometimes.
Improved	Slobber dribbles down my bulldog Murphy's mouth when he gets excited.

Vague	The girl moved across the ice in a nice fashion.
Improved	The tiny girl in pigtails glided smoothly across the ice.
Vague	The weather is terrible this morning.
Improved	It's five degrees below zero and the fog is wet and thick.
Vague	Bothered by a leg problem, the football player didn't move well.
Improved	Hobbled by a swollen ankle, the halfback ran at half speed.
Vague	That young person just left with my glasses.
Improved	That tow-headed ten-year-old just stole my sunglasses.

ONLINE ACTIVITY: DESCRIPTIVE LANGUAGE

For further suggestions on using descriptive language, go online to St. Cloud State University's writing website LEO (Literacy Education Online): http://leo.stcloudstate.edu/#develop.

When you arrive, click on "I'd like to work on sensory details," which will bring up a number of suggestions for replacing vague, general wording with more specific, interesting language. Read the examples carefully, and apply what you learn to the upcoming exercise and to your first draft.

REVISION ACTIVITY 1.12

Revise the following vaguely worded sentences by replacing general words with more specific ones and weak verbs with more vivid ones. Then review your latest draft and replace vague language with more descriptive visual words.

Example	We left to go downtown and take care of some business.
Revised	My best friend and I left school at noon to order our class rings from the downtown jewelry store.

1. There is a funny smell coming from one part of the garage.

2. Melissa has a very strange hairdo.

3. That man is strong for his age.

4. The horses left from the starting gate and moved down the track.

5. The moon is beautiful tonight.

6. The girl waited for her date to arrive.

7. The boxer put his right glove in the other boxer's face and then did it again with the other hand.

8. After a long hike, the boy didn't feel great at all.

9. Your relative is quite small for her age.

10. The bird went up to the top of the tree and sat.

FINAL EDITING

Now that you have revised your paper to improve its content, organization, and wording, you are ready to give it a thorough proofreading to locate and correct any errors in punctuation, spelling, or grammar. No matter how interesting or well-developed a paper may be, if it is full of errors, readers become distracted.

PROOFREADING GUIDELINES

When proofreading a draft for errors, keep in mind the following general areas:

1. *Check to make sure that each sentence ends with a period.* A common problem among writers is to run pairs of sentences together rather than separating them with a period. (See the upcoming section on "Run-on Sentences.")

2. *Check to make sure you haven't left off any word endings.* Occasionally, writers will leave off an *ed* on a past tense verb, an *s* or *es* on a plural word, or an *ly* on an adverb such as "quickly" or "longingly." A quick check of word endings may uncover some omissions.

3. *Check your spelling carefully.* Misspelled words are the most common writing errors and the most troubling for readers. If you use a computer, learn to use the spelling check on your word processor. Also make a list of words that you frequently misspell, and work on spelling those words correctly. If you struggle with spelling, your instructor may refer you to the "Spelling" section in the appendix at the back of this book. The section gives you some basic spelling rules and includes lists of frequently misspelled words.

4. *Check your "internal" punctuation: the commas and apostrophes within your sentences.* Make sure you have inserted commas where you want readers to pause in a sentence, and apostrophes (') in contractions (you're, isn't) and possessive words (John's car, a week's salary). (See the upcoming section on "Comma Usage.")

5. *Check your use of subject pronouns (I, he, she, you, we, they).* Writers sometimes write "Me and my brother went fishing" instead of "My

brother and I went fishing," or "Marie, Harriet, and me are friends" instead of "Marie, Harriet, and I are friends," or "Me and her went to the mall together" instead of "She and I went to the mall together."

Of course, this checklist doesn't cover all of the types of errors you may run across in your writing, and it doesn't provide you with the rules and practice you may need to eliminate certain error tendencies. It does provide some direction in proofreading your drafts and correcting common errors. As you work through the book, you will learn the rules and gain the practice needed to eliminate most errors and to proofread accurately.

PROOFREADING ACTIVITY 1.13

In small groups, proofread the following student draft for errors in spelling, punctuation, or grammar, and make the necessary corrections.

Bloody Mary

When I was young, I was a little of a rebel. One day some of my friends came over and we were just hanging out chillin. One of my friends said let's go out late tonight and check out the cematery while my friends were excited I was a little intimated cause I knew all those storys about the cematery. I said I don't know if I can make it. They gave me a hard time, so I said what the heck, let's go to the cematery.

We snuck out of the house around 1:00 A.M. and walked all the way to the cematery. It was me, David, Jose, Frankie, and Mike. One friend said so what did we come here for. I said we came her to see if there was really Bloody Mary roaming the cematery, like we had always been told. One of my friends was really getting scared, he wanted to go home. We all agreed to stay strong, so started roaming the cematery we all had flashlights, thank God.

All of a sudden we could sense we weren't alone. Everyone wanted to go home, but we couldn't cause we were too scared and we were in the middle of the cematery. Then we heard an owl hooting. Everywhere we go, it looks like the owl is following us. Then all of a sudden we saw somebody on the other side of the cematery. Now this is too much for us to handle, so we just stayed still where we were for about twenty minutes. We all know what we saw, it was something white roaming the cematery we drop the flashlights and started running as fast as we can like an escape from prison.

Finally we made it home nobody mentioned what we saw, and the next day nobody wanted to talk about it. When someone said something, we go pale and stay silent for a while. Is there really a Bloody Mary? I don't know for sure, but on that day, something told me maybe those stories are true. I'll end by saying I'm a believer. Maybe I'll go once more to the cematery if I'm stupid enough, which I dout.

PROOFREADING ACTIVITY 1.14

Following the guidelines just presented, proofread your latest draft and correct any errors that you find. Your instructor may have you work through the upcoming sections on "Run-on Sentences" and "Comma Usage" before you proofread your paper. Also, exchange papers with a classmate and proofread each other's drafts.

When you finish correcting your paper, write or print out the final draft to share with your classmates and instructor.

JOURNAL ENTRY THREE

Under Journal Entry Three in your notebook, relate the kinds of errors you found in your draft and the corrections you made. What are some of your error tendencies to be aware of for future writing?

SENTENCE PROBLEMS

The most common punctuation problem comes from running pairs of sentences together. Two or more sentences run together without a period or capital letter are called a *run-on sentence*. In many cases, run-on sentences confuse readers and make writing more difficult to understand. The purpose of this section is to help you recognize the most common types of run-ons, to show you how to correct them, and to help you avoid them in the future.

RUN-ON SENTENCES

Here are some common features of run-on sentences:

1. A run-on sentence is usually two sentences run together without a period ending the first sentence or a capital letter beginning the second.

   EXAMPLE   June is a very spoiled child she expects to get her way at all times.

2. A run-on sentence that contains a comma between sentences is called a *comma splice*. A comma by itself does not separate sentences, and it does not replace a period.

   EXAMPLE   We never go into town during the week, it is too far from our farm.

3. The sentences within a run-on are usually closely related in meaning.

   EXAMPLE   Maria is doing well in algebra she has gotten Bs on all her tests.

4. Most run-on sentences follow certain patterns. A pronoun that replaces the subject of the first sentence often begins the second

sentence within a run-on: he, she, it, they, you, we, or I. The following common "introductory" words also frequently begin the second sentence in a run-on: the, then, there, that, this, these, and those.

Here are some examples of run-on sentences in which the underlined pronoun or introductory word begins the second sentence within the run-on sentence:

EXAMPLES   Ted's parents spoil him <u>they</u> give him money to brush his teeth.

Sylvia came to class early <u>she</u> wanted to study her notes.

The tides at the beach were unpredictable and very strong, <u>they</u> made swimming dangerous.

John went for a long walk around the lake in the park <u>then</u> he took a nap before going to work.

Getting to the museum is difficult, <u>there</u> is one route that I would recommend.

5. To correct run-on sentences, you either need to separate the sentences with a period and capital letter, or combine them with a joining word.

As a rule, you *separate longer sentences with a period and combine shorter run-on sentences with a joining word.* Here are corrected versions of the run-on sentences.

EXAMPLES   Ted's parents spoil him <u>because</u> they give him money to brush his teeth.

Sylvia came to class early, <u>for</u> she wanted to study her notes.

John went for a long walk around the lake in the park. Then he took a nap before going to work.

Getting to the museum is difficult, <u>but</u> there is one route that I would recommend.

RUN-ON ACTIVITY 1.15

Most of the following sentences are run together. Correct the run-on sentences by putting a period after the first sentence and capitalizing the second sentence, or by combining the sentences with a joining word. *As a general rule, separate longer run-on sentences with a period, and connect the shorter sentences with joining words.* When you finish, proofread your latest draft for run-on sentences and make the necessary corrections.

EXAMPLE   The bear backed into its cave, it was frightened by the flames.

REVISED   The bear backed into its cave because it was frightened by the flames.

EXAMPLE   I have tried to ignore your annoying habit of cracking your toes in class I must now ask you to stop before I go crazy.

REVISED   I have tried to ignore your annoying habit of cracking your toes in class. I must now ask you to stop before I go crazy.

1. Your mother is one of the nicest people I have ever met she is always smiling and has something nice to say.

2. None of the classes that I am taking this semester requires a lot of homework, that gives me more time to work in the evenings.

3. My car always smells like burning oil after I have driven it for a while I wonder if I might have a small oil leak in the manifold.

4. Sarah's baby sleeps almost every night from 9:00 or 10:00 p.m. until 6:00 a.m. in the morning, it is unusual for him to wake up in the middle of the night.

5. Before we were married, Patrice and I fought a lot we don't fight much now that we're married.

6. Please take the cat outside, she is scratching the carpet like she wants to go to the bathroom.

7. The United Nations Security Council rejected the United States proposal for a pre-emptive strike against Iraq by a vote of three to two the three dissenting nations were France, Russia, and Germany.

8. Eighteen-wheel truck rigs rumble down Highway 98 between DuPaw and Forkland at speeds of 80 mph, the highway patrol just seem to ignore them.

9. I seldom win an argument with my sister she always gets in the last word.

10. If you're not used to taking 1:00 p.m. classes, I'd suggest you not enroll in them, they come right after lunch, and I find myself falling asleep every class.

11. Crosstown driving is hectic between 4:00 and 6:00 p.m. during commuter rush time there is no north-south freeway in the city, so commuters have to negotiate the stoplight-laden boulevards that are choked with traffic.

12. Recent studies indicate that high fiber diets don't reduce the risk of colon cancer, heredity is still the primary factor in whether a person contracts the disease.

COMMA USAGE

The purpose of using commas in your writing is to make the meaning of each sentence clear to readers. Proper comma usage establishes the reading rhythm of a sentence by indicating to readers where to pause, and by separating words or phrases whose meaning would be ambiguous if they were run together. Improper comma usage, on the other hand, can destroy sentence rhythm and confuse readers.

BASIC COMMA RULES

The following basic comma rules will serve you well for punctuating sentences effectively. A few additional rules will be covered later in the book.

1. *Commas in series:* Three or more words or groups of words in a series should be separated by commas. Words in a series are usually joined by *conjunctions,* such as *and, but,* or *or.*

   EXAMPLES   I enjoy hiking, fishing, and reading.

   Marie likes to jog in the morning, after lunch, after work, or in the early evening.

   Jorge is excited about the debate, prepared to argue his case, and determined to do well.

   Samantha works on Saturdays but relaxes on Sundays.

   (No comma needed because there are only *two* groups of words joined by *but:* "works on Saturdays" *but* "relaxes on Sundays.")

2. *Commas in compound sentences:* In a sentence containing two complete sentences *(independent clauses)* joined by a *conjunction*—and, but, so, or, yet, for,—a comma goes after the word before the conjunction.

   EXAMPLES   Teddy is planning on going to the curriculum meeting after school, but she may change her plans if her tooth continues to ache.

   Those bugs on the ceiling are coming in through the broken window screen, so I think we'd better buy a new one.

   The rain has flooded all of the streets around the college, and it is impossible to park anywhere near campus.

3. *Introductory groups of words:* If a sentence begins with an introductory group of words, a comma sets off the introduction. Introductory phrases and clauses often begin with a *preposition* (in, on, by, with, between, through, for example), a *subordinate conjunction* (when, while, as,

unless, although, because, if, after, before), or a word that ends in *ing* or *ed* (working, hoping, troubled, amazed).

EXAMPLES   On your way out of the auditorium, please lock the double doors in the back.

In the middle of her greatest season, Maribel broke her pitching hand.

If you have finished mowing the lawn, please give me some help with the laundry.

Because I have over 100 pages of botany to read tonight, I can't go to the concert.

Looking at her watch every few minutes, Marcela waited impatiently for her date to arrive.

Alarmed at how quickly his hair was falling out, Marvin bought a wig.

Shouting at the top of her lungs, Tanisha attracted the judge's attention.

4. *Before "who" or "which" clauses:* Insert commas before and after a group of words beginning with a *who* or *which* that is used to identify a specific person or thing. If the group of words beginning with *who* or *which* ends the sentence, insert a comma only before the *who* or *which*.

EXAMPLES   Emily Rebraca, who is the first girl in her family to attend college, will graduate in June.

The women's chess team, which was formed last semester, has more than fifty members.

I'd like you to meet Latham George, who transferred to Memphis State from Louisiana Tech.

The Grand Canyon, which is located in Arizona, is one of the seven natural wonders of the world.

COMMA ACTIVITY 1.16

Insert commas in the following sentences where they are needed in series, in compound sentences, after introductory groups of words, and before and after "who" and "which" clauses. When you finish, proofread your latest draft for correct comma usage.

EXAMPLE   In the back of the bus, we found snakes, frogs, and lizards.

1. When the college administration first proposed that a new basketball arena be built on campus most students were not enthusiastic.

2. It wasn't that they didn't like the men's and women's basketball teams which had been quite successful for many years.

3. The problem was the seating arrangement at the current downtown arena and the lack of student seats.

4. At the downtown arena where the team had played for years eleven thousand five hundred of the twelve thousand seats were sold to the general public.

5. That left only five hundred seats for a student body of fifteen thousand so most students never had a chance to get season tickets.

6. In addition the five hundred student seats were high in a corner of the arena which made spectating difficult.

7. If the new arena was going to have the same discriminatory seating policy the students were not going to support it which meant it probably wouldn't get built.

8. The administration realized they were going to have to make some changes so they proposed that three thousand seats in the new twelve-thousand–seat arena be designated for student seating and the student section would be near the floor and the center of the court.

9. The proposal was well-received by students and the student council voted to approve the construction of the arena.

10. The new SaveMart Center Arena which will be situated adjacent to the student dormitories is located ideally for students to walk to the games which will cut down on traffic and parking congestion.

11. Perhaps the people who are most pleased are the college's basketball players who have longed for a huge student following to bring energy to the building and fire up the players.

12. Funded by a state bond individual donors and large businesses the arena will be under construction for two years and the first basketball season in the arena will be in 2004–2005.

13. The arena will be a multipurpose facility although college basketball will be the primary activity and main revenue source for the school.

14. Along with men's and women's basketball the women's volleyball team will also play in the arena and special events such as concerts political rallies and guest lectures will be held on occasion.

15. The arena will cost over $50 million to build but over half of that funding will come of course from national business conglomerates like Pepsi Cola and SaveMart.

JOURNAL ENTRY FOUR

Under Journal Entry Four in your notebook, evaluate the writing process you used to write your main paper for this unit. What things did you find most useful in the process? What would you want to do similarly when writing your next paper? What might you do differently?

WRITING REVIEW

At the end of each unit, you will apply what you have learned to a final writing assignment. For this unit, you will write a second personal experience paper, this one based on a more recent experience.

To write your paper, follow the steps presented, which summarize the writing process for this unit.

WRITING PROCESS

1. Select an experience-related topic from your recent past. To select a topic, consider the following:

   a. What particular experience in my recent life really stands out?

   b. What experience did I learn something from that may be of interest or value to my classmates?

   c. What recent experience have I had that may be similar to something my classmates may have gone through, and to which they can relate?

   d. What recent experience would I most like to spend some time thinking and writing about?

2. When you have selected a topic, reflect on the experience before writing by considering the following:

   a. Picture the experience in your mind and recall when and where it occurred, who was involved, and what exactly happened.

   b. Try to remember your thoughts and feelings at different times in the experience in order to share them with your readers.

   c. Reflect on the significance of the experience. What did you learn that has helped you (or may help you in the future)? How can you best express what you learned to your classmates? What do you want them to take from the paper?

STUDENT SAMPLE IDEAS   I think I'll write about an experience during my freshman year in college. Actually, I'll have to include a few experiences within my freshman year, all of which I learned a similar lesson from. I'll tie all of these experiences together so they are parts of one bigger learning experience, which they were.

The experiences that stand out include a meeting in my dormitory, the first day of swim practice, a discussion in English class, and a freshman queen competition. All had the same effect on me: humbling. It was hard realizing I wasn't as popular, smart, talented, or good looking as I thought, and it was a hard lesson. It might be good to share with classmates who have had similar experiences.

3. After you have reflected on the experience, write the first draft of your paper following these guidelines:

   a. Your classmates are your reading audience for the paper. Keep them in mind as you write, and your purpose for writing about this particular topic: why are you writing to them about this particular experience?

   b. Write without great concern for your wording or an occasional error. In a first draft, don't labor with a sentence to get the wording. "Just write." You'll probably change it anyway in a future draft.

   c. Keep the elements of narration in mind as you write: providing a setting, including and bringing to life the important people, telling the story with your audience in mind, and concluding with the resolution: what you learned, gained, or lost from the experience or the relationship.

   d. Change paragraphs as you move to different parts of the experience: different times, places, or incidents.

College Experience

STUDENT DRAFT   I went from a high school of one hundred and fifty graduating seniors to a college of twenty thousand students my freshman year. I had been something of a big wheel in high school, and I was about to get a real shock coming out of the shelter of my small-town life.

The first defining experience I recall was a meeting of my classmates on the same dormitory floor. We got together to elect floor officers and discuss rules and regulations. I was surprised by how confident and articulate many of the girls were. I felt overmatched by their brains and good looks, so I sat in a corner and kept quiet. Needless to say, I wasn't nominated for any office, and I left the meeting a bit shaken. I sure didn't feel like the former senior class president of my high school.

A similar experience occurred in an English class. We had all read the same short story by Flannery O'Conner, but students in the class came up with insights and connections I hadn't begun to make. It was a lively and interesting discussion, but I was frightened stiff that the instructor would call on me. No one would have recognized me as a top ten student at Grimly High School.

The old swimming pool was one place I could regain my confidence, I thought. No way. Being an all-league swimmer where I came from was nothing compared to the talent on the college team. Some of these girls were the best in the state. I was put in a lane with about ten other "B" level swimmers, and that was clearly where I belonged.

A final humbling experience was something I'd always looked forward to in high school—popularity contests. A number of freshman girls were nominated for something called "Dream Court" to be a part of college homecoming activities. Posters of girls nominated by different clubs and dorms started going up around campus, and needless to say, my face wasn't among them. I wasn't nominated or, to my knowledge, even considered for nomination by anyone. I wasn't that pretty or popular.

Needless to say, my freshman year was rough. My whole life I felt I had a pretty good idea of who I was, and one semester in college changed all of that. I lost all confidence, and for a long time I went into a shell. No one got to know me because I didn't know who I was myself.

Then after feeling sorry for myself for a long time, I went in the other direction and foolishly decided to make a name for myself. I joined everything that I could, kissed up to every popular girl and boy, tried to talk and laugh louder than anyone, and tried to be the life of the party by out-drinking everyone. After a couple months of this, one of the few friends I had on campus asked me the question that needed asking: "Who are you trying to be?" That really got me thinking.

My freshman year was a mess, and I'd never want to relive it. However, it was a year I had to go through to understand a few things. No matter where I'd gone to college, there would be people who were smarter, better looking, and more talented than me. My first two reactions to that realization—first, to go into a shell, and second, to try to be something that I wasn't—were I think pretty natural reactions. I don't fault myself for either because I learned from both.

What I learned were a few basic things that have helped me rediscover myself. First, I know I'm basically a pretty good person, and that's the most important thing. Second, although I'll never be the smartest, prettiest, or most talented, I know I have what it takes to be successful as long as I work at it. Third, I know I can be myself and make friends and enjoy life. It takes time to get to know people and make friends in a new environment, and I had wanted it all to happen overnight.

As a sophomore, I am a different person than as a freshman. Actually, I'm the same person with a year's experience and understanding. I may now appear as confident and sound as articulate as the girls that I met at the first meeting a year ago. I may even intimidate some of them as I was intimidated. Thousands of freshmen surely go through experiences similar to mine, and like me, most of them will have to learn the hard way. Maybe that's why I've become a peer counselor at the college. When I talk to a freshman who is down in the dumps, I can say to her in all honesty, "Hey, I've been there. I know how you're feeling. It's going to get better."

4. When you finish your first draft, evaluate it for possible revisions by applying the following guidelines. Next, exchange drafts with a classmate and make revision suggestions. Then write the second draft of your paper, including any revisions you feel will make it better.

   a. Can readers clearly picture where and when the experience took place, and what actually happened?

   b. Have you highlighted for readers the most important parts of the experience or relationship and shared with them your thoughts and feelings as the experience or relationship unfolds?

   c. In the conclusion, have you revealed the significance of the experience to your readers and passed on what you learned?

   d. Can you improve some first-draft sentences by making them more concrete (visually descriptive), more concise, smoother, or clearer?

   e. Does your paragraphing help readers move smoothly through the experience? Do you change paragraphs as you move to different times, places, or incidents, and have you avoided extremely long or short paragraphs?

5. After you have written your second draft, proofread it carefully for errors by covering the following areas:

   a. Read each sentence to make sure you have a period at the end. Check in particular for run-on sentences that need punctuating.

   b. Check your word endings, and in particular the *ed* endings on all regular past tense verbs.

   c. Check your spelling carefully, and use the spelling check on your word processor.

   d. Check your use of commas in words in series, in compound sentences, and after introductory groups of words; and make sure you have used apostrophes in contractions (don't, it's) and possessive words (cat's tail, Ralph's notebook). If you have included dialogue, make sure you have introduced the speakers (Julia said, Mike shouted) and put quotation marks (" ") around the spoken words.

   e. Check your use of subject pronouns (I, he, she, we, they, you), and make sure you haven't begun any sentences incorrectly with "Me and my mother," or "The Gomez twins and me," or "Ralph and her," or "The Williamses and them."

6. When you have proofread your paper and corrected all errors, write or print out your final draft. Share copies with classmates and your instructor.

Writing about Relationships

During our lives, we form relationships with a variety of people: parents, brothers, sisters, grandparents, husbands, wives, children, friends, teachers, coworkers, neighbors, classmates, and so on. The quality of our relationships with people, particularly those most prominent in our lives, greatly influences how we view ourselves, how we think and feel about different things, how we respond to other people, and our general welfare and happiness.

Writers often write about people who have influenced their lives, and the impact that they have made. The person may have been a positive influence—a loving mother, an understanding counselor, a protective big brother, a caring teacher, a lifelong friend—or a negative influence—an alcoholic parent, an absentee father, a school bully, an overbearing boss. Some relationships change over time, getting better or worse, or growing stronger or weaker, and others are full of ambivalence, such as the love-hate relationship that may exist between siblings or spouses.

In Unit Two, you write about people in your life who have made or continue to make an impact. The purpose of your writing is to think more deeply about relationships with different people, to analyze the impact of those relationships on your life, to understand your role in the relationships, and to understand better other people's attitudes and behavior toward you.

Writing about relationships also allows you to bring special people to life for readers by using examples and situations that reveal much about the relationship and the person. Through the use of description, examples, and incidents, you help readers best understand the person and your feelings toward him or her.

PREWRITING

Prewriting includes everything that you do before writing the first draft of a paper. For example, your prewriting for the personal experience paper in Unit One included considering different experiences to write about, sharing experiences with classmates to get feedback and ideas, reflecting on your experience to understand it better, and considering your purpose for writing and how your reading audience would react. By the time you began your first draft, you had done considerable preparation.

Prewriting activities differ from writer to writer, and there are a number of different activities presented in the text. You may have also discovered effective prewriting activities in other classes or through your personal writing experience. The more prewriting options you are familiar with, the better you can tailor your prewriting to the writing task at hand.

PREWRITING GUIDELINES

For any prewriting work that you do, the following guidelines should help:

1. Think seriously about what you want to write about. Topic selection is crucial to writing something that you will enjoy working on and others will find interesting to read. Spend time thinking about possible topics, and select one that interests you and that may interest your readers.

2. Try generating some ideas to include in your first draft. As you dig into your topic, you may find that you have lots of ideas on the subject. If you discover you don't really have much to write about, you may want to change topics.

   The following prewriting activities help writers generate ideas for their papers:

   Making lists of a few main points to include helps writers get started and continue their writing.

   Brainstorming ideas—considering any thought that comes to mind on a topic—is a useful individual or group activity for coming up with main ideas as well as details and examples.

Outlining a draft to include main ideas and some supporting material provides both an organizational framework and plenty to write about.

Mapping or clustering—an informal type of outlining by diagram— helps writers to analyze their topic in ever-increasing detail.

Free writing—writing whatever comes to mind about a topic without concern for order or logic—helps writers discover what they may know about a topic, or helps them find a topic to write about.

Asking and answering questions about the topic, such as who is involved, what happened, when did it happen, where did it happen, how did it happen, and why did it happen, can help writers generate a lot of material for a draft and analyze a topic in some depth.

You will have opportunities to try out different prewriting activities as you work through the writing assignments in the text. You may find one particular activity that suits you well, different activities for different kinds of writing you do, or a mixture of activities that become your personal prewriting routine.

3. Determine your reading audience for the paper (the people you think would enjoy or benefit from reading it) and your purpose for writing (why you are writing about this topic for this particular audience). Writers write for many reasons: to entertain, inform, influence, amuse, provoke, challenge, educate, or some combination. During your prewriting, consider what your purpose is for writing, and keep that purpose in mind as you write your draft.

In your writing outside of school, of course, topic selection and audience are dictated by your circumstances. You usually write—whether it be a friendly letter, a complaint, an editorial, or an application—for a purpose: to bring a friend up to date on your life, to get money back on a defective product, to support the school bond election, or to get a job interview. You usually write for a definite audience: the friend, the manufacturing company, the voters, the hiring employer. Outside the classroom, you write when you have a reason to do so. The main purpose of this text is to help you write effectively in those situations as well as in your college career.

TOPIC SELECTION

For this unit's writing assignment, you will write about a person whom you know well and about your relationship with him or her. Select a person who has made or continues to make an impact on your life, whether good, bad, or mixed. This may be a person you love, respect, dislike, fear, envy, or admire, or have a range of feelings toward. Select someone who, for better or worse, has influenced your life.

STUDENT TOPIC SELECTION SAMPLE

I might write about my young daughter, who is the brightest spot in my life right now. She makes me want to keep going and try to succeed and be a good mother. My own mother is a big influence. Without her I don't think I could make it being a single mother, and she has always been there. The father of my child is someone who has influenced my life, but in a sad and bad way. I'd never get involved with someone like him again. My continuation school counselor also played a big role. I probably wouldn't be here if it wasn't for him encouraging me and making me feel I could succeed.

GROUP ACTIVITY 2.1

In small groups, talk about some of the people who have influenced your life. Feel free to ask questions to help classmates explore their relationships with other people. The purpose of the activity is to help you decide on the person you want to write about and consider some of the things you may want to say.

When you finish, select the person you are going to write about, or keep a couple of people in mind if you are still undecided.

ASKING AND ANSWERING QUESTIONS

Once you have selected a person to write about, your next prewriting task is to generate some ideas that you may include in your paper. The following questions will help you explore your topic and list some of the ideas you may include in your first draft:

1. In a sentence, how would you characterize your relationship with this person?

2. What are your feelings towards this person, and why do you think you feel this way?

3. What are three or four qualities or traits that this person possesses?

4. What is at least one example or incident that would show readers each quality or trait?

5. In what way or ways has this person made an impact on your life (for example, by pushing you to work hard, by always being there for you when you need help, by criticizing everything you do, by loving you the way you are, by giving you good advice, by constantly picking on you, etc.)?

6. What are some examples or incidents that would show readers the way or ways in which the person has made an impact on your life?

STUDENT SAMPLE RESPONSES TO QUESTIONS

1. My dad is the greatest person I know.

2. I really love and respect him.

3/4. Hard working (works two jobs, 12 hours a day)

Caring (always wanting to know how I am doing in school and sports)

Funny (always liked playing jokes on me, such as sneaking up and scaring me)

Always has time (always played ball with me, let me work on cars with him)

5/6. I'm a hard worker (go to school and have a part-time job)

My job choice (I'm taking auto mechanics courses, and will go to work for my dad.)

Love of the outdoors (enjoy camping, fishing, hiking because of my dad)

Love of family (I know I will be a good father because of him.)

PREWRITING ACTIVITY 2.2

Write answers to the six questions provided to help you think more deeply about your topic and to generate some ideas for your paper.

AUDIENCE AND PURPOSE

Two things to consider for any writing you do are the people you are writing for and your purpose for writing. For your upcoming paper, consider the following:

1. Your reading audience is your classmates. As you write about this person in your life, what do you need to keep in mind about your readers that may influence the things that you include, or the way in which you write about your subject?

2. What might your purpose be in writing about this particular person for your classmates? Is there anything they might learn? Is there anything they might understand better about you? Or do you just want them to know something about this special person and why he or she is so special?

STUDENT SAMPLE RESPONSE I'm writing about my dad because I'm really proud of him, and I don't mind my classmates knowing about it. I think they will see what a great dad he is, and that's what I want to show, and also how having a great dad can make your life better and make you a better person. I will also let my dad read the paper.

GROUP ACTIVITY 2.3

Read the following essay, "Dad" by Andrew Malcolm. In small groups, answer these questions:

1. What readers do you think Malcolm may be writing for primarily? Do you think he is writing for a very general audience or a more specific group of readers, and why?

2. What do you think Malcolm's purpose(s) may have been in writing about his father?

3. How does Malcolm feel about his father, and what did he learn from him?

4. How did Malcolm use examples from his life to show his relationship with his dad?

Dad
Andrew H. Malcolm

The first memory I have of him—of anything, really—is his strength. It was in the late afternoon in a house under construction near ours. The unfinished wood floors had large, terrifying holes whose yawning darkness I knew led to nowhere good. His powerful hands, then age thirty-three, wrapped all the way around my tiny arms, then age four, and easily swung me up to his shoulders to command all I surveyed.

The relationship between a son and his father changes over time. It may grow and flourish in mutual maturity. It may sour in resented dependence or independence. With many children living in single-parent homes today, it may not even exist.

But to a little boy right after World War II, a father seemed a god with strange strengths and uncanny powers enabling him to do and know things that no mortal could do or know. Amazing things, like putting a bicycle chain back on, just like that. Or building a hamster cage. Or guiding a jigsaw so it formed the letter F; I learned the alphabet that way in those pretelevision days, one letter or number every other evening plus a review of the collection. (The vowels we painted red because they were special somehow.)

He seemed to know what I thought before I did. "You look like you could use a cheeseburger and a chocolate shake," he would say on hot Sunday afternoons. When, at the age of five, I broke a neighbor's garage window with a wild curveball and waited in fear for ten days to make the announcement, he seemed to know about it already and to have been waiting for something.

There were, of course, rules to learn. First came the handshake. None of those fishy little finger grips, but a good firm squeeze accompanied by an equally strong gaze into the other's eyes. "The first thing anyone knows about you is your handshake," he would say. And we'd practice it each night on his return from work, the serious toddler in the battered Cleveland Indians cap running up to the giant father to shake hands again and again until it was firm enough.

When my cat killed a bird, he defused the anger of a nine-year-old with a little chat about something called "instinked." The next year, when my dog got run over and the weight of sorrow was just too immense to stand, he was there, too, with his big arms and his own tears and some thoughts on the natural order of life and death, although what was natural about a speeding car that didn't stop always escaped me.

As time passed, there were other rules to learn. "Always do your best." "Do it now." "NEVER LIE!" And, most important, "You can do whatever you have to do." By my teens, he wasn't telling me what to do anymore, which was scary and heady at the same time. He provided perspective, not telling me what was around the great corner of life but letting me know there was a lot more than just today and the next, which I hadn't thought of.

When the most important girl in the world—I forget her name now—turned down a movie date, he just happened to walk by the kitchen phone. "This may be hard to believe right now," he said, "but someday you won't even remember her name."

One day, I realize now, there was a change. I wasn't trying to please him so much as I was trying to impress him. I never asked him to come to my football games. He had a high-pressure career, and it meant driving through most of Friday night. But for all the big games, when I looked over at the sideline, there was that familiar fedora. And, by God, did the opposing team captain ever get a firm handshake and a gaze he would remember.

Then, a school fact contradicted something he said. Impossible that he could be wrong, but there it was in the book. These accumulated over time, along with personal experiences, to buttress my own developing sense of values. And I could tell we had each taken our own, perfectly normal paths.

I began to see, too, his blind spots, his prejudices, and his weaknesses. I never threw these up at him. He hadn't to me, and, anyway, he seemed to need protection. I stopped asking his advice; the experiences he drew from no longer seemed relevant to the decisions I had to make. On the phone, he would go on about politics at times, why he would vote the way he did or why some incumbent was a jerk. And I would roll my eyes to the ceiling and smile a little, though I hid it in my voice.

He volunteered advice for a while. But then, in more recent years, politics and issues gave way to talk of empty errands and, always, to ailments—his friends', my mother's, and his own, which were serious and included heart disease. He had a bedside oxygen tank, and he would ostentatiously retire there during my visits, asking my help in easing his body onto the mattress. "You have very strong arms," he once noted.

From his bed, he showed me the many sores and scars on his misshapen body and all the bottles of medicine. He talked of the pain and craved much sympathy. He got some. But the scene was not attractive. He told me, as the doctor had, that his condition would only deteriorate. "Sometimes," he confided, "I would just like to lie down and go to sleep and not wake up."

After much thought and practice ("You can do whatever you have to do"), one night last winter, I sat down by his bed and remembered for an instant those terrifying dark holes in another house thirty-five years before. I told my father how much I loved him. I described all the things people were doing for him. But, I said, he kept eating poorly, hiding in his room, and violating other doctors' orders. No amount of love could make someone else care about life, I said: It was a two-way street. He wasn't doing his best. The decision was his.

He said he knew how hard my words had been to say and how proud he was of me. "I had the best teacher," I said. "You can do whatever you have to do." He smiled a little and we shook hands, firmly, for the last time.

Several days later, at about 4 a.m., my mother heard Dad shuffling about their dark room. "I have some things I have to do," he said. He paid a bundle of bills. He composed for my mother a long list of legal and financial what-to-do's "in case of emergency." And he wrote me a note.

Then he walked back to his bed and laid himself down. He went to sleep, naturally. And he did not wake up.

JOURNAL ENTRY FIVE

Under Journal Entry Five in your notebook, relate how prepared you are to write your first draft. What prewriting activities, if any, were most helpful in preparing you to write?

FIRST DRAFTS

Now that you have selected a topic and done considerable prewriting work, you are ready to write the first draft of your paper. Consider the following suggestions for writing your draft:

FIRST-DRAFT GUIDELINES

1. *Make use of your prewriting plans.* From your prewriting, you have a basic idea of what you want to write, something to help you get

started and continue writing. However, feel free to add ideas that come to mind and to change other things that you aren't satisfied with. Your prewriting plan provides a general direction to follow rather than an unchangeable course. You will probably discover new things to write as you go.

2. *Don't worry about perfect wording.* Get your ideas down using the wording that comes to you first. Don't labor endlessly over a sentence to make it "perfect." You will revise and improve your wording in the next draft.

3. *Don't worry about making some mistakes.* You can take care of a misspelled word or an omitted comma when you edit your writing. Now is not the time to worry about mistakes. A first draft should flow fairly smoothly. If you are constantly looking for errors to correct, you may not concentrate on the content of your writing, which is most important.

4. *Keep in mind that writing is a recursive process.* Writers continually go back and reread what they've written in the last sentence or paragraph to keep them on track, to help them generate new ideas, and to make sure their sentences follow logically one to the next. Often, ideas that writers include in a draft come to them as they write. Much of the momentum for generating new ideas comes from going back and rereading what you've already written. Try doing that if it isn't yet a natural part of your writing process.

5. *Providing good examples is critical* for showing readers what the person you are writing about is like and your relationship with him or her. Each time you present a quality the person possesses or something about your relationship, try to include an example.

6. *Keep in mind your audience and purpose.* Your reading audience for this paper is your classmates, and your purpose is whatever you want it to be. While keeping your readers and your purpose in mind is important, don't write every sentence with the thought "What are my classmates going to think of this?" or "Does this sentence tie in to my purpose?" Such thoughts will slow your writing and perhaps keep you from writing what you really want. Remember, when you rewrite your draft, you can make changes that will make your paper more interesting for readers or more true to your purpose, *which might even change as you write.*

Before writing your first draft, read the following student draft and notice how the writer uses examples to help the reader understand her situation.

Roommate

STUDENT SAMPLE
DRAFT
I was really looking forward to going away to school and living in the dorms. I was lucky, or I thought I was lucky, to already know my college roommate. I didn't really know her well, she was from another town, but our parents were friends from childhood, and we had competed in volleyball against each other in high school, so I had spent some time with her. I soon discovered I didn't know her at all.

To say she was moody is not strong enough. She came to college with the idea that she would have this great social life. She showed me all the dresses she had brought for going out every weekend. When she didn't get dates and when the weekends started dragging, she would get very depressed and not want to talk at all. She would go into like a depression, and I had no idea what to do for her.

As the semester went on, and her social life wasn't great, she started getting more and more possessive of me. She wanted me to do everything with her and drop anything I was doing to spend time with her. I started making other friends in the dorms, and that bothered her. It was like I was betraying her or something. And when one of my friends visited for the weekend and I didn't include her in what we did, she screamed at me afterward, and then pouted for days after my friend left. I couldn't believe it. I spent less and less time with her and started hanging out with other girls.

Then things got weirder. I'd wake up at night sometimes and she would be lying in bed just staring at me. I'd say, "What's wrong?" and she'd just roll over and not say anything. It gave me the creeps. Other nights I'd wake up and she wasn't in the room. She'd come in the middle of the night and bang the door shut and I'd say, "Where were you?" "Just driving around," she'd mutter. I never knew where she went or what she did.

Like I said, she was moody, and after pouting and being mad at me, she'd turn around and cry and hug me and say I was her only friend. So I'd try to be nice to her, but it wouldn't take long before she started bugging me again. The friends I made didn't really like having her around because she was so unpredictable and into herself, and I quit spending much time in the room, avoiding her when I could.

It was the longest semester I'd ever had, and I was miserable a lot of the time because of my roommate. I kept thinking maybe all this was my fault because she'd lay such a guilt trip on me, like it was my fault she was miserable most of the time. I didn't know how to deal with it, and I think now that she really needed some counseling or psychological help, but all I knew was she was ruining my year.

The hardest thing I had to do was tell her I wasn't going to live with her the next semester, and even after all the signals I'd sent, she still went ballistic when I told her. She told her mom all kinds of lies about me and her mom called my mom and it was a mess. However, my mom knew the story, I'd talked to her a thousand times, and she supported me all the way.

I moved out next semester into an apartment with the girls I'd become friends with, and my life changed completely. Just coming home to our apartment every day was wonderful. Never again will I live with someone I don't know, and now I know how living with the wrong person can ruin your college experience, at least for a while. I also realize that I'm not responsible for making someone else happy. They have to figure that out for themselves. And I'm glad I finally confronted her and moved out. It was a hard thing to do, but it made me stronger.

After that semester I would see her once in a while at a party, and she was usually half drunk. We never spoke. I lost track of her after that year, and I hope that she got some help. She was in bad shape, but all I could think of was she wasn't making me miserable any more.

DRAFTING ACTIVITY 2.4

Write the first draft of your personal relationship paper. Divide your paper into paragraphs as you move to new areas: a new example, a different idea, a new quality or trait, etc.

REVISIONS

After you have written your first draft, set it aside for a while before reading it over. It is often easier to see both the flaws and the strengths in a paper after you have distanced yourself from it for a while. Some sentences that looked fine to you when you wrote them may now appear rather awkward or wordy. You may find sentences or even paragraphs that seem out of place where they are located. Or you will discover a particular statement—My *aunt dresses strangely*—that is in need of a good example, or you will think of a better example than the one you used.

In each "Revisions" section, you are provided a set of guidelines to help you analyze your first draft and those of your classmates. You also read and analyze a student draft in the text before working on your own draft. Next, you are given one or two "mini-lessons" in specific writing areas—"Paragraphing" and "Using Examples" in this section—that will help you revise your draft. Finally, you look at some suggestions for improving the wording of your sentences, and apply those suggestions to your draft.

That may seem like a lot of revision activities for one paper. However, many of the things that are covered in the lessons and activities will become ingrained in your writing process, and before long you will analyze and revise your drafts effectively with little direction.

REVISION GUIDELINES

As you reread your first draft, apply the following revision suggestions:

1. *Additions:* Read your draft, looking for places where you might add an example or incident to help reveal to readers more clearly the person you are writing about or your relationship with him or her. (See the upcoming section on "Using Examples.")

2. *Improved wording:* Read each sentence to see if a change in wording would make it clearer or smoother. (See upcoming section on "Wording Problems.")

3. *Paragraphing:* Check to see if you have divided your paper into paragraphs as you move to new ideas in your paper. If you have not paragraphed your paper, read your draft and find places where you might end one paragraph and begin another: a new idea, a different point, an example, a conclusion. (See the upcoming section on "Paragraphing.")

4. *Improved organization:* Read your draft to see if any sentences or paragraphs seem out of place, and decide whether they would fit better somewhere else in the paper, with other sentences (or a paragraph) more closely related to them.

5. *Audience and purpose:* Reread your draft with your reading audience—your classmates—and your purpose in mind. Consider making changes that would make the paper more interesting or informative to your classmates, and that would help you accomplish your purpose for writing.

REVISION ACTIVITY 2.5

In small groups, read the following student draft and apply the suggestions for revision, noting what you like about the draft, and the kinds of changes that would make the next draft more effective. Next, your instructor may have you provide copies of your draft for your classmates to evaluate in the same manner, discussing each student's draft.

My Dad

Student Sample Draft   I would like to write about a person who has been there for me in the bad and the good times. I have known this person my whole life. This special person in my life is my dad. I think I was blessed with the largest gift of life by having such a loving and caring father.

As I was growing up, my dad was always there to help me out with my schoolwork. Even though my dad read very little English, he did the best he could to help me.

When I was in elementary I played the clarinet in the school band. I remember my dad taking me to all my school concerts. I would get so embarrassed when my clarinet squeaked, I had to stop playing for a moment and look at my dad for a look of encouragement.

It is very hard for me to be away from my dad for a long period of time. When I was a junior in high school, my parents and I went to Mexico. When it came time for me to return to school after winter break, our van didn't work. My dad sent me back to California with my uncle.

I cried and begged for him not to send me back. I didn't want to leave without him. I was only sixteen and felt very frightened to be by myself without his guidance. I felt like my whole life was falling apart. I was scared and thinking the worst being that I came on an airplane.

I was in California for five weeks. I spent my seventeenth birthday alone and felt very lonely and depressed because I had always spent my birthday with my family.

When my family arrived from Mexico, my dad threw me a big surprise party. He bought me a small cake, and gave me two little teddy bears hugging, symbolizing the father and daughter aspect. My dad promised me he would never make me be without him again for a long period of time.

My dad has been the strength in my life. I thank God every day for blessing me with a wonderful father. Without him I would not have been able to accomplish most of my short-term goals. I love my dad very much.

REVISION ACTIVITY 2.6

After considering your classmates' suggestions and your own evaluation, write the next draft of your personal relationship paper, including all changes you think will improve the paper. (Before rewriting, your instructor may have you work through the upcoming sections on "Paragraphing" and "Using Examples.")

JOURNAL ENTRY SIX

Under Journal Entry Six in your notebook, record the kinds of changes you made from your first draft to your second. How do you feel they improved your paper?

PARAGRAPHING

Among students in a class, experience with paragraphing varies greatly. You may already be quite sophisticated in your paragraphing skills, you may have some understanding of paragraphing but little experience, or you may vaguely recollect writing paragraphs in elementary or high school. Your instructor will determine how much time you need to spend on paragraphing instruction as he or she becomes more familiar with your writing.

Basic Paragraphing

Paragraphing is not an exact science. Two writers may paragraph the same paper in somewhat different ways. However, there are some general rules that apply to most paragraphing you will do.

1. *Develop one idea in a paragraph.* Generally speaking, all of the sentences in a paragraph relate to one idea. For example, if a paragraph begins with the sentence, "Training horses is hard work," the rest of the sentences in the paragraph would reveal how hard the work is. When the sentence "Although training horses is hard work, it can be quite profitable" appears, it is probably time to move to the next paragraph to develop the new idea.

2. *Change paragraphs when you move to something new in a paper.* A different point, a different event or time, a new step, a different example, or a different aspect of your topic usually triggers a new paragraph. For example, if you are writing about a good friend, you might devote a separate paragraph to each quality or trait—good-natured, loyal, shy—and a separate paragraph to each of the ways he or she has influenced your life—taught you to be loyal, helped you through some rough times.

3. *Although paragraphs vary in length, as a rule avoid writing overly long or short paragraphs.* Readers can get bogged down in paragraphs that run on too long and may get little out of a paragraph of a sentence or two. Long paragraphs can usually be divided effectively, and short paragraphs can be combined with other related paragraphs or lengthened through more development.

PARAGRAPHING ACTIVITY 2.7

In small groups, read the following essay, "Only Daughter" by Sandra Cisneros, and discuss her paragraphing: what is contained in each paragraph, and why you think she changes paragraphs as she does. In addition, discuss the relationship between the writer and her father, the examples she uses to reveal that relationship, and the importance of the ending of the essay.

Only Daughter
Sandra Cisneros

Once, several years ago, when I was just starting out my writing career, I was asked to write my own contributor's note for an anthology I was part of. I wrote: "I am the only daughter in a family of six sons. *That* explains everything."

Well, I've thought about that ever since, and yes, it explains a lot to me, but for the reader's sake I should have written: "I am the only daughter of a Mexican father and a Mexican-American mother." Or: "I am the only daughter of a working-class family of nine." All of these had everything to do with who I am today.

I was/am the only daughter and *only* a daughter. Being an only daughter in a family of six sons forced me by circumstance to spend a lot of time by myself because my brothers felt it beneath them to play with a *girl* in public. But that aloneness, that loneliness, was good for a would-be writer—it allowed me time to think and think, to imagine, to read and prepare myself.

Being only a daughter for my father meant my destiny would lead me to become someone's wife. That's what he believed. But when I was in the fifth grade and shared my plans for college with him, I was sure he understood. I remember my father saying, "*Que bueno, ni'ja*, that's good." That meant a lot to me, especially since my brothers thought the idea hilarious. What I didn't realize was that my father thought college was good for girls—good for finding a husband. After four years in college and two more in graduate school, and still no husband, my father shakes his head even now and says I wasted all that education.

In retrospect, I'm lucky my father believed daughters were meant for husbands. It meant it didn't matter if I majored in something silly like English. After all, I'd find a nice professional eventually, right? This allowed me the liberty to putter about embroidering my little poems and stories without my father interrupting with so much as a "What's that you're writing?"

But the truth is, I wanted him to interrupt. I wanted my father to understand what it was I was scribbling, to introduce me as "My only daughter, the writer." Not as "This is only my daughter. She teaches." *Es maestra*—teacher. Not even *profesora*.

In a sense, everything I have ever written has been for him, to win his approval even though I know my father can't read English words, even though my father's only reading includes the brown-ink *Esto* sports magazines from Mexico City and the bloody *¡Alarma!* magazines that feature yet another sighting of *La Virgen de Guadalupe* on a tortilla or a wife's revenge on her philandering husband by bashing his skull in with a *molcajete* (a kitchen mortar made of volcanic rock). Or the *fotonovelas*, the little picture paperbacks with tragedy and trauma erupting from the characters' mouths in bubbles.

My father represents, then, the public majority. A public who is uninterested in reading, and yet one whom I am writing about and for, and privately trying to woo.

When we were growing up in Chicago, we moved a lot because of my father. He suffered bouts of nostalgia. Then we'd have to let go of our flat, store the furniture with mother's relatives, load the station wagon with baggage and bologna sandwiches, and head south. To Mexico City.

We came back, of course. To yet another Chicago flat, another Chicago neighborhood, another Catholic school. Each time, my father would seek out the parish priest in order to get a tuition break, and complain or boast: "I have seven sons."

He meant *siete hijos*, seven children, but he translated it as "sons." "I have seven sons." To anyone who would listen. The Sears Roebuck employee who sold us the washing machine. The short-order cook where my father ate his ham-and-eggs breakfasts. "I have seven sons." As if he deserved a from the state.

My papa. He didn't mean anything by that mistranslation, I'm sure. But somehow I could feel myself being erased. I'd tug my father's sleeve and whisper: "Not seven sons. Six! and *one daughter*."

When my oldest brother graduated from medical school, he fulfilled my father's dream that we study hard and use this—our heads, instead of this—our hands. Even now my father's hands are thick and yellow, stubbed by a history of hammer and nails and twine and coils and springs. "Use this," my father said, tapping his head, "and not this," showing us those hands. He always looked tired when he said it.

Wasn't college an investment? And hadn't I spent all those years in college? And if I didn't marry, what was it all for? Why would anyone go to college and then choose to be poor? Especially someone who had always been poor.

Last year, after ten years of writing professionally, the financial rewards started to trickle in. My second National Endowment for the Arts Fellowship. A guest professorship at the University of California, Berkeley. My book, which sold to a major New York publishing house.

At Christmas, I flew home to Chicago. The house was throbbing, same as always; hot *tamales* and sweet *tamales* hissing in my mother's pressure cooker, and everybody—my mother, six brothers, wives, babies, aunts, cousins—talking too loud and at the same time, like in a Fellini film, because that's just how we are.

I went upstairs to my father's room. One of my stories had just been translated into Spanish and published in an anthology of Chicano writing, and I wanted to show it to him. Ever since he recovered from a stroke two years ago, my father likes to spend his leisure hours horizontally. And that's how I found him, watching a Pedro Infante movie on Galavision and eating rice pudding.

There was a glass filmed with milk on the bedside table. There were several vials of pills and balled Kleenex. And on the floor, one black sock and a plastic urinal that I didn't want to look at but looked at anyway. Pedro Infante was about to burst into song, and my father was laughing.

I'm not sure if it was because my story was translated into Spanish, or because it was published in Mexico, or perhaps because the story dealt with Tepeyac, the *colonia* my father was raised in and the house he grew up in, but at any rate, my father punched the mute button on his remote control and read my story.

I sat on the bed next to my father and waited. He read it very slowly. As if he were reading each line over and over. He laughed at all the right places and read lines he liked out loud. He pointed and asked questions: "Is this So-and-so?" "Yes," I said. He kept reading.

When he was finally finished, after what seemed like hours, my father looked up and asked: "Where can we get more copies of this for the relatives?"

Of all the wonderful things that happened to me last year, that was the most wonderful.

PARAGRAPHING ACTIVITY 2.8

Following the suggestions presented earlier in this chapter, divide each of the following papers into paragraphs. Then reread the first (or second) draft of your paper, and make any paragraphing changes that you feel will improve the paper's effectiveness, including dividing overly long paragraphs and combining or developing very short paragraphs.

My Coach

I went out for wrestling my junior and senior years of high school. I hadn't done any sports until then, but some of my friends wrestled, so I decided to try it out. When I first met the coach he seemed like a pretty tough guy, and he was. He expected a lot out of you and worked you hard. But I also got to know my coach as a person, and he was one of the best people I ever knew. I was going through a hard time at home, with my dad having left my mom and sisters. He had done it before, and we didn't know when or if he'd come back. It was really hard on my mom, who had to work a lot and take care of us too, and I had to help out more around the house. There was a lot of strain at home. Wrestling became something to look forward to, and I became pretty good at it. Coach always encouraged me and said I had a lot of potential. He didn't cut me any slack, but I didn't mind working hard, and having someone say "Good job" and encouraging me felt good, something I never got from my dad. Coach was always encouraging all the guys and getting them to improve, and we had a good team because of him. My senior year was the best, and I was undefeated going into the league championships. I was picked to win, and our team had a good chance to take it all. In addition, the league championships were in our home gym, so we'd have the crowd behind us. The only problem I had in wrestling was I always struggled to make weight, because I wasn't a natural at the 145 pound class. I would rather have wrestled up a weight, but one of our best wrestlers was there, so I stayed a 145 and worked to keep my weight down. The day before the championship, I pretty much starved myself to make sure I made weight, and I came in three pounds under on match day. The trouble is, I felt a little weak, and hoped it wouldn't hurt me. I went through my first three matches undefeated, but I hadn't pinned anyone, which I usually could do. The championship match was a tough one, against a guy I'd barely beat in duels. It was a close match, but I could feel he was staying strong and I was getting weaker near the end. He ended up beating me 5 to 4, and my dream season was over. I had lost the match and let my team down and all the people who came to watch. Most of all, I felt I'd let my coach down, and I just sat on the mat, stunned. It was quiet in the gym, and I just sat there. Then coach was there by my side, and he picked me up and lifted me up over his head, like I had won, and then he gave me a big hug. "You did a great job, Isaiah," he said. "You gave it your best and just ran into a tough guy today. You've got nothing to be ashamed of." Then the other guys on the team came out to the mat and hugged me, and I had tears. That was the end of wrestling, but not my relationship with coach. I'd still come by his office and see him and talk to him, and he always had time for me. One day he said, "Isaiah, next year, if you're interested, you can come back and help me shape up the team. You can come to practice when you have time, and I can use you to demonstrate." That's when I really knew coach cared about me more than just as one of his wrestlers. He cared about me as a person, and wanted to stay in my life. I said, "Sure, coach," and now after my second year in college, I still go back to the gym and work out with the wrestling team, and sometimes go to matches with them.

An Understanding Mom

When I was in tenth grade, I had my first drink of alcohol. My mom would have been mad if she found out, but sooner or later she would find out anyway, and I would be in more trouble. When I was in tenth grade, I went to parties with my girlfriends. There was alcohol there, but I chose not to drink. My friends would drink and they would offer me some, but I just couldn't do it. Besides that, if my mom found out, she would never let me go out with my friends, and she would lose trust in me. I think that having a mother's trust is very important because once you lose that trust, you may never get it back. Then there was this one party that I had gone to with friends, and it was out in the country. Everything was going well, and people were drinking and having a good time. Then one of my friends offered me a beer. At first I was like, "No," but then I thought I would try some just to see how it tasted. I didn't like it. It tasted sick, and I was like, "How can you drink this?" She told me it's because it was my first beer that I had, and it tastes sick at first. I ended up having more, but not to the point where I was drunk and passed out. Everyone who was there was drunk and didn't know what he or she was doing. My friends were going to stay there because they were friends with the girl that was throwing the party. I didn't want to stay, so I called my mom and had her pick me up. My mom picked me up, and as we were driving, she asked me if I had drunk anything, and I told her, "No," and she didn't say anything, so I figured that she believed me, but for some odd reason I felt that she knew I was lying. When I got home, I went straight to bed and fell asleep. The next day as we were eating breakfast, my mom brought up if I drank again. She asked me, "So you didn't drink yesterday," and I told her, "No," and she said that she was proud of me. Inside I felt bad because I lied to my mom again, and I had never lied to my mom about anything. Later on that day, I told her that I had drunk beer at the party, and she looked at me and said, "I know it," and I was like, "What do you mean you knew that I drank?" She said that she could smell it on me. I felt bad deep down inside because she had caught me in a lie. I was grounded for a week, and I couldn't go out with my friends. My mom and I had a talk later on that day, and she was talking about her life when she was younger and how she was in my position, and she said that she was proud of me that I didn't get in the car with someone who was drinking. She was glad that I called her and had her pick me up. I kept going to parties after that, but didn't drink, and still had fun. My mom, instead of jumping on me and making me feel ashamed, had punished me fairly and even told me some of the things she had done as a teenager. She didn't lay a guilt trip on me, and she even said some positive things, like my not getting in a car with someone who had been drinking. I thought my mom handled the situation great, and it made me feel even closer to her and made me want to please her more. All I could ask of a mom is to treat me fairly and be understanding when I have some problems, and that's what my mom did. I didn't get away with anything, but I wasn't made to feel like a bad person or a bad daughter. I thank my mom for that.

USING EXAMPLES

Writers often clarify their ideas and capture their readers' interest by using examples. Examples often provide a human interest element to your writing and show readers exactly what you mean. A timely example will have readers responding, "I understand," or "That makes it clearer."

For example, a student may write, "My three-year-old daughter is a real character." What does that mean to readers? What does a "real character" do? Are people "real characters" in different ways? Notice how the following example personalizes and clarifies the student's statement:

My three-year-old daughter is a real character. For example, she likes to walk around with lampshades on her head. She also prefers walking backwards to forwards when there are people around to notice. She loves making strange sounds with her mouth and tongue, and she has at least twenty different grunting, chirping, cackling, and blowing sounds she makes. She also starts laughing wildly for no reason that I know of, until she has all of us laughing with her.

For another example, a student wrote, "Malcolm can intimidate people without even trying." What does that mean to readers? Maybe we think we can picture Malcolm, but we're just guessing. We need examples:

Malcolm can intimidate people without really trying. For example, when he walks into a room, all 6'5", 350 pounds of him, people tend to back up and stare. And when he talks in that loud, deep voice, he gets your attention. In addition, he has this scowl on his face a lot of the time, although it's just his normal look. Unless you get to know him, you wouldn't know Malcolm is one of the nicest people around.

Guidelines for Using Examples

The following guidelines will help you use examples effectively in your writing:

1. *Use examples to clarify general statements, statements that by themselves don't tell readers enough to get a clear picture or understanding.*

   For example, the following general statements need to be followed by examples:

   The swimming pool at my old high school is in terrible shape. (Describe it.)

   My uncle has the weirdest sense of humor. (Give examples.)

   It seems like Melinda can get away with anything. (Give an example.)

   I would call Freddie a sly flirt. (Explain what you mean.)

   A good back massage does wonders for me. (Describe what it does.)

2. *Use examples to help readers understand exactly what you mean:*

   Vitamin C is truly a wonder drug. (Give examples of what it can do.)

   The Arkansas State football program is a sleeping giant. (Explain what you mean.)

   Aunt Thelma is a bridge junkie. (Give examples.)

3. *Use examples to help convince readers that you are right or correct:*

   Six-cylinder engines can get better gas mileage than four-cylinder. (Convince us.)

   The best time to buy stocks is during a recession. (Prove it.)

   Drinking diet soda is as good for you as drinking water. (Convince us.)

   This summer's heat wave is caused by global warming. (Provide evidence.)

REVISION ACTIVITY 2.9

Read the following paragraph. Insert examples in places where they would help clarify what the writer means and create interest for readers. Make up your own examples.

Uncle Rob was a scary old man to my sister and me when we were little. First, his face was sort of frightening looking. Second, he would scare us with stories about what happened to little kids who visited him. Third, he loved to hide behind doors and then jump out and say "boo" when we'd open them, make strange sounds when we were napping and then tell us the house was haunted, or jump up and down on the roof to make us think there were monsters up there. He just loved scaring us to death.

REVISION ACTIVITY 2.10

Reread your latest draft and see whether you have provided good examples to clarify general statements and make your paper more interesting. Add examples where you think they would help, or change examples if you think of a better one.

SENTENCE WORDING

Like most writers, an important part of your draft revision process is improving your sentence wording. When you first struggle to express a thought, the words seldom come out as smoothly or clearly as you may wish. Writers share the task of reworking first-draft sentences, and the result is usually a more clearly and concisely worded paper.

Wording Problems

The following wording problems are common in first-draft sentences:

1. *Wordiness:* using more words than necessary to express a thought. This often occurs in first drafts as writers get down their ideas in whatever words come to them.

FIRST DRAFT	I am late for school because of the fact that my car wouldn't start.
REVISED	I am late for school because my car wouldn't start.
FIRST DRAFT	The reason why I did well on my test was because I studied hard for it.
REVISED	I did well on my test because I studied hard.

2. *Awkward phrasing:* using words and phrases that don't tie together smoothly and logically. Awkward phrasing is again the result of writers trying out their ideas on paper for the first time.

FIRST DRAFT   Lunch could be gotten in the cafeteria in the hours between eleven and two o'clock.

REVISED   The cafeteria is open for lunch between eleven and two o'clock.

FIRST DRAFT   Although we went to the swap meet, but we didn't buy anything.

REVISED   Although we went to the swap meet, we didn't buy anything.

3. *Poor word choice:* not using the best word to express a thought. With first drafts, writers use some words that don't quite hit the mark, but for lack of a better word at the time, they move on and rethink the word during the revision process.

FIRST DRAFT   We were excited about a lot of different stuff in the intramural track meet.

REVISED   We were excited about participating in different events in the intramural track meet.

FIRST DRAFT   Jonathan had learned all his children to use a computer.

REVISED   Jonathan had taught all his children to use a computer.

ONLINE ACTIVITY: ELIMINATING WORDINESS

There are some excellent suggestions and exercises on eliminating wordiness in your sentences at the online site for Purdue University's Resources for Writers. Go online to http://owl.english.purdue.edu/handouts/general/gl_concise.html.

When you arrive, read the ten suggestions for eliminating wordiness in your sentences. Next, click on the underlined "exercises" near the top of the page, which takes you to a group of activities for eliminating wordiness. Do the three exercises, and then apply what you learn, along with the text's suggestions, to the upcoming exercise and to your first draft.

SENTENCE REVISION ACTIVITY 2.11

The following first-draft sentences need revising. The sentences have problems with wordiness, awkward phrasing, and poor word choices. Revise and rewrite each sentence to make it smoother and clearer. Then reread your latest draft and revise sentences to make them smoother and clearer, and to eliminate wordiness.

FIRST DRAFT   My goal is to lose six pounds of body weight.

REVISED   My goal is to lose six pounds.

FIRST DRAFT   On the left side of the ring my name is on it in initials.

REVISED   On the left side of the ring are my initials.

1. The main reason why I like my job is the fact that it is so close to home.

2. I would be glad if I did well enough in college to gain my goal.

3. To avoid bad luck, parents want their children on New Year's Day to be on their very best behavior and to avoid the use of vulgar expressions in China.

4. If I could look into the future ten years from now, I would like to see a pretty image of myself as a successful person.

5. Almost all of the credits from Kings River College are able to be transferred to the school of your choosing, plus it is much less money to go there.

6. You do want to be happy for the rest of your life until you die because if you're not happy with what you're doing, then you're going to be miserable for the rest of your entire life.

7. I have been to hospitals and seen sick kids, and I would like to help them, for instance, kids with AIDS, cancer, bad burns, and a variety of sicknesses.

8. Everything was better for my family before my father died, especially for my mother, because she would always cry and remember him on special occasions like on Christmas and Thanksgiving.

9. College is not like high school, because you can choose your classes at the best time of day for you.

10. I want a house with lots of rooms, but I want one room that has mirrors all around, on the floor, on the ceiling, just everywhere.

FINAL EDITING

Now that you have revised your paper for content and wording improvement, you are ready to proofread the latest draft for any remaining errors. When proofreading, pay particular attention to those areas where writers typically have problems, such as run-on sentences, misspellings, or comma omissions. Your goal is to identify and correct any errors to produce an error-free final draft for readers.

PROOFREADING GUIDELINES

As you check your paper for errors, be sure to cover the following areas:

1. *Make sure you have a period at the end of each sentence.* Look in particular for sentences that are run together without a period or that are separated by a comma instead of a period. If you have problems with run-ons, review the upcoming section on "Run-on Sentences" before proofreading.

2. *Make sure you haven't left off any word endings.* Since your paper is probably written in the past tense, check to make sure you have an *ed* ending on all regular past tense verbs. If you need some work on *ed* endings with past tense verbs or on spelling irregular verbs correctly, refer to the "Correct Usage" section in the Appendix at the back of this book, which deals with regular and irregular past tense verbs.

3. *Check each sentence carefully for misspelled words.* Check the spelling of any word that doesn't appear right to you, and check your use of homophones such as there/their/they're, its/it's, and your/you're. Use the spelling check on your word processor.

4. *Check the internal punctuation of each sentence.* Make sure you have used commas in series of three or more words or groups of words, before conjunctions (and, so, but, or, for, yet) in a compound sentence, after introductory groups of words, and with "who" or "which" clauses. Also make sure you haven't inserted commas where they aren't needed. If you included any conversation in your paper, check your use of quotation marks. (See the upcoming section on "Quotation Marks.")

5. *Check your use of subject pronouns.* Make sure you have used the proper subject pronouns—I, he, she, they, we, you—and haven't begun sentences with "My sister and me," "Me and my cousins," "Frances's mother and her," or "The Smiths and them." (See the upcoming section on "Subject Pronouns.")

EDITING ACTIVITY 2.12

In small groups and following the guidelines presented, proofread the following student draft for errors and make the necessary corrections.

My Girlfriend

STUDENT SAMPLE DRAFT   I met the most special person in my life when I was in second grade. She use to sit next to me in class, but I didn't talk to her because I was to shy and scared. We didn't talk or anything we didn't even become friends until the seventh grade when I started to hang out with her brother Charles. We were good friends back then, now he's in jail. I ended up going out with Tamyra in the seventh grade, we lasted two weeks until she left me. I ended up hating her for leaving me but I couldn't do anything about it.

Our first year in high school we started going out again. We became good friends as well. I don't know why she went out with me, that was when I started getting in trouble. I started drinking and partying with an older crowd, which was a big mistake. I didn't care about anything at the time.

Tamyra left me again because she seen the way I was. I told her lies to get her back and it worked. I lied a lot to her and she kept coming back to me. I'm not proud of that but I didn't want to lose her. I kept doing all those bad things behind her back. We stayed that way for a long time until she found out again. That's when she told me that I had to choose between her and my friends. I didn't know what to do at the time so I left for a few months.

When I came back six months later a lot of my friends were in jail or getting out of jail. That's when I made my decision. I had decided not to end up like my friends and chose to stay with my girlfriend. She looked out for me more then my friends did anyway.

Now I have new friends and a better life. It's been five years and I'm still with Tamyra. If she had never made me chose between her and my friends I don't think that I would be here today. I would probably be out getting into some kind of trouble.

EDITING ACTIVITY 2.13

Proofread your latest draft for errors and make necessary corrections. Your instructor may have you go over the upcoming sections on "Punctuation" and "Correct Usage" before proofreading.

When you have corrected any errors, write or print out the final draft of your paper to share with classmates and your instructor.

JOURNAL ENTRY SEVEN

Under Journal Entry Seven in your notebook, record the kinds of errors, if any, you identified and corrected in your draft. What particular kinds of errors do you still need to work on eliminating in your writing?

SENTENCE PROBLEMS

This section reviews what you learned about run-on sentences in Unit One. Because run-on sentences are an ongoing problem for many writers, they will be covered at different times throughout the text.

Run-on Sentences

Here is a summary of points on run-on sentences presented in Unit One.

1. A run-on sentence is usually two sentences run together without a period. (Sholanda doesn't need to work on run-on sentence correction she never runs on sentences in her writing.)

2. Often sentences within a run-on are separated incorrectly by a comma. (Jules enjoys long walks in the morning, he usually takes his cocker spaniel with him.)

3. A pronoun (I, he, she, you, we, they, it) most frequently begins the second sentence within a run-on sentence. The following introductory words also begin the second sentence of many run-ons: there, then, the, that, this, those, these.

4. To correct run-on sentences, put a period after the first sentence or combine the sentences with a joining word, such as *and, but, so, yet, because, until, before, although, unless.* As a general rule, separate longer run-on sentences and combine shorter ones.

RUN-ON ACTIVITY 2.14

Correct any run-on sentences in the following paragraph by either inserting a period at the end of a complete sentence and capitalizing the first letter of the next sentence, or by combining the two sentences within the run-on sentence with a joining word, such as *and, but, so,* or *for.*

EXAMPLE   The college band has to sit behind the end zone at football games there is no room for them in the stands. They are pretty upset about losing their seats on the south side of the stadium, those seats have now been reserved for spectators for the visiting team.

REVISED   The college band has to sit behind the end zone at football games, *for* there is no room for them in the stands. They are pretty upset about losing their seats on the south side of the stadium. Those seats have now been reserved for spectators for the visiting team.

The cost of health insurance went up dramatically this year, in some areas of the state, it went up by as much as 30%. Many employers, particularly in the public sector, did not have enough money to pay the full additional cost of premiums they passed some of that cost onto employees. Negotiations over health insurance have been long and drawn out this year. Both employers and employees are looking for ways to cut costs, they are looking at higher deductible rates and larger co-payments for office calls and prescription drugs. They are also looking to get into larger employee insurance pools, joining employees from a number of different public agencies across the state, to help drive down costs. There is no good solution to the increases in health care costs, people need health insurance, and employers have an obligation to provide it.

PUNCTUATION

Because you may have included some dialogue (conversation) in your personal relationship paper, check the proper use of quotation marks in this section.

Quotation Marks

In any paper you write, you may on occasion want to include the actual words that someone said to add interest to your paper. Another time, you may want to quote an expert on a subject to provide support for a position you've taken. To show that a person is talking in your paper, you need to do two things:

1. Put *quotation marks* (" ") around the spoken words.

2. Make reference to the person speaking.

Here are some examples of direct quotations correctly punctuated.

EXAMPLES John said, "Where are you going with my hammer?"

"I don't want to go shopping in these curlers," said Harriet.

Alvin interrupted Mary by saying, "Stop telling those flattering lies about me."

My mother said, "You have always had a bad temper. Remember the time you threw your brother out the window?"

"I want you to go," Mike insisted. "We need you to liven up the party."

"Alice's biggest weakness," her sister admitted, "is that she can't say 'no.'"

Here are the basic rules for punctuating direct quotations, as demonstrated in the example sentences, and a word about indirect quotations.

1. Quotation marks go around only the spoken words: John said, "Where are you going?"

2. Quotation marks always go *outside* of end marks: Maria replied, "I ~ am going home."

3. The reference to the speaker may come at the beginning, in the middle, or at the end of a quote. A comma always separates the reference to the speaker from the quote itself: "I don't believe," said Mark, "that we have met."

4. If a quote contains two or more sentences together, the quotation marks are placed in front of the first sentence and after the last sentence only: Juan said, "I am very tired. I am also hungry and thirsty."

5. A comma comes after the last word in a quote only if the sentence continues after the quote. Otherwise, an end mark is used: "You are a good friend," said Julia.

6. If the reference to the speaker is in the middle of a quote, the quoted words on both sides of the reference are in quotation marks. (See rule 3.)

7. When you change speakers in a paper, you usually begin a new paragraph.

8. Direct quotations are the exact words of the speaker. An *indirect quotation* tells what the speaker said *as told by the writer*: Jack said that he needs a second job. Mary told me that she was tired of school. Indirect quotations are *not put in quotation marks* because they are not the words of a speaker.

QUOTATION ACTIVITY 2.15

Most of the following sentences are direct quotations that need punctuating with quotation marks. Punctuate the quotations correctly following the rules just given. If a sentence is an indirect quotation, don't put it in quotes. When you finish, check your latest draft for correct usage of quotation marks.

EXAMPLE   If you don't stop biting your nails, you'll draw blood said Claire.

REVISED   "If you don't stop biting your nails, you'll draw blood," said Claire.

1. Hank said Please bring me a glass of Alka-Seltzer.

2. The trouble with school said Muriel is the classes.

3. I know what I'm going to do after my last final whispered Allyson.

4. Freda admitted I have very oily hair. I have to wash it twice a day.

5. That's a beautiful ring exclaimed Bob Where did you buy it?

6. No one said Millie is leaving this house. We have a mess to clean up!

7. Charlotte said that her nephew from Miami would arrive by bus.

8. Teddy said My niece will be on the same bus as your nephew.

9. Maria said that you would help me with my algebra.

10. Will you please help me with my lab report for botany? asked Freddie.

CORRECT USAGE

Each "Correct Usage" section presents some basic rules of grammar to help you eliminate problems you may have in a paper. Since your paper for this unit involves other people, this section covers the proper use of subject pronouns in your writing.

Subject Pronouns

The following basic rules will help you use subject pronouns correctly in your writing:

1. Subject pronouns are always the same: I, he, she, we, you, it, they.

2. The following pronouns are *not* used as subjects: me, him, her, us, them, myself, herself, himself, ourselves, yourself, themselves.

3. The most common subject pronoun errors involve compound subjects.

   INCORRECT   John and <u>me</u> went skating. Mary and <u>him</u> are a couple.

   The Ludlow family and <u>them</u> met for brunch.
   Felix, Katerina, and <u>her</u> look great together.

4. A good technique for selecting the correct pronoun form with compound subjects is to consider the pronoun by itself. For example, in the sentence "John and me went skating," would you say, "Me went skating"? In the sentence "The Ludlow family and them met for brunch," would you say, "Them met for brunch"? The incorrect forms stand out badly by themselves, and the correct forms—*I* and *they*—sound correct.

EXAMPLES	

INCORRECT	Jonathan, Syd, and me like tuna sandwiches.
CORRECT	Jonathan, Syd, and I like tuna sandwiches.
INCORRECT	Samantha and him are excellent mechanics.
CORRECT	Samantha and he are excellent mechanics.
INCORRECT	Fran's mother and her don't want to go shopping in the rain.
CORRECT	Fran's mother and she don't want to go shopping in the rain.
INCORRECT	Alice, Alex, and them did well on the fitness test.
CORRECT	Alice, Alex, and they did well on the fitness test.

SUBJECT PRONOUN ACTIVITY 2.16

Underline the correct subject pronoun in each of the following sentences. Then proofread your latest draft for correct usage of subject pronouns.

EXAMPLES   Sue and (<u>I</u>, me) belong to the same business sorority.

I don't think that you and (<u>she</u>, her) really hate each other.

1. The Smiths, the Gonzaleses, and (we, us) will meet at the bottom of the mountain.

2. Shirley, (he, him), and (I, me) are studying together tonight.

3. Fred and (they, them) quit their jobs on the same day.

4. Do you think that Gladys, Thelma, and (she, her) are triplets?

5. I'm tired of wandering around the museum, but Gwen and (they, them) certainly aren't.

6. Are you and (they, them) still obligated to attend the supermarket opening?

7. Matty and (I, me) don't have anything in common.

8. Phil, my brothers, and (I, me) went ice skating at Mill Pond.

9. (We, Us) and (they, them) are archrivals in bocce ball.

10. (She, Her) and (he, him) don't see eye to eye on anything.

JOURNAL ENTRY EIGHT

Under Journal Entry Eight, relate how useful the grammar usage activities are for you. Can you apply the things you learn to your writing? Are you learning things that you didn't know or had forgotten, or are you just reviewing what you already knew?

WRITING REVIEW

At the end of each unit you apply what you have learned to a final writing assignment. For this unit, you will write a second personal relationship paper about a person who made a different impact on your life than the first person you wrote about.

WRITING PROCESS

To write your paper, follow the steps presented, which summarize the writing process for this unit.

1. Write about a person that has made a very different impact on your life than the first person you wrote about. Write about someone you know well and your relationship with him or her.

2. Once you have selected a person to write about, your next prewriting task is to generate some ideas that you may include in your paper. Answer the following questions to help you explore your topic and list some of the ideas you may include in your first draft.

   a. In a sentence, how would you characterize your relationship with this person?

   b. What are your feelings toward this person, and why do you think you feel this way?

   c. What are three or four qualities or traits that this person possesses?

   d. What is at least one example or incident that would show readers each quality or trait?

   e. In what way or ways has this person made an impact on your life (for example, by pushing you to work hard, by always being there for you when you need help, by criticizing everything you do, by loving you the way you are, by giving you good advice, by constantly picking on you, etc.)?

   f. What are some examples or incidents that would show readers the way or ways in which the person has made an impact on your life?

   g. What do I want to keep in mind about my readers (classmates) as I think about my topic, and what might be my purpose in writing to them about this particular person?

3. When you finish your prewriting work, write the first draft of your paper following these guidelines:

   a. *Make use of your prewriting plans.* From your prewriting, you have a basic idea of what you want to write, something to help you get started and continue writing. However, feel free to add ideas that come to mind and to change other things that you aren't satisfied with. Your prewriting plan provides a general direction to follow rather than an unchangeable direction. You will probably discover new things to write as you go.

   b. *Don't worry about perfect wording.* Get your ideas down using the wording that comes to you first. Don't labor endlessly over a sentence to make it "perfect." You will revise and improve your wording in the next draft.

c. *Don't worry about making some mistakes.* You can take care of a misspelled word or an omitted comma when you edit your writing. Now is not the time to worry about mistakes. A first draft should flow fairly smoothly, and if you are constantly looking for errors to correct, you will spend more time than you need and not concentrate on the content of your writing, which is most important.

d. *Keep in mind that writing is a recursive process.* Writers continually go back and reread what they've written in the last sentence or paragraph to keep them on track, to help them generate new ideas, and to make sure their sentences follow logically one to the next. Often, ideas that writers include in a draft are not in their minds when they start but come to them as they write. Much of the momentum for generating new ideas comes from going back and rereading what you've already written. All writers do it.

e. *Providing good examples is critical for showing readers what the person you are writing about is like and your relationship with him or her.* Each time you provide a quality the person possesses or something about your relationship, try to include an example.

f. *Keep in mind your audience and purpose.* Your reading audience for this paper is your classmates, and your purpose is whatever you want it to be. While you should have your readers and purpose in mind as you write your first draft, don't write every sentence with the thought, "What are my classmates going to think of this?" or "Does this sentence tie in to my purpose?" Such thoughts will slow your writing and perhaps keep you from writing what you really want. Remember, when you rewrite your draft, you can go back and make changes that you think will make your paper more interesting for readers or more true to your purpose, *which might even change as you write.*

Uncle Prine

STUDENT SAMPLE   My family didn't visit Uncle Prine and his wife that often, but when we did it was always memorable. My brother and I were young when we visited them, between the years of six and twelve, when we still could be scared by adults. Uncle Prine was an expert at scaring children.

He must have been in his sixties, although he looked even older. He had a red face, big ears, a big nose with veins in it, a sly grin, and eyes that I can only describe as crazy looking: very blue but kind of wild looking like a crazy person. I remember he used to sit out on their old front porch in a rocking chair, and any time my brother and I went outside, we had to go past Uncle Prine.

He'd always call us over, that crazy look in his eyes, and I knew he was going to say something scary. I remember one time he said, "You kids watch out playing out back. There are snakes back there that crawl out from under the house and bite little kids. They'll get you!" We'd get all scared and stand very still and after a while, he'd let out this cackling laugh and say "Gotcha!" and just keep laughing. I guess we knew then that he was teasing, but he never said so, so we always played out back with an eye out for those snakes.

Another time my family had gone somewhere and come back to the house. I ran up to the house fast because I had to go to the bathroom. When I ran across the front porch, Uncle Prine said, "Where ya going sissy so fast?" "Gotta go to the bathroom," I said. "Wouldn't do that," said Uncle Prine. "There's a lion in the bathroom, he's been in there all morning, and he'll eat you up." Being young, I didn't think about how impossible that was, that a lion would somehow be in Uncle Prine's bathroom, but it scared me so bad that I just stood there and wet my pants. I started crying and Uncle Prine let out a hoot. My mother scolded him for scaring me like that, but Uncle Prine just sat there with that sly grin and those crazy eyes.

One day mom told us that Uncle Prine had passed away from cancer and we were going to see Aunt Sarah. We went, and it seemed strange not seeing Uncle Prine sitting in that chair on the porch waiting for us. I missed him in a way because as a kid, getting a good scare wasn't the worst thing in the world, and that was his way I guess of paying attention to us. Years later I still remember him very well because he gave me some of the best scares of my childhood, and what I also remember is how much he seemed to enjoy it and how he would laugh and laugh. I guess he was just like a big kid himself.

4. When you finish your first draft, set it aside for a while, and then reread it, applying the following revision suggestions:

a. *Additions:* Read your draft, looking for places where you might add an example or incident to help reveal to readers more clearly the person you are writing about or your relationship with him or her.

b. *Improved wording:* Read each sentence to see if a change in wording would make it clearer or smoother.

c. *Paragraphing:* Check to see if you have divided your paper into paragraphs as you move to new ideas in your paper. If you have not paragraphed your paper, read your draft and find places where you might end one paragraph and begin another: a new idea, a different point, an example, a conclusion.

d. *Improved organization:* Read your draft to see if any sentences or paragraphs seem out of place, and decide whether they would fit better somewhere else in the paper, with other sentences (or a paragraph) related to them.

e. *Audience and purpose:* Reread your draft with your reading audience—your classmates—and your purpose in mind. Consider making changes that would make the paper more interesting or informative to your classmates, and that would help you accomplish your purpose for writing.

5. Write the second draft of your paper, including all revisions that you feel will improve it.

6. When you've finished your latest draft, proofread it carefully for errors, applying the following guidelines for error correction, and make the necessary corrections:

a. *Make sure you have a period at the end of each sentence.* Look in particular for sentences that are run together without a period or that are separated by a comma instead of a period. If you have problems with run-ons, review the section on "Run-on Sentences" before proofreading.

b. *Make sure you haven't left off any word endings.* Since your paper is probably written in the past tense, check to make sure you have an *ed* ending on all regular past tense verbs. If you need some work on *ed* endings with past tense verbs or on spelling irregular verbs correctly, refer to the "Correct Usage" section in the Appendix at the back of the book, which deals with regular and irregular past tense verbs.

c. *Check each sentence carefully for misspelled words.* Check the spelling of any word that doesn't appear right to you, and check your use of homonyms such as there/their/they're, its/it's, and your/you're. Use the spelling check on your word processor.

d. *Check the internal punctuation of each sentence.* Make sure you have used commas in series of three or more words or groups of words, before conjunctions (and, so, but, or, for, yet) in a compound sentence, and after introductory groups of words. Also make sure you haven't inserted commas where they aren't needed. If you included any conversation in your paper, check your use of quotation marks. (See the section on "Quotation Marks" in this unit.)

e. *Check your use of subject pronouns.* Make sure you have used the proper subject pronouns—I, he, she, they, we, you—and haven't begun sentences with "My sister and me," "Me and my cousins," "Franny's mother and her," or "The Smiths and them." (See the section on "Subject Pronouns" in this unit.)

7. After you have corrected any errors, write the final error-free draft of your paper to share with your classmates and instructor.

Writing about Opinions

Every day we make judgments and decisions based on our *opinions*: our beliefs about what is right or best, based on our experience and knowledge. Our opinions help us decide where to eat lunch, what to watch on television, what clothes to buy, what to do on a Saturday night, whom to vote for, what jobs to apply for, and whom to spend time with. Our opinions affect most of what we do and say.

Writing about opinions gives you the opportunity to accomplish a number of things: to consider seriously a particular opinion you hold; to provide support for an opinion to convince readers of its merit; to use effective examples to help provide that support; and to employ opening, middle, and concluding paragraphs to introduce, support, and reinforce your opinion. In addition, you will include a *thesis statement*, which expresses your opinion on a particular topic, and organize your essay in a way that you will also find useful for future writing.

For readers, the merit of your opinion is often based on the quality of support you provide, and a well-supported opinion can influence people. A main purpose of this unit is to help you learn to provide strong, believable support for your opinions. You will also learn the value of differing opinions, to respect opinions different from your own, and to evaluate and even reconsider your opinions when exposed to different viewpoints.

PREWRITING

For most writers, prewriting usually includes deciding on a topic and what to write about it. Prewriting often includes generating ideas for a paper and organizing them in some manner. Through prewriting, thought, and planning, writers often answer the following questions:

1. What am I going to write about?

2. What approach do I want to take?

3. What may I want to include in my writing?

4. How might I best organize my ideas?

5. Who should read my writing, and why?

While most writers consider these types of questions during prewriting, they don't all follow the same process. Some may deal with questions in tandem (such as deciding on the topic and approach together), others may give some questions much thought (such as topic selection) and other questions little or none (such as organization), and still others may not find answers to all questions during prewriting—waiting, for example, to discover the best organizational plan during drafting. You create your personal prewriting process by discovering what works best for you, which may differ depending on the writing task.

Your prewriting activities for this unit include selecting a topic, generating a thesis statement based on your opinion about the topic, listing ideas to include in your paper, and considering how to organize your ideas most effectively. Rather than providing you with a rigid formula, the prewriting activities give you strategies for finding the best ways to put your thoughts on paper.

THESIS STATEMENT

While the term *thesis statement* may sound rather formal or imposing, your *thesis* for an essay is simply the viewpoint you are going to express and support on a particular topic. For example, if you are writing about the college cafeteria, depending on your opinion, your *thesis* might be, "The college cafeteria is a convenient place to get a healthy, inexpensive lunch," or, "For my money, I'd rather go off campus to any fast food restaurant than eat at the college cafeteria." Whatever your thesis statement is, it reflects the opinion on the topic that you are going to develop in your essay.

A *thesis statement* provides direction for all writers, whether writing a letter ("Just writing to let you know how finals went") or a lengthy research paper ("Based on extensive research, I have concluded that the hole in the ozone layer over the North Pole does not pose an environmental threat"). For much of the writing you do, a clear writing focus, which the thesis provides, benefits both you and your readers. To that end, it is important to decide on a tentative thesis statement early in the writing process.

The following points clarify what a thesis is and what it does:

1. A thesis expresses *the main idea* you want to develop on your topic. It often expresses your *opinion* on the topic.

2. Your thesis determines the way in which you develop a topic in a paper. You write your paper *in support* of your thesis.

3. Without a thesis, a paper may lack direction. A thesis provides a *controlling idea* to tie your thoughts together and to help readers understand your intent.

4. There is no right or wrong thesis; it reflects the way you think or feel about a particular topic. A paper's effectiveness rests strongly on how well you *support* your thesis.

Here are examples of thesis statements students have generated to express their opinion on a variety of topics. Notice that for the same topic, writers have come up with different thesis statements, which would lead to very different papers.

Topic	hybrid cars
Thesis	In an energy-conscious world, hybrid cars will dominate the market within ten years.
Thesis	While an improvement over gas guzzling cars, hybrids are not the answer to our vehicle pollution problem.
Thesis	Hybrid cars deliver far less than they promise.
Topic	daylight saving time
Thesis	I'd like to live on daylight saving time all year around.
Thesis	For a nocturnal person, daylight saving is a disaster.
Thesis	Daylight saving has both advantages and disadvantages.
Topic	gun control
Thesis	Gun control laws are a threat to every law-abiding American.
Thesis	Gun control is the only way to reduce violent crime in America.
Thesis	The only effective gun control is the elimination of handguns.
Topic	*The Office* TV series
Thesis	*The Office* is the best television comedy today.

THESIS   *The Office* is a quirky television comedy that misses the mark.

THESIS   The success of *The Office* rests on the shoulders of its talented star Steve Carell.

THESIS CONSIDERATION

Deciding on a thesis for your topic is an important part of the writing process. Not only does the thesis help you develop your paper, it reveals to readers how you think or feel about a topic. Whatever time you may spend deciding on a thesis is well spent.

When thinking about a thesis for a specific topic, consider the following:

1. *What is my opinion on the topic?* Don't worry about how other people may feel, or what you think readers might want to hear. Your thesis reflects your own belief.

2. *How could I best support my thesis in a paper?* No matter how strongly you feel about a topic, the effectiveness of your paper depends on how convincingly you can support your thesis. For example, you may believe that there are other human-like creatures on other planets in the universe, but to convince a skeptical reading audience, you must provide some strong, believable support.

THESIS ACTIVITY 3.1

Considering the questions just presented, write thesis statements that express your opinion on any five of the following topics. (Fill in each blank with your specific choice of topics.)

EXAMPLES   TOPIC   a particular hobby (writing songs)

THESIS   Writing songs is my one creative outlet.

1. TOPIC   a particular town (_____)

   THESIS   _____

2. TOPIC   a particular team (_____)

   THESIS   _____

3. TOPIC   a particular TV program (_____)

   THESIS   _____

4. TOPIC   a particular job (_____)

   THESIS   _____

5. Topic   a particular holiday (_____)

Thesis   _____

6. Topic   a particular school (_____)

Thesis   _____

7. Topic   a particular type of music (_____)

Thesis   _____

8. Topic   a particular pet (_____)

Thesis   _____

9. Topic   a particular restaurant (_____)

Thesis   _____

10. Topic   a particular book or movie (_____)

Thesis   _____

TOPIC SELECTION

For your writing assignment for this unit, select a topic following these guidelines:

1. Choose a specific topic that interests you and that you have an opinion on. You may select a topic from the previous activity, or another of your choice.

2. Choose a topic that you are knowledgeable about.

3. Choose a topic that might interest your classmates, the reading audience for your paper.

TOPIC SELECTION ACTIVITY 3.2

In small groups, share with classmates different topic ideas and your opinion on each. Discuss differing opinions on the same topics, and analyze where these opinions come from: why people feel or believe the way they do. The purpose of the group activity is to help you decide on a topic, and to discuss and understand better differing opinions that people hold.

TOPIC SELECTION ACTIVITY 3.3

After you have finished the group activity, decide on a topic for your upcoming paper and the opinion that you want to support. After you have selected a topic, write a tentative thesis statement for your paper—a sentence expressing your opinion on the topic.

STUDENT SAMPLE   Since I returned to college after many years, I was interested in what college would be like twenty years later. I think I'd like to write about what college is like from my perspective as an older returning student. It might interest my classmates to view college through my eyes, whether they are my age or younger, and compare it with their own experience.

TOPIC	Returning to college as an older student.
OPINION	A lot of things have changed.
THESIS STATEMENT	In the twenty years since I last attended college, a lot of changes have occurred.

LISTING IDEAS

Now that you have selected a topic, formed your opinion, and written a tentative thesis statement, you can consider the kinds of support you might include in your paper. One way that writers generate support for a thesis is to make a list of supporting ideas.

Listing your supporting points is beneficial in different ways:

1. You have a number of points to develop in your draft, which will help you get started and continue writing.

2. From your list, you can decide on an organization of your paper: the best order for presenting your supporting points in the draft.

3. After listing your supporting points, you can consider how you might develop each point in a paragraph, or you can come up with specific examples to use.

STUDENT SAMPLE   The returning student who wrote about what college is like listed the following points to support her thesis:

THESIS	In the twenty years since I last attended college, a lot of changes have occurred.

SUPPORTING POINTS

1. A more ethnically diverse group of students

2. A wider age range of students

3. Much better food on campus

4. The big impact of computers

5. My change in attitude

After listing these supporting points, she put them in the order she wanted to present them in the paper, and she added some examples after each point to include in her first draft.

Supporting points in writing order, followed by examples:

1. A wider age range of students (students my age and older, students in their twenties and thirties, many married and working)

2. A more ethnically diverse group of students (more foreign students, especially from Asia and the Middle East, and more African-American and Latino students)

3. The big impact of computers (all library files computerized, computers in composition and business classrooms, open computer labs around campus, Internet access)

4. Much better food (cafeteria more like a food court today, with all kinds of ethnic foods and franchised restaurants)

5. My change in attitude (more serious and motivated, more career direction than when I was young)

As you can see, by making a list of points, you generate ideas to support your opinion, you have some ideas to develop in individual paragraphs, you have an organizational plan for your paper, and you have some examples for developing each supporting point. A simple prewriting technique like listing can pay great dividends.

LISTING ACTIVITY 3.4

For your writing topic, do the following prewriting work:

1. Make a list of four or five points to support your opinion (thesis support).

2. Decide on the best order to present your supporting points in the paper, considering their similarity and relative importance (you might save the most important point for last, or lead and conclude with the most important points).

3. After each point, list some examples you might include in your draft.

AUDIENCE AND PURPOSE

Once again, your audience for your opinion paper is your classmates. When considering your reading audience, and your purpose for writing to them, keep these questions in mind:

1. How much do my classmates know about my topic? Can I write about it as if they have similar knowledge, or do I need to make sure to clarify some things that may be new to them?

2. What might my classmates' opinion be on my topic? Might some students feel very differently than I do? Might there be a range of different

opinions on the topic? How might I take into consideration my classmates' opinions as I am presenting and supporting my own?

3. What is my purpose in sharing my opinion with my classmates? What
do I want them to get out of the paper? Do I hope that they will learn
something they may not know? Do I want to try to convince them of
the merit of my opinion? Or do I want them to get to know me better
by understanding my opinion on this topic?

**STUDENT SAMPLE
RESPONSE**

1. Since many of my classmates are younger than I am, they probably
won't know what school was like twenty years ago, so I'll have to
make sure to show the differences clearly.

2. Since many of my classmates are younger than I am, they probably don't
have an opinion on this topic, or at least I'll assume that as I write.

3. I'm not really trying to convince anyone of anything, so I guess my
purpose is to inform and to show students how much college has
changed in some ways, but as I think about it, I think I will try to convince them in the ending that it has changed for the better. *In fact, I
might change my thesis sentence to include that thought.*

AUDIENCE ACTIVITY 3.5

Discuss with a classmate your topic and opinion, and provide answers to
the questions under "Audience and Purpose." Get feedback from your
classmate, who is a representative of the reading audience for your paper.

JOURNAL ENTRY NINE

Under Journal Entry Nine in your notebook, relate how the prewriting
activities for your opinion paper have helped you prepare to write. What
particular activities, if any, did you find most useful?

FIRST DRAFTS

After selecting a topic, forming an opinion, generating a thesis sentence for
your paper, listing and ordering supporting points, and adding examples
under each point, you are ready to write your first draft. To write a paper
in support of a thesis, consider the following suggestions:

THESIS-DIRECTED DRAFT

1. Write your draft in three parts: a beginning, a middle, and ending.

BEGINNING   In an introductory paragraph or two, introduce your
topic, create some interest for readers (so they will want

to continue reading), and include your thesis sentence expressing your opinion on the topic.

MIDDLE   Present the supporting points for your thesis, which tell *why* you believe as you do. As a general rule, present and develop each supporting point in a separate paragraph, using examples from your prewriting to help develop each paragraph.

ENDING   In a paragraph or two, conclude your paper by leaving readers with a sense of completion. You might reinforce your thesis in some manner, summarize your supporting points, or emphasize a particularly important point. Make sure through your ending that readers understand your purpose for writing.

2. As you write your draft, feel free to add ideas you didn't think of during prewriting, or to revise your organizational plan. Drafting is a process of discovery, and your prewriting work, while important, provides a general road map rather than a precise route to follow.

3. Keep your thesis in mind as you write. Everything in your draft should be related in some way to supporting your opinion expressed in the thesis sentence.

4. Keep your audience (classmates) and purpose in mind as you write: what do you want them to get out of the paper?

5. As with all first drafts, your goal is to get your ideas on paper, so don't be concerned about perfect wording or an occasional error.

ONLINE ACTIVITY: PREWRITING TIPS

For further prewriting tips to help you get started with your writing, go to Purdue University's Resources for Writers online address http://owl. english.purdue.edu/handouts/general/index.html.

When you reach the website, scroll down to "Planning/Starting to Write." You will find three different "planning/invention" sites that provide a range of prewriting and writing suggestions to help you get started. Read the suggestions and make note of those that seem particularly useful. Try applying them to your upcoming draft.

DRAFTING ACTIVITY 3.6

Before writing your first draft, read the following essay by "What's the Deal with iPods?" Monica Early. In small groups, do the following:

1. Identify the opening paragraph(s) and the thesis sentence expressing the author's opinion. Discuss what is accomplished in the paper's opening.

2. Identify each supporting point in the middle paragraphs, and the examples clarifying each point.

3. Identify the concluding paragraph(s), and discuss what is accomplished.

What's the Deal with iPods?
Monica Early

Television commercials show all sorts of people walking down the street listening to music on their iPods. They're jumping around, looking perfectly ridiculous, each in rhythm, we assume, to the iPod music only they can hear.

The commercials try to convince us that carrying around an iPod is the greatest thing going, and we should all rush out and get ours. I for one am not scurrying to any Circuit City to plunk down a few hundred bucks for yet another techno marvel. I frankly have no use for iPods, and I think they can be harmful.

The first assumption with iPods that I don't buy is that we need to be entertained constantly. Walking down the street or up the escalator, sitting in the airport or on the bus, we always need to have music in our ears. But that's not enough. We also need to see the videos that go with the music. In short, by carrying around our iPod, we can watch MTV everywhere, all the time! Is that what Americans really need?

Carrying around an iPod constantly may tune in the music, but it tunes out the world. Wherever we are, there is so much around us to take in: people, sights, sounds, happenings, natural and architectural wonders. How much do we miss out on, and how much do our senses of observation diminish, when we are encased in an insular musical bubble?

iPods are yet another techno innovation that further isolates us from our fellow humans. Today we can sit in front of a computer at work all day, or even work from home, plug in our iPod whenever we are out and about, turn on the TV when we get home, and spend the day literally plugged into some kind of machine or gadget. It's little wonder that parents and kids and spouses have trouble communicating and that we don't get to know our neighbors or fellow workers very well. We are living more and more in our own little electronic worlds.

iPods are yet another example of the advertising world creating a demand for something we don't need. Who wouldn't want to have a gadget where you can store over 3,000 songs? Not that you'd ever listen to one tenth of them. It's just such a cool idea, something that gadget-crazy Americans buy into as they are bombarded by iPod commercials day and night.

iPod listening/viewing, like most television we watch, is anti-educational. It is a passive, non-intellectual activity that requires no thinking. It's the kind of thing that, taken to the nth degree, turns your brain to mush. It's the antithesis of reading a book or magazine, and it takes time away from doing either. Too much mouth candy ruins your teeth. What does too much ear candy do? I suppose we'll find out.

DRAFTING ACTIVITY 3.7

Write the first draft of your opinion paper.

REVISIONS

After writing your first draft, set it aside for a while before starting the revision process. After leaving it for a while, you generally view your draft more objectively and make more and better revisions. Set your draft aside for an hour or overnight, and you will find things to improve that you wouldn't have noticed otherwise.

REVISION GUIDELINES

As you read and evaluate your first draft, consider the following revision guidelines:

1. Evaluate your beginning. Have you introduced your topic, created some interest for readers, and included your thesis sentence? (See the upcoming section on "Openings and Conclusions.")

2. Evaluate your middle paragraphs. Do they provide strong supporting points for your thesis? Is each supporting point developed in a separate paragraph? Are there examples, details, or explanations you might add to improve any paragraph?

3. Evaluate the order in which you have presented your ideas. Would any sentence(s) or paragraph(s) make better sense in a different location? Would your supporting points be more effective in a different order?

4. Read each sentence and consider how it might be revised to improve its smoothness, clarity, or conciseness. Evaluate your sentence variety and make revisions, if necessary, to improve the variety. (See the upcoming section on "Guidelines for Improving Sentence Variety.")

5. Evaluate your paragraphing to make sure that you have a distinct opening, middle, and ending to your draft; that you have developed your supporting points in separate paragraphs; that the sentences within each paragraph are related; and that you don't have any overly long or short paragraphs.

6. Evaluate your ending. Does it give readers a sense of completion? Does it help accomplish your purpose? Does it relate to your thesis statement in some way?

7. Reread your draft, keeping in mind your audience (classmates) and purpose (what you want them to get out of the paper). What changes might you make to accomplish your purpose better or to make the paper more interesting or worthwhile for your readers?

REVISION ACTIVITY 3.8

In small groups, read and evaluate the following student draft by applying the revision guidelines. Be prepared to share your revision suggestions with the class.

When you finish, evaluate each group member's draft in the same manner and provide revision suggestions.

House Music

People enjoy listening to many different kinds of music. They listen to it in their car, while they're exercising, or even taking a shower and thinking that they're going to be the next American Idol.

There are so many different famous names out there, like Kanye West, J.Lo, Faith Hill, and Enrique Iglesias, and they all sing different kinds of music. Many people enjoy listening to these types of music, but my favorite kind of music is House or trans.

I need music that I can actually dance to and that I want to dance to. House music is really fast beats all going at the same time, so you always have to be moving, unlike rap. I don't know what kind of dance you do or even if there is a dance for rap.

A lot of people go to raves, which are all-age events that play house music all night long. They get very tiring though. Most of the clubs also play a lot of House music because it's a music that everyone dances to.

It's a kind of music that when I hear it, it will make me want to get up and dance. To some people, it gives them a big, fat headache. I tell them I could sleep to this kind of music. I guess everyone has a different taste in music, but House is my favorite.

REVISION ACTIVITY 3.9

Write the second draft of your paper, including all of the revisions you have noted for improvement. You may also find other things to revise during the drafting process. (Your instructor may have you go over the upcoming sections on "Paragraphing" and "Sentence Revision" before you write the draft.)

JOURNAL ENTRY TEN

In your notebook under Journal Entry Ten, relate the kinds of changes you made from your first draft and how you feel they improved the paper. In addition, relate your revision process. Do you make revisions while you are reading the draft as you happen upon things that need changing, do you read all the way through the draft, highlight areas that you want to change, and then go back and make all the revisions, or do you use some other process?

PARAGRAPHING

Each unit presents some paragraphing instruction to apply to the paper you are working on. Since you are writing opening and concluding paragraphs for the current paper, this section gives you some help in those areas.

Openings and Conclusions

Two of the most important parts of a paper are its opening and conclusion. If you get off to a good start, readers will continue to read your paper with interest. If you conclude strongly, they are left with a favorable final impression.

The following suggestions, and lots of practice, will help you begin and end your papers effectively. To write effective *openings*:

1. Motivate readers to read further by introducing your topic in an interesting way: through a brief personal experience, an anecdote, an interesting quotation, a provoking fact, or an example of how readers are affected by the topic.

2. Let readers know what lies ahead by presenting your thesis: the opinion you are going to develop in the paper.

3. Keep your opening relatively short—a paragraph or two—since it is an introduction leading into the heart of your paper.

4. Through your opening, you may "hook" or "lose" your readers' attention. Write your opening to capture their interest and ensure their understanding of your topic and opinion.

To write effective *conclusions*:

1. Leave readers with something you want them to remember: the importance of the topic, the importance of their involvement in something, your purpose for writing, a crucial point, a memorable example, a prediction for the future, a thought to ponder, a possible solution to a problem.

2. Your conclusion should follow logically from what has preceded it in your paper. Therefore, you may not decide how you will end a paper until you've written everything but the conclusion.

3. Give readers something new in the conclusion—more than just a summary of what has come before. Make the conclusion worth their reading.

4. Think of the conclusion as your "last shot" with your readers. If they remember little else other than the conclusion, what will they be left with?

5. A brief, hurried conclusion is a common first draft problem. You may want to take a break before writing it, then return with renewed energy, and give it the time and effort it deserves.

The following sample openings and conclusions reveal the variety of ways in which writers begin and end their papers, and may also give you some ideas for your own essay. As you read each opening, determine the topic for the essay and the writer's opinion on the topic (thesis statement).

Buying Furnishings for a House
(written for future home renters or owners)

OPENING   When my husband and I rented our first house, we were excited about getting rid of some of our junk furnishings and replacing them with nicer things. Our first acquisition was a beautiful entertainment center that we bought on sale.

When we put the three-piece unit in our family room, it swallowed up a lot of space. It made the room look tiny and took away from our seating space. Unfortunately, we were stuck with it because it was a "no return" sales item. That was one of many lessons we learned as we began to furnish our house. There are a lot of costly mistakes that can be made when furnishing a house, and you need to take it slowly.

(**Middle paragraphs** cover a number of points on furnishing a house wisely: taking measurements, taking into account the whole room, considering color schemes, considering decor themes, weighing deferred payment options, never purchasing non-returnables.)

CONCLUSION   Above all else, make sure to take your time in furnishing your home. Most of what you buy may be with you for many years, so taking a few months to find just the right chair or picture is worth the effort. Furnishing a home can also be expensive, so it makes sense to spread out your acquisitions over a few years rather than building up a huge debt. My husband and I now view furnishing our home as a longtime project, something that we will enjoy doing for many years. That is a great difference from those first months of shopping, when we made hurried and ill-advised decisions. We learned the hard way.

Recycling Paper
(written to a college audience)

OPENING   Americans throw away millions of tons of paper a year: newspapers, magazines, paper bags, letters, and envelopes. All of this paper represents thousands of trees that are cut annually from our dwindling U.S. forest lands. Our national forests don't have to be devastated, however, if we recycle our paper instead of throwing it away. With the recycling programs that are available today throughout the country, no American should ever throw away a piece of paper again.

(**Middle paragraphs** cover a number of different paper recycling programs available in most towns, the profits individuals can make by recycling their paper products, and ways to start up paper recycling programs in towns that don't have them.)

CONCLUSION   College students can make as big a contribution to saving our forests as anyone. Too often we throw away our notes, papers, handouts, returned tests, flier, and student newspapers. Every college should have a number of paper "drop" stations on campus for recycling. The student council could be in charge of the program, and profits from selling the recycled paper could go to the student body. If your college doesn't have a recycling program, take the lead in getting one started, and once it is in place, carry the message to local K–12 school districts. Students can play a big role in helping to preserve U.S. forests for future generations.

Time for a Change
(letter to the editor of a local newspaper)

OPENING   Coach Mabry has had three years to turn the college basketball program around, and the team isn't any better than when she came in 1992. The last two years she has had her own recruits to work with, so she can't blame the "carry-over" players that Coach Forney recruited previously. It's time for a change in basketball coaches because under Coach Mabry, the women's basketball program is stagnating.

(**Middle paragraphs** cover the negative ramifications: poor attendance at games, lack of interest in the program among students, lack of financial support from boosters, program in the red, and the program losing its previous national reputation.)

CONCLUSION   Division I coaches are hired with the understanding that losing seasons bring about firings. That's the nature of the business and one reason that they are paid considerably more than other college instructors. No one should feel sorry for Coach Mabry. She has had her chance, she's made over $100,000 a year, and she hasn't produced. It's time to give someone else a chance before the college basketball program goes into cardiac arrest. There are plenty of excellent coaches in the country who would love the chance to revive our once outstanding program. It can be outstanding again, but not with Coach Mabry at the helm.

New College Drop Date
(written to a board of trustees)

OPENING   The change in the college's semester drop date from the twelfth week to the sixth week was instituted quietly this fall and went practically unnoticed by students. Then when the sixth week of the new semester crept closer and teachers began notifying their classes, it began to sink in with students that the new date was going to create some serious problems. The six-week drop date is clearly not in the best interests of most students, and it should be changed back to the original twelve-week date.

(**Middle paragraphs** cover the reasons why the writer opposes the new drop date: not enough time for students to make up their minds, not enough testing at that point for students to evaluate their standing, negative effects on financial aid for students who drop classes that early, will lead to higher college dropout rate, will lead to poorer GPAs, and will hinder students' chances of transferring successfully.)

CONCLUSION   For all of these reasons, the six-week drop date is bad for most students and should be changed. It is not surprising that students were not involved in discussions on changing the drop date or on its effects. If we had been, I don't believe the date would have been changed.

True, the six-week drop date may make life easier for instructors, but does the board make decisions based on what is easy for instructors or what is best for students? Please reconsider this hastily made change and do what is best for students: Return the drop date to the twelfth week. There is plenty of time to make that change for the fall semester of 1997. Thank you.

PARAGRAPHING ACTIVITY 3.10

Read the following essay, "Smoking in the Girls' Room" by Alyssa Tiant. In small groups discuss the following:

1. What is accomplished in the opening of the essay?

2. What is the thesis for the essay—Tiant's opinion on high school girls smoking—and where is it found?

3. Identify the supporting points for the thesis and the examples that develop each point. How are the supporting points and examples paragraphed?

4. What is accomplished in the conclusion of the essay?

5. Do you agree with Tiant's opinion, and why?

Smoking in the Girls' Room
Alyssa Tiant

Alright, I admit it. I was one of those girls who snuck a smoke or two in the girls' bathroom in high school. I was a high school rebel of sorts, and it was a wonderful act of defiance to puff on a cig, on the school grounds no less, in violation of numerous high school rules. Of course, it wasn't any fun if someone didn't see me do it. A smoking rebel without an audience is, well, just a smoker.

The point is, today I read these studies showing that not only are high school girls smoking more, they have surpassed boys in numbers. And people just don't understand, what with all we know about how bad smoking is for us. How could girls be so foolish? But I do understand, because I've been there. In reality, smoking for most girls isn't about smoking at all. It's about the really screwed-up world of being a teenage girl in high school.

You see, a lot of girls just don't fit into the high school success mold. They aren't beautiful, they aren't super-smart achievers, they aren't athletic, they aren't rich. They aren't really noticed, except in negative ways, or by the loser boys who don't fit in either.

So what does smoking have to do with anything? It makes a simple statement: I don't give a damn. I don't give a damn what you think of me, I don't give a damn about high school, I don't give a damn about being on the outside, I don't give a damn what this cancer stick is doing to me. The cigarette dangling from my lips says it all.

But why smoking? Aren't there other ways to express oneself? Truth be told, smoking is the best. This cigarette I'm lighting says I'm cool, I'm reckless, I'm rebellious, I'm defiant, I'm tough, I'm even sexy. I'll bet despite your 4.0 GPA or your cheerleader's sweater or your prom queen crown or your volleyball trophy, you'd really like to be as cool as me. I'm Rizzo in *Grease* and you Sandys make me sick.

Of course, most of these girls do give a damn, as did I. I would have traded places with the popular girls in a minute and I envied them more than I hated them. And in their eyes, I probably looked more pathetic than cool. More likely, they didn't even notice me. Was I actually poisoning my body for nothing?

That of course is hindsight, and no one lives in the moment more than high school girls. "Smoking might give me cancer in thirty years?" they ask rhetorically. "Like I care what happens thirty years from now. Pass me a Marlboro and be quiet. Besides, who wants to live in this screwed-up world for thirty more years?"

Yes, smoking is stupid. Even when I was doing it I knew it was stupid, and fortunately I didn't get hooked on nicotine before I developed enough self-esteem to realize I didn't need smoking. And today I could go back to high school and tell girls not to smoke and that it doesn't prove a thing or make anything better, but they'd pay no attention to me. I wouldn't have either. Smoking helped get me through high school. That may sound like a huge exaggeration, but it's the truth. And it's the truth for a lot of other girls. Like I said, it really has nothing to do with smoking.

PARAGRAPHING ACTIVITY 3.11

Review the opening and concluding paragraphs of your latest draft, and make any revisions that will add to their interest and effectiveness.

SENTENCE REVISION

In the first two units, you worked on improving first-draft sentences by eliminating unnecessary words, smoothing out awkward phrasing, replacing questionable word choices, and using concrete, visual language. Another consideration in sentence revision is *sentence variety:* using a variety of sentence structures and joining words to express your thoughts most effectively. In this section you begin working with a number of different sentence structures.

Guidelines for Improving Sentence Variety

By using a variety of sentence structures and joining words, you make your writing interesting for readers and express yourself most effectively. Some of the most common sentence problems are described here, with suggestions for solving them.

1. *Overreliance on a particular sentence structure:* You may find that you are using simple sentences (one subject, one verb) to the exclusion of other types.

   EXAMPLE   At 7:00 a.m. it was cool and breezy in Turlock. However, by 10:00 a.m. the breeze had stopped. The temperature began rising slowly. By 3:00 p.m. the temperature had reached 100 degrees. Then the breeze came up again at about 7:00 p.m. By 10:00 p.m. it was cool and windy. There was a 40-degree difference between the high and low for the day.

   Check your sentences to see if you have relied on a particular sentence structure to the exclusion of others: simple (one subject, one verb); compound (two sentences joined by *and, but, so, or, yet, for*); or complex (sentences joined or beginning with *because, if, while, unless, although, before, after*). Revise sentences to include a variety of simple, compound, and complex sentences.

2. *Overreliance on one or two joining words:* You may be using *and* to the exclusion of other options.

   EXAMPLE   A blue jay built her nest in a hanging plant on our apartment patio, and we inspected it occasionally, and a couple neighborhood cats also kept watch. The nest was about six feet above the ground, and we didn't worry about the cats. The blue jay would return regularly, and she would dive-bomb the cats and scare them away. One day the blue jay didn't return to the nest, and we never saw her again after that. After a couple months we took down the nest and threw the unhatched eggs away.

Check your sentences to see if you have relied on one or two joining words exclusively, such as *and, so,* or *because.* If you have, replace the overused word with other appropriate word choices.

3. *Overreliance on short or long sentences:* You may be using too many long sentences (as in the following sample paragraph) or too many short sentences (as in the paragraph example from number 1 about the weather).

EXAMPLE   I feel very uncomfortable in my Psychology II class this semester because it is a small class, and everyone is expected to participate in discussions. There are a number of older students in the class, some of whom have obviously taken a few psychology courses, and they frequently talk in jargon that I can't understand and make references to books I haven't read and psychological experiments that I've never heard of. When I do speak up in class, my observations and opinions sound pretty weak to me, and I'm sure these older students feel the same way although they don't reveal it and are always very considerate of the other students like myself, which is the one thing that makes the class tolerable.

Check the lengths of your sentences to see if you have too many short sentences (which can hurt the flow of your paper) or overly long sentences (which readers can get lost in or bored with). Revise groups of short sentences by combining them with joining words or developing their content. Revise overly long sentences by dividing them into two or more complete sentences (which may involve deleting some joining words).

SENTENCE REVISION ACTIVITY 3.12

Revise the following first-draft paragraphs by varying sentence structures, replacing overused joining words, combining very short sentences, and dividing overly long sentences. Add, delete, and move words around any way you wish. Possible wording options include coordinate conjunctions (and, but, so, for, or, yet) or subordinate conjunctions (although, because, since, if, unless, until, when, before, after, while, who, which, that).

Gretchen wanted to move out of the dorms, but she didn't know anyone to share an apartment with. She decided to look in the paper for "roommates wanted" ads, but she was leery about living with strangers. She finally decided to check out one ad because the apartment was in walking distance to the school, and because there were three girls who needed one roommate, and that would mean dividing the rent four ways, which was the cheapest way to go.

Gretchen went to the apartment and met the girls. They were a year older than she was and seemed nice. Their apartment looked clean and was nicely furnished. Her rent would be $150 a month and her share of the utility bill $50. Although she knew little about the girls, Gretchen decided to move in with them although she would have to buy a bicycle to go to and from classes. Although her mother was concerned about the move, Gretchen felt she had made the right decision. She moved her belongings from the dorm. She got her cleaning deposit back. She said farewell to her dormitory friends. She said good-bye to her floor supervisor.

SENTENCE REVISION ACTIVITY 3.13

Review the sentences in your latest draft and, if necessary, make revisions to include more sentence variety, replace overused joining words, combine pairs or groups of short sentences, and divide overly long sentences.

Combining Sentences

Practice in combining sentences has proven successful in helping students develop their sentence-writing skills. The Appendix includes a number of combining activities for students who could benefit from working with a variety of simple, compound, and complex sentence structures. Your instructor may assign these activities throughout the course to give you regular sentence-combining practice.

WORDING PROBLEM REVIEW

Here is a review from Unit Two of some common first-draft wording problems:

1. *Wordiness:* using more words than necessary to express a thought.

   EXAMPLE   The hailstones that had collected on the lawn in front of the house gave the appearance of snow to anyone who saw them on the lawn.

   REVISED   The hailstones on the front lawn of the house looked like snow.

2. *Awkward phrasing:* using words and phrases that don't fit together smoothly or logically.

   EXAMPLE   Because we've lived in weather where the temperature is cold all our lives, so we are used to dressing the proper way.

   REVISED   Because we've lived with cold weather all our lives, we're used to dressing warmly.

3. *Poor word choice:* using an incorrect or questionable word to express a thought.

   EXAMPLE   Your speech on positive thinking transpired all of us.

   REVISED   Your speech on positive thinking inspired all of us.

REVISION ACTIVITY 3.14

The following first-draft sentences need revising because of problems with wordiness, awkward phrasing, and poor word choices. Revise each sentence to make it smoother and clearer. Then evaluate your first (or second) draft sentences a final time.

EXAMPLE   John had a bald spot that parted his hair in the middle that was black. *(wordy, awkward, poor word choice)*

REVISED   John had a bald spot in the middle of his black hair.

1. The first thing is to let the oil settle down on the oil pan and let the oil cool down right there.

2. In football you don't have to have that good of an endurance to play it.

3. We went to a good show, and we saw it last weekend together.

4. Even though I am his cousin, but he doesn't let me borrow his notes.

5. From all of the dish washing, your hands are pruning and aging with rapidity.

6. It's hot outside tonight with very few breezes.

7. The doctor told my dad I was on time to stop the infection from spreading.

8. By looking at their patio from north to south, it is 12 feet by 12 feet.

9. The accident almost cost me to lose my life.

10. I was curious to see what a group of cats' behaviors were together, so I followed that group of cats.

FINAL EDITING

The last step in the writing process is to proofread your paper for any remaining errors. By this time in the course you are probably aware of your error tendencies, so pay particular attention to those areas.

This section introduces two new considerations that give some writers problems: sentence fragments and subject-verb agreement. You may want to cover these topics before proofreading your latest draft.

PROOFREADING GUIDELINES

1. *Make sure you have a period at the end of each complete sentence.* Check in particular for run-on sentences and for sentence fragments that need correcting. (See the upcoming section on "Fragments" in this unit.)

2. *Check your word endings to make sure you haven't inadvertently left off an* s *on a plural word, an* ed *on a past tense verb, or an* ly *on an adverb. Also make sure that your present tense verb endings agree with their subjects.* (See the upcoming section on "Subjects and Verbs" in this unit.)

3. *Check your spelling carefully, and look up any words you are uncertain of. Also make sure you have made the correct homophone choices among words such as* there/their/they're, your/you're, no/know, its/it's, *and* through/threw. (Check the sections on these confusing homonyms under "Spelling" in the Appendix.) *Also be sure to use the spelling check in your word processing program.*

4. *Check your internal punctuation, including comma usage in series of words, compound sentences, and after introductory groups of words; apostrophes in contractions and possessives; and quotation marks with dialogue.* (If you have any problems with contractions, see the "Spelling" section in the Appendix.)

5. *Check your use of pronouns in compound subjects (Marsha and I, Ross and she, my mother and I, he and I, the Williamses and they).*

EDITING ACTIVITY 3.15

In small groups, proofread the following student draft for errors and make the necessary corrections.

Then, following the guidelines presented, proofread your latest draft for errors, and make the necessary corrections. (Your instructor may have you cover the upcoming sections on "Fragments" and "Subjects and Verbs" before you proofread.)

Finally, write or print out the final error-free draft of your paper to share with your instructor and classmates.

The Best Holiday

Christmas has to be the best holiday of the year. I can remember when I was ten years old it was Christmas Eve and everyone was asleep but me. I had snuck out of my room to look at the gifts, I had crawled under the tree and started grabbing my gifts.

I thought that I was so smart I had planed to put all my gifts in one spot so that the next day I would go strate to them and not have to go under the tree. But I did not count on my dad being up that late and he caught me he made me put them back and sent me to bed. However, I could not sleep I could only think of the next day when all my famile would come over for dinner.

The way we did it was half of the family you know the ones you really like would come over for breakfast, and we would eat. After that we would open the gifts from them. After they would go home and my mom would get all the stuff ready for dinner. Then all my other relatives would show up to eat then we would open there gifts, talk, and play.

The reason that particular Christmas stands out is that year started a bad tradition that I just broke last year which is the Christmas tree falling on me. It started when I went under the tree to get the cat out it jump into the tree and throw the tree off balance, and it fell. The next year a bulb fell off, so I turned it back on, and as I turned to leave, the tree fell on me and kept doing so every year until last. So I'm looking forward to next year and hoping the tree doesn't hit me again.

JOURNAL ENTRY ELEVEN

Under Journal Entry Eleven, record the kinds of recurring errors you still have to watch out for in your writing. In addition, relate how much error correction you do during the drafting process. How much do you do during the final proofreading?

SENTENCE PROBLEMS

In the first units, you worked on identifying and correcting run-on sentences in your writing. A less frequent but equally troublesome problem is the *sentence fragment*, which is covered in this section.

Fragments

Here are some common features of sentence fragments:

1. A fragment is an incomplete sentence. While a sentence expresses a complete idea and makes sense by itself, a fragment does not.

    EXAMPLES   The man walking down the freeway.

    Because it has been snowing all weekend.

    Driving to school in an old Volkswagen bus.

2. A fragment often leaves the reader with an unanswered question.

    EXAMPLES   The girl standing in the fountain. *(What happened to her?)*

    If you do all your homework tonight. *(What will happen?)*

    Whenever I start to apologize to you. *(What happens?)*

3. Fragments are often separate thoughts that belong in one sentence.

    EXAMPLES   (FRAGMENTS UNDERLINED)

    If you want a ride to school tomorrow. You can give me a call.

    I hope the game is over. Before it starts raining hard.

4. Since fragments are incorrect sentence structures that confuse readers, they need to be revised to form complete sentences. To correct a sentence fragment, either add words to the fragment to make it a sentence, or connect it to the sentence that it belongs with.

EXAMPLE   The girl standing in the fountain.

REVISED   The girl standing in the fountain is cooling her feet.

EXAMPLE   After we pay this month's bills. We'll have little money left for entertainment.

REVISED   After we pay this month's bills, we'll have little money left for entertainment.

EXAMPLE   You can always take the bus to the downtown library. If you can't get a ride from your sister.

REVISED   You can always take the bus to the downtown library if you can't get a ride from your sister.

FRAGMENT ACTIVITY 3.16

The following paragraph contains a number of fragments. Some are the result of a sentence being incorrectly split into a sentence and a fragment, and others are missing the words to form a complete sentence. Rewrite the paragraph and correct all fragments by uniting split sentences and by adding words to fragments that are incomplete. When you finish, check your latest draft for fragments and make the necessary corrections.

EXAMPLE   Patricia was interested in fashion merchandising. Because she loved to buy clothes. Expensive clothes in particular.

REVISED   Patricia was interested in fashion merchandising because she loved to buy clothes. She liked expensive clothes in particular.

It was a bad time to be looking for apartments. Because they were scarce and rent was high. A one-bedroom apartment cost $300 a month. Maria and Henry were hoping to find a two-bedroom apartment. Since she was expecting a baby in April. They needed to live closer to the campus. Because Henry didn't own a car. The only two-bedroom place they found was renting for $350. They decided to take it. Although the payments would be difficult. Could survive until Henry graduated in June. They moved their belongings into the apartment. They felt everything would work out. Unless Henry's grant application was not accepted.

CORRECT USAGE

Writers sometimes make grammatical errors within a sentence that distract readers. Knowledge of the basic rules of grammar helps writers eliminate such errors. This section introduces the basic rules for subject-verb identification and agreement that every writer should know.

Subjects and Verbs

As a general rule, every sentence you write contains a subject and a verb. The *subject* is who or what the sentence is about, and the *verb* tells what the subject is doing or joins the subject with words that describe it. To understand subject-verb agreement, you need to be able to identify these main sentence parts.

Subject-Verb Identification

The following sentences have their subjects underlined once and the verbs twice. Notice that in each sentence, the *subject* is who or what the sentence is about, and the *verb* tells what the subject is doing.

EXAMPLES   The dolphin leaped through the air. (*The sentence is about a* dolphin. Leaped *tells what the dolphin did.*)

The doctor made house calls. (*The sentence is about a* doctor. Made *house calls tells what he did.*)

The boulders tumbled down the mountain. (*The sentence is about* boulders. Tumbled *tells what they did.*)

A second way of finding the subject and verb is to locate the verb first and then the subject. To find the verb, look for the *action* in the sentence: running, thinking, talking, looking, touching, and so on. To find the subject, ask, "Who or what is doing the action?" Here are more examples.

EXAMPLES   The raisins shrivel in the sun. (*The action is* shrivel. *What is shriveling? The* raisins.)

Jogging builds Jolene's stamina. (*The action is* builds. *What builds?* Jogging.)

Clyde hates sardines and anchovies. (*The action is* hates. *Who hates?* Clyde.)

SUBJECT-VERB ACTIVITY 3.17

Underline the subject once and the verb twice in the following sentences. Either find out what the sentence is about (the subject) and what the subject is doing (the verb), or look for the action in the sentence (the verb) and find who or what is doing it (the subject).

EXAMPLES   The <u>noose</u> <u>tightened</u> around his neck.

The <u>skier</u> <u>fell</u> off the ski lift.

1. Juanita's ankle aches from roller skating.

2. The tarantula crawled inside Felix's sleeping bag.

3. Aunt Lottie from Toledo cracks walnuts on her head.

4. Ashes from the volcano covered the city.

5. Knitting relaxes Jose.

6. Today the stock market dropped to a record low.

7. Sal often thinks about joining the circus.

8. A fire spreading from a tool shed destroyed the family's belongings.

9. The countries in the Middle East negotiated a new peace treaty.

10. The rats chewed through the pantry wall.

11. High interest rates in March and April killed Fred's chances for a loan.

12. The hockey team from Calgary practices at 4:00 a.m. every day.

13. The opportunity for fame escaped Alice.

14. The poetry competition between classes ends today.

15. Ink blots from his fountain pen stained Rasheed's shirt pocket.

Subject-Verb Agreement

The following rules for subject-verb agreement will help you use the correct present tense verb forms.

1. The subject of a sentence can be *singular* (one of anything) or *plural* (more than one of anything). The plural of most words is formed by adding *s* or *es*: cats, dogs, dresses, boxes.

2. There are two forms of present tense verbs: one ends in *s* and one does not (ride/rides, fight/fights, sing/sings).

3. When you use a present tense verb, you must select the correct form of the verb to agree with the subject. If the subject of the sentence is *singular*, use the form that ends in *s*. If the subject is *plural*, use the form that does *not* end in *s*.

   a. *Singular subject:* present tense verb ends in *s*.

   b. *Plural subject:* present tense verb does not end in *s*.

   EXAMPLES   (SUBJECT UNDERLINED ONCE, VERB UNDERLINED TWICE)

   SINGULAR
   SUBJECT   The <u>elm tree</u> <u>sheds</u> its leaves in early December.

PLURAL SUBJECT	The <u>elm trees</u> <u>shed</u> their leaves in early December.
SINGULAR SUBJECT	Your <u>aunt</u> <u>believes</u> in reincarnation.
PLURAL SUBJECT	Your <u>aunts</u> <u>believe</u> in reincarnation.

4. There are a few exceptions to the basic subject-verb agreement rules. With the singular subject pronouns *I* and *you*, the verb does *not* end in *s*: I enjoy roller-skating; you prefer skateboarding. Verbs such as *dress, press, regress,* and *impress* end in *s* with a plural subject—The Johnson girls dress alike—and in *es* with a singular subject—Sarah dresses very differently from her twin sister.

SUBJECT-VERB AGREEMENT ACTIVITY 3.18

Underline the correct form of the present tense verb in parentheses that agrees with the subject of the sentence.

EXAMPLES   Your uncle (build, <u>builds</u>) huge sand castles.

Your uncles (<u>build</u>, builds) huge sand castles.

1. Juanita often (practice, practices) her baton twirling three nights a week.

2. The girls (practice, practices) karate in the school's gymnastics room.

3. My nephew from New Orleans (believe, believes) in extraterrestrial beings.

4. My nieces (believe, believes) that my nephew is crazy.

5. The pole-vaulters from Central College (warm, warms) up for their event by using a trampoline.

6. The high jumper from Drake University (warm, warms) up for her event by doing stretching exercises.

7. The city newspapers that I subscribe to (do, does) a lousy job of covering campus activities.

8. The college newspaper (do, does) a great job of covering city events.

9. That pickle on your hamburger (look, looks) like it's been nibbled on by a rat.

10. Those olives (look, looks) like they've been dehydrated.

11. Your dentist (need, needs) braces on his lower teeth.

12. Most physicians that I know (need, needs) to take better care of their own health.

13. Your success (prove, proves) that hard work sometimes pays off.

14. My recent failures in math (prove, proves) that hard work isn't always enough.

15. A savings account (are, is) one thing I need to open immediately.

16. Savings accounts (are, is) great if you have anything to put into them.

Subject-Verb Variations
Here are some variations in the subject-verb pattern that often create agreement problems for writers.

1. *Separated subject and verb:* The subject and verb are separated by a group of words, most often a *prepositional phrase,* that confuses the agreement situation. *Solution:* Ignore any words between a subject and verb when making decisions about agreement.

PREPOSITIONAL PHRASES *(PREPOSITIONS ITALICIZED)*

after the game	*from* his room
against his will	*in* the boat
among the roses	*into* the water
around the house	*of* the three churches
before the test	*on* the table
behind the batter	*to* the ground
between the lines	*through* the mail
for good mileage	*with* her friends

EXAMPLES   (SUBJECT AND VERB UNDERLINED, PREPOSITIONAL PHRASES CROSSED OUT)

<u>One</u> ~~of the women teachers~~ <u>smokes</u> a pipe in the lounge.

The <u>aroma</u> ~~of barbecuing steaks~~ <u>nauseates</u> Herman.

<u>Men</u> ~~in the back of the room by the pencil sharpener~~ <u>look</u> threatening.

<u>Each</u> ~~of the sixteen yellow raincoats~~ <u>has</u> a flaw in it.

2. *Sentences beginning with* there *plus a form of* to be: Sentences beginning with *there is, there are, there was,* and *there were* cause writers problems because the subject comes *after* the verb. *Solution:* Because *there* is never the subject in a *there + to be* sentence, find the subject after the verb and use *is* or *was* with singular subjects and *are* or *were* with plural subjects.

EXAMPLES   (SUBJECTS AND VERBS UNDERLINED)

There <u>is</u> a <u>snake</u> in the basement.

There <u>are</u> sixteen <u>ways</u> to cook potatoes.

There <u>was</u> <u>no one</u> home at the Garcia's.

There <u>were</u> no Christmas <u>trees</u> left in the lot when I went shopping.

3. *Compound verbs:* If a sentence has a single subject and two or more main verbs (compound verb), each main verb must agree with the subject.

EXAMPLES   (SUBJECTS AND VERBS UNDERLINED)

<u>Mavis</u> <u>jogs</u> to work, <u>does</u> aerobics on her lunch hour, and <u>lifts</u> weights at night.

My <u>uncles</u> <u>make</u> great chili and <u>serve</u> it in old tin cans.

<u>G Street</u> <u>winds</u> around our suburb and then <u>dead-ends</u> by the canal.

<u>Sarah and Clyde</u> <u>love</u> to fight and <u>love</u> to make up even more.

SUBJECT-VERB AGREEMENT ACTIVITY 3.19

Underline the subject in each of the following sentences, and then circle the verb in parentheses that *agrees* with the subject. When you finish, proofread your latest draft for any subject-verb agreement problems.

EXAMPLE   <u>One</u> of my goldfish (look, <u>looks</u>) ill.

1. Sarah and Jesus (dances, dance) smoothly together.

2. No one in the audience (understand, understands) the plot of the Fellini movie.

3. The huge planes (circles, circle) the runway in the fog.

4. The french fries from the Happy Hamburger (is, are) greasy.

5. The children from Grant School (appears, appear) bored after Act One of *The Great Anchovy.*

6. There (is, are) something about you that I like.

7. Before the election, the mayor (hires, hire) his campaign manager and (prepares, prepare) his speech.

8. Tryouts for the philharmonic orchestra (begins, begin) on Monday.

9. Julia and Fred (seems, seem) surprised by the attention from the press.

10. The students from Sweden and Israel (speaks, speak) and (writes, write) excellent English.

11. In the back of your locker (lies, lie) a pair of stinky sweat socks.

12. The view across the bay from the middle of the bridge (was, were) magnificent.

13. There (is, are) one of the Daffney twins, but I (don't, doesn't) know the whereabouts of her sister.

14. There (is, are) no good reason for you to miss the farewell party for Gonzo.

15. From the looks of your car, it (needs, need) a good wash and wax job.

JOURNAL ENTRY TWELVE

Under Journal Entry Twelve in your notebook, relate what you learned through the writing process and activities in this unit that may help you for future writing that you do.

WRITING REVIEW

In the "Writing Review" section at the end of each unit, you work more independently on a paper and apply what you have learned during the unit. For this assignment, you will be writing a particular kind of opinion paper called a *critique*.

WRITING A CRITIQUE

A *critique* is an essay written to evaluate a particular writing: an essay, an article in a magazine, an editorial, or a book. When you write a *critique*, you are expressing your opinion on the writing: what you liked or didn't like about it, how well it was written, whether you agree with the author.

Writing an effective critique requires a close and careful reading of the essay you are evaluating. To that end, consider the following suggestions:

1. What is the topic of the essay you are evaluating and what is the author's viewpoint?

2. What should be included from the essay in your critique to summarize its content effectively?

3. Evaluate the author's support for her viewpoint on the topic. How well does she substantiate her assertions? How believable is her support?

4. What is your viewpoint on the essay: the thesis you will support in your paper?

5. What do you believe the author's purpose was in writing the essay, and how well did she accomplish it?

To prepare for your upcoming writing assignment, read the following sample essay and apply the preceding questions to help you evaluate it.

Snubbing the Kyoto Protocol
Cynthia Watts

SAMPLE READING FOR ANALYSIS The Kyoto Protocol is a worldwide agreement entered into by most countries of the world to work together to decrease global warming and its negative effects. Championed by the Clinton administration through environmental spokesperson Vice President Al Gore, it has been rejected by President Bush, whose administration has refused to participate.

Scientists have agreed for years that our atmosphere is getting warmer due to man-made pollutants that form a blanket in the atmosphere and don't allow heat to escape as it naturally would. How else could we account for the fact that the polar icecaps are melting at an unprecedented rate, that the oceans' waters are warming and rising as a result, and that the majority of the hottest days in recorded history have occurred in the past ten years?

Should we care that our atmosphere is warming? Definitely. Rising oceans can result in the displacement of millions of people whose ocean-side communities and farmlands would be permanently flooded. Changes in climate can negatively affect agriculture across the world, whose crops depend on the natural climate of the area. Overheating the planet could destroy millions of acres of farmland.

Global warming is also warming the currents that run through the oceans, which is paradoxically resulting in colder temperatures in places such as Northern Europe, where the warmer currents meet the colder northern waters, resulting in increased rain and snowfall. Global warming is also being viewed as the possible culprit behind the exceptional climatological upheavals we've seen in recent years, such as the devastating 2003 tsunami and Hurricane Katrina, one of three powerful hurricanes that have prowled the Gulf of Mexico in the last three years.

Whether global warming is responsible for every climatological problem we are facing is beside the point. There is enough evidence of its negative impact to convince most of the nations of the world to band together to do something about it. Then why on earth is President Bush thumbing his nose at the Kyoto Protocol and sending the message to other countries that the United States isn't going to cooperate in combating global warming? Why is the Bush administration turning its back on a worldwide anti-pollution effort that the Clinton administration embraced?

The chief cause of global warming is the millions of tons of hydrocarbons pumped into the atmosphere by the emissions of automobiles and heavy industries. Reversing global warming would require governmental regulation of the auto, coal, and oil industries that Bush isn't willing to commit to. He claims that such regulation would hurt the U.S. economy, but in reality, he doesn't want to offend the industry magnates that helped put him in the White House. In addition, how can you regulate and police the very industry that you and your family are a major part of: big oil? The fox, unfortunately, is guarding the henhouse.

It is unconscionable for the Bush administration not to support the Kyoto Protocol and take a leadership role in combating global warming and its disastrous environmental effects. Bush's response to critics has been similar to his response to worldwide criticism of the Iraqi war: We are right and the world is wrong. When it comes to global warming, the world has it right and the Bush administration is dead wrong.

Why Americans aren't in an uproar over Bush's horrible environmental position on global warming probably lies in the fact that the very worst results of global warming lie in the future. We tend not to worry about environmental issues until the situation becomes dire, like the destructive pollution of America's lakes and rivers in the 1980s. But if we do nothing about global warming now, and the Bush administration is doing just that, we may be leaving our children and grandchildren with an environmental catastrophe of hideous proportions.

Perhaps the crowning blow for the Bush administration was a recent meeting of six former heads of the EPA (federal Environmental Protection Agency), five of whom served under Republican presidents, who unanimously stated that global warming was a serious issue and the Bush administration was not doing enough to combat it. Their purpose was obvious: to get Bush to change course dramatically on global warming. Unfortunately, Bush doesn't listen to environmental experts, he listens to the big polluters who write his campaign checks: the auto, coal, and oil industry magnates. And if Americans don't get angry over this environmental outrage, and express their outrage in a big way, nothing is going to change for at least another three years. And the planet will keep getting hotter and hotter as Bush continues to fiddle.

WRITING PROCESS

1. Select an essay from this text or a magazine or newspaper article or editorial to write a critique on, and generate a thesis following these suggestions:

   a. Choose a reading to critique that you are interested in and can form a definite opinion on. Read several essays and articles to find the best one for you.

b. Write a tentative thesis statement: a sentence expressing your overall opinion of the reading that you will support throughout your paper.

c. Your audience for the paper is your classmates. What purpose might you have in writing to them about this particular topic? What might they get out of the paper?

STUDENT SAMPLE IDEAS   I read an article about global warming that I found interesting. I agree with the author that global warming is a big problem and that the Bush administration isn't doing anything about it. Since I'm interested in the topic, I'm going to write a critique on the essay.

TOPIC   The article "Snubbing the Kyoto Protocol"

THESIS STATEMENT   The essay "Snubbing the Kyoto Protocol" presents a good case for the dangers of global warming, but I wonder if Americans really care enough to get involved.

2. To prepare to write your critique, do the following:

a. Read the essay you are critiquing carefully and apply the questions for evaluation from the section on "Writing a Critique."

b. Decide how you are best going to support your thesis in the critique: what you are going to use from the essay you are critiquing to support your opinion.

STUDENT SAMPLE   Thesis: The essay "Snubbing the Kyoto Protocol" presents a good case for the dangers of global warming, but I wonder if Americans really care enough to get involved.

a. The topic of the essay is global warming and the author believes it is a serious problem and the Bush administration is doing little to combat it. She gives good examples of the effects of global warming and some evidence that President Bush is neglecting the problem. I agree with the article and feel the author makes her points, but I'm not sure that people are too upset about global warming, including myself, and I'm not sure she accomplished her purpose, which I think was to get people activated.

b. I'll present the author's evidence of global warming and her evidence that Bush isn't doing anything about it.

3. When you have completed your prewriting work, write the first draft of your paper following these guidelines:

a. Present the topic of the essay you are critiquing and the author's viewpoint on the topic at the beginning of the paper so that readers have a clear understanding of what they are reading about. Then present your thesis statement: your overall opinion of the essay you are critiquing.

b. The content of the essay you are critiquing forms the basis for your paper, and presenting and evaluating the content in support of your thesis fills the middle part of the paper.

c. Have a clear purpose for your conclusion, something you want to leave readers with: a final positive (or negative) comment on the essay you are critiquing to reinforce your thesis; a question or concern you want to leave readers with relating to the essay; something to reinforce what you feel is most important for readers to take from your critique; a comment to make readers consider further the topic of the essay.

d. Keep your thesis (your opinion on the topic) in mind as you write to provide focus throughout the paper.

e. Keep your audience (classmates) in mind as you write, and your purpose: what you want them to get out of the paper.

f. Don't worry about perfect wording or making an occasional error. Revision and editing lie ahead.

Before you begin your draft, read the following critique of the essay "Snubbing the Kyoto Protocol" to gain a better understanding of critique writing.

The Kyoto Protocol
Torrey Allen

The article "Snubbing the Kyoto Protocol" is an indictment of President Bush's administration for not supporting the Kyoto Protocol, an agreement among most nations to reduce global warming and its negative impacts. While the Clinton administration supported the Kyoto Protocol and played a leadership role in combating global warming, the Bush administration has virtually ignored the problem and not cooperated with the participating nations, according to author Cynthia Watts. The essay presents a good case for the dangers of global warming, but I wonder if Americans really care enough to get involved.

Why would anyone not support a worldwide effort to reduce global warming, writer Watts questions. She provides evidence of global warming—melting icecaps; warming, rising ocean waters; abrupt climatological changes—and possible effects—the flooding of farmlands and oceanside communities worldwide, the negative impact of climate changes on agriculture, perhaps even the disastrous natural disasters such as tsunamis and hurricanes that have been occurring at an alarming rate.

While Watts expects us to accept her evidence and the effects of global warming without presenting any real proof, enough has been written on the topic in recent years to substantiate what she says. It is difficult not to agree with her assessment that global warming is a problem that needs addressing.

To explain why President Bush doesn't support the Kyoto Protocol, Watts offers two reasons. First, Bush doesn't want to regulate the industries such as coal and oil that emit a lot of the hydrocarbons into the atmosphere that cause global warming. These industry leaders are big Bush contributors, claims Watts, and he and his family are a part of big oil themselves. Second, Bush claims that it would hurt the economy to move too fast on global warming. Watts doesn't explain her reasoning.

Watts doesn't provide support for her assertion about Bush's relationship with the coal and oil industries, but with the Bush family in the oil business, it's not hard to believe. She also expects readers to accept that these industries are major global warming polluters without providing evidence, but their contribution wouldn't be surprising. If reducing global warming would hurt the U.S. economy, I'd like to know how and to what extent, but even then, what's more important: today's economy or the environmental future of our planet?

Watts's best evidence against the Bush administration's position is that recently six former heads of the federal Environmental Protection Agency, five of them serving under Republican presidents, stated together publicly that global warming was a serious problem and that the Bush administration wasn't doing enough. It's difficult not to believe these experts, and at least five of them aren't playing partisan politics. In addition, why would most of the nations of the world band together to fight global warming if it wasn't a serious problem?

While I agree with Watts that global warming is a problem and the president's position on the issue is terrible, I'm afraid I'm one of those Americans that Watts mentions in her essay: the ones who don't get too excited until the effects of global warming are at our doorstep. But will it be too late by then to change course? I too want the president to support the Kyoto Protocol and be a leader against global warming, but I also suspect that isn't going to happen. Unfortunately, I'm not enraged enough to do much. But that's not Watts's fault. Her essay didn't rouse me to action, but I'm not sure what she could have said that would.

4. When you finish your first draft, set it aside for a while before evaluating it. Then read the draft carefully for possible revisions, following these guidelines:

   a. Is your opening a strong part of your paper? Do you introduce your topic in an interesting way and clearly state your thesis? How might you improve the opening?

b. Do you support your thesis well in the middle paragraphs? Do you present the most important material from the essay you are critiquing and provide your personal evaluation in keeping with your thesis? What might you add or revise to improve your middle paragraphs?

c. Is your paper paragraphed effectively? Are the opening, middle, and endings paragraphed separately? Do you develop different points from the essay you are critiquing in separate paragraphs? Are the sentences within each paragraph related? Do you have any overly long paragraphs that need dividing or short paragraphs that need combining or developing further?

d. Is your paper organized effectively? Have you presented the main points from the essay you are critiquing in the best possible order? Are there any sentences or paragraphs that would fit more logically in a different location?

e. Do you have a strong conclusion to your paper? Does it leave readers with a sense of completion and help you accomplish your purpose?

f. Revise the wording of individual sentences to make them clearer, smoother, more concise, and more concrete (visual). Check your sentences to see if you can improve their structural variety, replace overused joining words, combine pairs or groups of short sentences, or divide overly long sentences.

g. Evaluate the overall impact of your paper on your reading audience. What can you do to make it more interesting, more informative, or more convincing?

5. Following the proofreading guidelines in this unit, proofread your draft carefully for errors and make the necessary corrections.

6. Write or print out the final draft of your paper, and share it with your instructor and classmates.

Unit 4

Writing
to
Compare

As you write papers for this course, you use different thought processes that help you develop both your thinking and writing skills. Good thinking leads to good writing, and good writing requires a lot of thought: What am I going to write about? What will my approach be? How will I best support it? How can I capture and maintain my readers' interest? How shall I conclude my paper? What can I do to improve my paper? No act of communication requires more thinking and decision making than writing, and that is why writing is so valuable to a person's intellectual growth.

As you continue to write and revise your papers, you draw upon and expand your ability to recollect, to analyze, to compare, to evaluate, to organize, to draw conclusions, to persuade, and to create. In short, you are developing thinking skills that will help you in other college courses, in your future career, and in everyday life.

In your writing for this unit, you draw upon your comparative skills to evaluate similar subjects, consider their relative value, and decide which one you would recommend to readers. The tasks involved in writing a comparative paper include identifying the most important factors to compare, evaluating those factors, determining the relative value of each, and making decisions based on your evaluation. During the planning and writing process, you will use different thinking skills—comparing, evaluating, classifying, and drawing conclusions—that are beneficial for most decision making you will do.

Comparing subjects and making decisions are familiar acts to all of us. We decide where to live, what to eat, where to shop, where to go to school, what team to root for, and whom to vote for based on comparing and evaluating our choices. Sometimes the process is quite simple—choosing chocolate swirl ice cream over strawberry or vanilla. Sometimes it can be complicated—deciding which college to attend or what kind of car to buy. For your upcoming writing assignment, you will compare subjects to provide readers with the best information and advice for making their own decisions.

PREWRITING

For most people, writing a comparative paper requires some planning. You decide what subjects you want to compare, the factors you want to compare them by, what you might need to find out to provide the best comparison, and how best to organize your paper to accomplish your purpose.

While some writers prefer making a detailed outline before writing, others prefer beginning with a general idea and using the drafting process to help discover their direction. People who tend to plan and organize their writing in detail often do the same with other aspects of their lives. People who are less organized and more spontaneous tend to do less detailed planning. In the end, there is no one best way to prepare for writing a paper. Most writers ultimately settle on an approach that works well for them and is true to their nature.

For your prewriting work for the upcoming writing assignment, you do some things that are particularly important for making comparisons—deciding on factors to compare and weighing the value of those factors—and others that are useful for any writing—generating material for your first draft and considering how to organize it. The purpose of all prewriting work is to prepare you for writing your first draft, and anything you do toward that end is beneficial.

TOPIC SELECTION

To select your writing topic for the unit, consider these suggestions:

1. What topics do I know the most about? Cars? Sports? Fashion? Computers? Politics? Religion? Music?

2. What subjects could I compare that might help readers make a decision or choice? Different college majors? Different teachers teaching the same course? Different stereo systems? Different schools? Different college soccer programs? Different cars? Different places to shop? Different Thai restaurants? Different living situations? Different candidates running for political office?

3. What specific subjects would I compare? Which two or three restaurants? Which brands of jogging shoes? Which colleges? Which instructors? Which clothing stores? Which brands of stereos? Which word processing programs? Which SUVs? Which ways of cooking ribs? Which political candidates? Which religions?

4. What would my purpose be in making this particular comparison? To help readers decide what to buy? Where to shop? Where to enroll? Where to work? What teacher or course to take? What to believe? What course of action to take? Whom to vote for?

5. What reading audience would be most interested in the subjects I am comparing? Sports enthusiasts? Model car collectors? Women who love to shop for children's clothes? Classmates who are transferring to another college? Consider the best reading audience for your topic.

TOPIC SELECTION ACTIVITY 4.1

In small groups, discuss possible topics for comparison that different group members offer. In particular, try to identify topics that classmates are interested in or would like to have more information on.

TOPIC SELECTION ACTIVITY 4.2

Applying the topic selection suggestions presented, do the following:

1. Select a topic for your comparison paper. Take your time and decide on a topic that interests you, that you are knowledgeable about, and that would interest some of your classmates. Select a topic that you may know more about than some of your classmates so that they will learn from your comparison.

2. Decide which similar subjects you want to compare within your topic, selecting two to four subjects. (For example, comparing living in the dormitories to living in an apartment while attending college is a useful two-subject comparison, while comparing three or four different kinds of car stereo systems may be most useful.)

3. Make sure that you are comparing "apples to apples." Comparing sports utility vehicles (SUVs) to sports cars is not a similar comparison.

Instead, you would compare different makes and models of SUVs in a paper, or you would compare different makes and models of sports cars in a different paper.

4. Depending on your topic, you may write this paper primarily for a particular group of classmates: those interested in shopping for children's clothes, or those who may be interested in space shuttles. Decide what group of classmates in particular you may direct your paper toward.

STUDENT SAMPLE DRAFT

What shall I compare? I know a lot about car stereos. I've owned enough of them, and I could compare three or four different brands that people might consider buying. This might interest classmates who own cars and are into music. I've taken classes from three different math teachers at the college, and they are very different. I could compare them for other students so they would know what to expect when they had them. This might interest classmates who still have some math ahead of them.

I could compare college to high school because they are very different, but I'm not sure what my purpose would be. And my classmates have also gone through both experiences. That's not an "apples to apples" comparison anyway, is it? I could compare some movies that I've seen recently and recommend them to people who haven't seen them, but that sounds boring.

I keep going back to my first topic: comparing car stereos. That topic interests me, and I know there are always people who are shopping for car stereo systems.

TOPIC   Comparing car stereo systems

SUBJECTS FOR COMPARISON   Alpine, Pioneer, Sanyo

AUDIENCE   Classmates who own cars and like music

PURPOSE   To recommend the best car stereo system for their money

FACTORS TO COMPARE

When you make comparisons and draw conclusions, you consider different factors, some of which may be more important than others. Then you draw your conclusions based on how your subjects compare on each factor, and on your overall evaluation of each subject.

For example, if you are looking for an apartment to rent, you might consider the following factors:

rent   tenants
size   condition
location

The apartment you ultimately select would probably meet your expectations in these five areas better than the apartments you compare it to. However, some factors may have figured more prominently in your decision than others. For example, if the rent was good and the apartment was within walking distance to campus, you might settle for something a little smaller or older than you would have preferred. Some factors may be more important than others.

To decide on the factors to compare your subjects on, follow these guidelines.

1. Your factors are the critical areas of comparison that readers should consider. For example, in comparing used guitars, your factors might include price, brand, condition, and looks. In comparing breeds of dogs, your factors might include price, looks, temperament, size, and gender. In comparing professional football teams, your factors might include team records, prominent players, coaches, relative age of players, and effects of free agency.

2. For your factors, select three to five important areas of comparison that you can cover thoroughly in a paper. For example, in buying a computer, there might be thirty different factors you could compare, but in a paper, you would include only the most critical ones, which might include price, reputation, performance speed, amount of memory, and accompanying software. Focus on those factors that would be most important to readers in making a decision.

PREWRITING ACTIVITY 4.3

In small groups, list four or five factors to compare for each of the following topics. Select those factors that would seem most important in deciding which subject is best.

1. comparing colleges to attend

2. comparing brands of running shoes to buy

3. comparing instructors who teach the same course

4. comparing malls to shop at

PREWRITING ACTIVITY 4.4

Applying the suggestions presented, decide on the factors you will include to compare subjects. Select three to five important areas of comparison from which you will draw your conclusions. Next, decide on the relative value of each factor. Are some more important than others? Should they receive more attention as you decide on your recommendation?

When you have decided on your factors, spend some time evaluating your different subjects for each factor. For example, let's say your topic is running shoes, and your subjects are Nike, Adidas, and Reebok shoes. If your factors include appearance, comfort, durability, and price, evaluate Nike, Adidas, and Reebok on each factor. Which brand looks the best? Which is most comfortable? Which lasts the longest? This will help prepare you to write your first draft.

Topic	Car stereo systems
Subjects To Compare	Alpine, Pioneer, Sanyo
Factors To Compare	Quality of sound Price Features Warranty

JOURNAL ENTRY THIRTEEN

Now that you have completed the prewriting activities, how well-prepared do you feel to write your first draft? Of the prewriting work you did, record in your journal what seemed most useful to you. What, if anything, could you have done without?

FIRST DRAFTS

After selecting your topic, deciding on the subjects to compare and the areas for comparison, and spending some time comparing your subjects on each factor, you are ready to write your first draft. Keep the following suggestions in mind.

DRAFTING GUIDELINES

1. Include an opening, middle, and ending as you did in the previous unit's paper. In the opening, introduce your topic in a way that helps readers understand your purpose: to help them make a particular decision or judgment regarding the topic. In the middle, compare your subjects based on the factors you have selected for comparison. In the ending, draw your conclusion for readers: what you would recommend based on the comparative information.

2. Organize your comparison in some manner: by comparing your subjects one factor at a time (how Alpine, Pioneer, and Sanyo stereos

compare in sound; how they compare in price; how they compare in features, and so on), or by evaluating one subject at a time on all factors (how Alpine fares regarding sound, price, features, warranty; how Pioneer fares regarding sound, price, features, warranty; how Sanyo fares regarding sound, price, features, warranty).

If you compare all subjects on one factor at a time, change paragraphs as you change factors. If you evaluate one subject at a time on all factors, change paragraphs as you change subjects.

3. Draw your conclusion (make your recommendation) for readers based on the comparative information you provide in the middle paragraphs.

You might draw an *unqualified* conclusion—meaning you would recommend the same choice to all readers:

- No one can go wrong in taking Dr. Allen for Calculus I at Kings College.

- The best place to buy boots in Clovis is Western Wear.

You might draw a *qualified* conclusion—giving readers choices based on their situation:

- If you are a math major, take Dr. Allen's Calculus I class, but if you are a nonmajor filling a requirement, take Dr. Fillmore's.

- If money is no object, buy your boots at Western Wear. If you are on a tight budget, go across the street to Boot World.

Keep your readers (classmates) in mind as you draw your conclusion and make recommendations, taking into account the differences among individuals.

4. Keep your purpose in mind as you write: to present the best comparative information and to draw the most reasonable conclusion for readers so they can make a wise decision or choice.

ONLINE ACTIVITY: PARTS OF A COMPOSITION

If you had a difficult time writing a particular part of your paper—the introduction, thesis statement, or conclusion—there is help online. Go to http://leo.stcloudstate.edu/#paperparts. When you arrive, you will see "I have problems with particular parts of a paper—introductions, thesis statements, conclusions" at the top. Click on the particular topic you would like help with, or take a look at all three. Apply what you learn to your upcoming draft. You may also want to refer to this site from time to time as you work on other papers.

DRAFTING ACTIVITY 4.5

Read the following student sample draft, "Car Stereo Systems," and the subsequent essay, "Born to be Different" by Camille Lewis. In small groups, discuss the following:

1. How does each writer introduce his or her topic?

2. What comparisons does each writer make in the middle paragraphs among or between subjects?

3. What conclusion does each writer draw at the end?

4. What was the purpose of each paper, and what reading audience do you think each was intended for?

Then write the first draft of your paper with the suggestions presented in mind.

Car Stereo Systems

STUDENT SAMPLE DRAFT   If you are in the market for a car stereo, there are a lot of options available. I've put in a few systems myself over the years, and basically you get what you pay for. However, there are some good buys out there, depending on what your particular needs are.

Three car stereo brands that represent the high-price to low-price range are Alpine, Pioneer, and Sanyo. Nakamichi ranks with Alpine in the high range; Kenwood, Panasonic, and Sony are in the medium range with Pioneer; and Kraco, Craig, and Realistic join Sanyo in the lower-priced range.

In sound quality, there's not much difference between Alpine and Pioneer. Their frequency response, sound/noise ratio, and dynamic range are similar. If I listened to one and then the other using the same speakers, I couldn't tell which was which. The Sanyo, however, and its lower-priced cousins don't sound as good. You get more noise with them as the volume increases, and their sound range isn't as great as the others.

In terms of features, all of the stereos offer DVD players and CD players. Digital display and programming are standard on the Alpine and Pioneer, but not on the Sanyo. Alpine and Pioneer also offer pull-out models, remote control, and channel memory, not available with Sanyo and other cheaper brands.

The warranty on the different brands has to do with the quality of components and construction. As might be expected, the Alpine has the longest warranty of three years on parts and service while the Pioneer has a one-year, parts-and-service warranty and Sanyo a 90-day to one-year, parts-only warranty. Clearly, the Alpine is better constructed, whereas the Pioneer and Sanyo are not going to hold up as well for as long a time.

The prices on the three models differ considerably. The Alpine models are priced from $500 to $1,500, Pioneer from $200 to $500, and Sanyo from $50 to $200. The range of prices within each brand reflects the different quality of models each offers. A $1,500 Alpine model would represent a state-of-the-art stereo of the finest craftsmanship, highest quality components, and the optimal number of features.

If I had money to burn, it would be great to have the $1,500 Alpine, knowing I've got about the best car stereo money can buy. However, not many people I know can afford one. For the money, I believe the best buy would be a mid-priced brand such as the Pioneer pull-out model with DVD and CD player, which you could get for under $300. You'd have good quality sound, the option to use tapes or CDs, and the security of being able to remove your stereo when you're parked. You could get the Pioneer even cheaper if you went with just a DVD or CD player and without the pull-out feature, if security isn't a problem.

Personally, I wouldn't recommend one of the lower-priced stereos like the Sanyo unless you aren't going to be in your car much or you really don't care about the quality of sound. Given the short warranty and lack of quality construction, you probably aren't going to be better off financially in the long run than if you'd bought a mid-priced stereo.

Finally, whatever you decide on, I'd recommend shopping around and looking for a good sale. Sale prices are more common on the mid-priced stereos since people who buy the more expensive ones aren't that price conscious and the cheaper stereos don't have much of a profit margin to discount. The only other consideration is whether you buy an American or foreign-brand stereo—both are available at every price range—and that's an individual choice.

Born to Be Different
Camille Lewis

Some years ago, when my children were very young, I cut a cartoon out of a magazine and taped it to my refrigerator. It showed a young couple welcoming friends over for Christmas. The hosts rather proudly announce that instead of dolls, they have given their little daughter her own set of tools. And sure enough, the second panel shows their little girl playing in her room, a wrench in one hand and a hammer in the other. But she's making the wrench say, "Would you like to go to the prom, Barbie?" and the hammer answer, "Oh, Ken! I'd love to!"

Oh my, did that cartoon strike a chord. I grew up with *Ms.* Magazine and the National Organization for Women and a firm belief that gender differences were *learned*, not inborn. Other parents may have believed that pink and baby dolls and kindergarten teaching were for girls, and blue and trucks and engineering were for boys, but by golly, *my* kids were going to be different. They were going to be raised free of all that harmful gender indoctrination. They were just going to be *people.*

I don't remember exactly when I began to suspect I was wrong. Maybe it was when my three-year-old son, raised in a "no weapons" household, bit his toast into a gun shape and tried to shoot the cat. Maybe it was when his younger brother nearly levitated out of his car seat, joyously crowing "backhoe!" upon spotting his first piece of earth-moving equipment. Maybe it was when my little daughter first lined up her stuffed animals and began teaching them their ABC's and bandaging their boo-boos.

It wasn't that my sons couldn't be sweet and sensitive, or that my daughter wasn't sometimes rowdy and boisterous. But I had to rethink my earlier assumptions. Despite my best efforts not to impose gender-specific expectations on them, my boys and my girl were, well, different. *Really* different.

Slowly and hesitantly, medical and psychological researchers have begun confirming my observations. The notion that the differences between the sexes (beyond the obvious anatomical ones) are biologically based is fraught with controversy. Such beliefs can easily be misinterpreted and used as the basis for harmful, oppressive stereotypes. They can be overstated and exaggerated into blanket statements about what men and women "can" and "can't" do; about what the genders are "good" and "bad" at. And yet, the unavoidable fact is that studies are making it ever clearer that, as groups, men and women differ in almost every measurable aspect. Learning about those differences helps us understand why men and women are simultaneously so attracted and fascinated, and yet so frequently stymied and frustrated, by the opposite sex. To dig into what it really means to be masculine and feminine helps to depersonalize our responses to one another's behavior—to avoid the "*My* perceptions and behaviors are normal; *yours* don't make sense" trap. Our differences are deep-rooted, hard-wired, and present from the moment of conception.

To begin with, let's look at something as basic as the anatomy of the brain. Typically, men have larger skulls and brains than women. But the sexes score equally well on intelligence tests. This apparent contradiction is explained by the fact that our brains are apportioned differently. Women have about 15 percent more "gray matter" than men. Gray matter, made up of nerve cells and the branches that connect them, allows the quick transference of thought from one part of the brain to another. This high concentration of gray matter helps explain women's ability to look at many sides of an argument at once, and to do several tasks (or hold several conversations) simultaneously.

Men's brains, on the other hand, have a more generous portion of "white matter." White matter, which is made up of neurons, actually inhibits the spread of information. It allows men to concentrate very narrowly on a specific task, without being distracted by thoughts that might conflict with the job at hand. In addition, men's larger skulls contain more cerebrospinal fluid, which cushions the brain. Scientists theorize that this reflects men's history of engaging in warfare and rough sports, activities which bring with them a high likelihood of having one's head banged about.

Our brains' very different makeup leads to our very different methods of interacting with the world around us. Simon Baron-Cohen, author of *The Essential Difference: Men, Women and the Extreme Male Brain,* has labeled the classic female mental process as "empathizing." He defines empathizing as "the drive to identify another person's emotions and thoughts, and to respond to these with an appropriate emotion." Empathizers are constantly measuring and responding to the surrounding emotional temperature. They are concerned about showing sensitivity to the people around them. This empathetic quality can be observed in virtually all aspects of women's lives: from the choice of typically female-dominated careers (nursing, elementary school teaching, social work) to reading matter popular mainly with women (romantic fiction, articles about relationships, advice columns about how people can get along better) to women's interaction with one another (which typically involves intimate discussion of relationships with friends and family, and sympathy for each others' concerns). So powerful is the empathizing mindset that it even affects how the typical female memory works. Ask a woman when a particular event happened, and she often pinpoints it in terms of an occurrence that had emotional content: "That was the summer my sister broke her leg," or "That was around the time Gene and Mary got into such an awful argument." Likewise, she is likely to bring her empathetic mind to bear on geography. She'll remember a particular address not as 11th and Market Streets but being "near the restaurant where we went on our anniversary," or "around the corner from Liz's old apartment."

In contrast, Baron-Cohen calls the typical male mindset "systemizing," which he defines as "the drive to analyze and explore a system, to extract underlying rules that govern the behavior of a system." A systemizer is less interested in how people feel than in how things work. Again, the systematic brain influences virtually all aspects of the typical man's life. Male-dominated professions (such as engineering, computer programming, auto repair, and mathematics) rely heavily on systems, formulas, and patterns, and very little on the ability to intuit another person's thoughts or emotions. Reading material most popular with men includes science fiction and history, as well as factual "how-to" magazines on such topics as computers, photography, home repair, and woodworking. When they get together with male friends, men are far less likely to engage in intimate conversation than they are to share an activity: watching or playing sports, working on a car, bowling, golfing, or fishing. Men's conversation is peppered with dates and addresses, illustrating their comfort with systems: "Back in 1996 when I was living in Boston . . ." or "The best way to the new stadium is to go all the way out Walnut Street to 33rd and then get on the bypass . . ."

One final way that men and women differ is in their typical responses to problem solving. Ironically, it may be this very activity—intended on both sides to eliminate problems—that creates the most conflict between partners of the opposite sex. To a woman, the process of solving a problem is all-important. Talking about a problem is a means of deepening the intimacy between her and her partner. The very anatomy of her brain, as well as her accompanying empathetic mindset, makes her want to consider all sides of a question and to explore various possible solutions. To have a partner who is willing to explore a problem with her is deeply satisfying. She interprets that willingness as an expression of the other's love and concern.

But men have an almost completely opposite approach when it comes to dealing with a problem. Everything in their mental makeup tells them to focus narrowly on the issue—solve it, and get it out of the way. The ability to fix a problem quickly and efficiently is, to them, a demonstration of their power and competence. When a man hears his female partner begin to describe a problem, his strongest impulse is to listen briefly and then tell her what to do about it. From his perspective, he has made a helpful and loving gesture; from hers, he's short-circuited a conversation that could have deepened and strengthened their relationship.

The challenge that confronts men and women is to put aside ideas of "better" and "worse" when it comes to their many differences. Our diverse brain development, our ways of interacting with the world, and our modes of dealing with problems all have their strong points. In some circumstances, a typically feminine approach may be more effective; in others, a classically masculine mode may have the advantage. Our differences aren't going to disappear: My daughter, now a middle-schooler, regularly tells me she loves me, while her teenage brothers express their affection by grabbing me in a headlock. Learning to understand and appreciate one another's gender-specific qualities is the key to more rich and rewarding lives together.

REVISIONS

During the revision process, you look at your draft through fresh eyes to evaluate what you've done well and what you might do better. Though you may write your first draft with little thought for readers, you evaluate and revise the draft with your readers clearly in mind. The effectiveness of your writing is based on how well they understand your thoughts and respond to them. The shift in emphasis from first to second draft is

from getting your ideas on paper to presenting them most effectively to
your readers.

REVISION GUIDELINES

As you read and evaluate your draft, consider these suggestions:

1. Evaluate the strength of your opening. Have you introduced your
   topic in an interesting way? Do readers know you are going to make
   a comparison that may eventually help them make a decision?

2. Evaluate the effectiveness of your comparisons. Can readers clearly see
   the differences (and similarities) among subjects in the important areas of
   comparison? Have you evaluated each subject in each area? Have you
   covered all of the most important factors that readers should consider?

3. Evaluate your ending. Do you draw a clear conclusion for readers
   based on your comparative information and on what you think is the
   best advice? Have you drawn an unqualified conclusion (one recommendation for everyone) or a qualified conclusion (different recommendations based on readers' needs), and does it make the most sense
   for your topic and readers?

4. Have you paragraphed your paper so that your opening, your areas of
   comparison, and your conclusion stand out for readers? Have you
   changed paragraphs as you compared different factors? Have you
   avoided extremely long or short paragraphs? Have you used *transitions* to tie your sentences and paragraphs together? (See the
   upcoming section on "Paragraph Transitions.")

5. Read each sentence carefully to see how you might make it clearer,
   more concise, smoother, or more concrete (visual). Check to see if you
   have varied your sentence structures, joining words, and sentence
   lengths. (See the upcoming review section on "Sentence Revision.")

REVISION ACTIVITY 4.6

In small groups, read and evaluate the following student first draft by
applying the revision guidelines presented and noting suggestions for
improvement.

Next, read and evaluate each classmate's draft—with group members
providing copies of their drafts—and make suggestions for possible revisions.

Living Options

STUDENT SAMPLE
DRAFT
Living in an apartment or living in a dorm provides almost the same
living style, except for a few differences. I have had the experience of
living in an apartment and a dorm. From what I can see, they have very

little difference. It would not make a difference as to where I lived as long as I had a place.

Having an apartment has some good qualities. In an apartment you have your own bathroom and don't have to share with anyone besides a roommate. Living in an apartment makes it easier to take a shower because you don't have to wait in line. Another thing is no waiting in line for the bathroom. You would always have to bring your shampoo and soap back and forth if living in a dorm. If you live in an apartment, you keep all your necessities in your bathroom. You also have more privacy. You don't have to hear the other college students doing other things besides homework. Lastly, you choose a person to live with as in a dorm, you get stuck with whoever it may be.

Living in a dorm is not too bad. You might not like your roommate, but you have many other students in the same building you get along with. It makes it easier when you need help with your homework, the reason being there are many other people who could help. If you live in an apartment, the only person to help is your roommate. Another good thing about living in a dorm is not having to clean the bathroom or the kitchen. Having an apartment means a lot more cleaning. In a dorm all you have to clean is your room. The best thing of all is you don't have to cook. You are able to eat at the cafeteria.

Based on what I have experienced, I would recommend an apartment for more quiet and reserved people. A dorm would be for someone who liked to socialize more. I would feel more comfortable living in an apartment. That is for the fact of more privacy. I would not mind cleaning and cooking for myself. The last reason would be because I am very strict as to whom I live with.

REVISION ACTIVITY 4.7

Evaluate your draft a final time, noting revisions you may want to make to improve your paper. (Your instructor may have you cover the upcoming sections on "Paragraph Transitions" and "Sentence Revision" before evaluating your draft.)

When you are ready, write your second draft, including all revisions you have noted for improving its content, organization, and wording.

JOURNAL ENTRY FOURTEEN

If you wrote your first draft on a computer, relate in your journal how much revising you did as you wrote. Did you write the entire first draft with little or no sentence revision, or did you do some sentence revision as you wrote the draft? What kinds of revisions did you make in the second draft to improve your paper?

PARAGRAPH TRANSITIONS

Writers use a variety of words called *transitions* to tie their sentences and paragraphs together effectively. The purpose of transitional wording is to help readers understand the relationship between different thoughts and also the relationship between different paragraphs.

You undoubtedly use some transitions in your writing already. The purpose of this section is to make you more aware of their value, to present the range of transitional wording available, and to help you use transitions more effectively in your writing.

Useful Transitions

The following transitional words and phrases are useful for most writing you do:

1. *Transitions that show movement in time, place, or sequence:* first, second, next, also, then, after, before, while, now, in the meantime, in conclusion, as you can see, finally, last, in summary.

2. *Transitions that connect supporting points, ideas, or examples:* first, second, also, another, in addition, additionally, furthermore, moreover, whereas, on top of that, beyond that, for example, for instance, such as, like.

3. *Transitions that show relationships between thoughts:* however, therefore, nevertheless, thus, despite, in spite of, on the contrary, on the other hand, consequently, moreover, frankly, honestly, confidentially, actually, truthfully, in fact, of course, in reality.

The following groupings of transitions will help you use them correctly and be aware of the options available.

Contrasting transitions	"Straight talk" transitions	"Adding" transitions
on the other hand	frankly	furthermore
however	honestly	moreover
nevertheless	confidentially	on top of that
on the contrary	actually	in addition
despite	in fact	beyond that
in spite of	truthfully	additionally
	of course	
	in reality	

(table continues on next page)

Comparative transitions	**"Example" transitions**	**Concluding transitions**
while	for example	in conclusion
whereas	for instance	as you can see
on the other hand	like	last
however	such as	in summary
whether		finally
		last but not least

Cause-effect transitions

therefore

thus

consequently

Transitions such as *however, therefore, furthermore,* and *nevertheless* are often preceded by a semicolon (;). The semicolon indicates the beginning of a new sentence closely related to the sentence preceding it. When you use a semicolon to separate two sentences, you do *not* capitalize the first letter of the second sentence.

EXAMPLES
I need to go Christmas shopping; however, I don't know when I will find time.

Louise is living at home this semester; therefore, she'll save the cost of renting an apartment.

Alicia got an A on her English final; furthermore, she passed biology after two previous attempts.

Felix bowled a score of 23 his first game; nevertheless, he had a good time.

TRANSITION ACTIVITY 4.8

In small groups, read the following paragraphs with their transitions underlined. For each underlined transition, come up with one or two optional transitions that could also be used effectively in place of the underlined transitions.

Getting across town from east to west can take time; <u>therefore,</u> you need to plan the best route and time to reach your destination. Herndon is probably the best east-west street to take at most times. <u>However,</u> at 5:00 rush hour, it gets very congested. <u>Consequently,</u> you may want to take Bullard Avenue at rush hour because it is less congested. <u>Furthermore,</u> Bullard has been worked on in the last year, so the road is very smooth.

<u>On the other hand,</u> there are a couple of routes, <u>like</u> Highway 168 and Highway 41, that may seem out of the way because they run more north- south. <u>Despite</u> their direction, they can ultimately deliver you to a westerly destination in a reasonable time because you can drive 70–75 miles per hour rather than 40–45 on Herndon or Bullard. <u>Moreover,</u> they are wide, beautiful new freeways that are easy and relaxing to drive on. <u>Therefore,</u> while you are taking a more round-about route and driving more miles on the freeways, you'll get there at about the same time and in a better mood.

<u>As you can see,</u> there are different options for getting from the west to the east side of town, <u>such as</u> Herndon, Bullard, Highway 168, or Highway 41. Herndon and Bullard are more direct routes <u>whereas</u> on the freeways, you drive faster and more relaxed. I've taken different routes, and the one I choose depends on my mood, the time of day, and how rushed I am. <u>Frankly,</u> there's no really good way to drive east to west in town, and until the county builds an east-to-west–running freeway, people who commute in that direction are going to be frustrated.

TRANSITION ACTIVITY 4.9

In small groups, read the following comparative essay, "Why America Can't Compete" by Leroy Crooks. Identify the transitions that he uses in each paragraph, and the purpose for each transition. Then discuss the questions at the end of the essay.

Then check your latest draft for transitional wording, and insert transitions wherever you think they would help connect ideas, sentences, or paragraphs.

Why America Can't Compete
Leroy Crooks

Recently I heard a grape farmer bemoaning the fact that the minimum wage was going up in California and that even paying the prevailing wage, it cost him a lot more to raise grapes than farmers in Mexico or Chile or China. How could American farmers, or any American producers or manufacturers, he wondered, compete in a global market where other countries are producing quality products for less? "American workers want more and more," he said, "and it's killing our chances to compete."

Well yes, American workers do want more, as the cost of housing, gaso-line, and health care skyrocket. Is the answer to competing with the Chinese, Japanese, Mexicans, or Chileans to cut back on wages so that our production costs are competitive with other nations? Well, who's the first volunteer to work for $1.00 an hour to make us more competitive? No takers, I'd imagine. The fact is, we can't compete with other nations in a number of markets, and that number is going to grow larger. What that says about America's future is scary to say the least.

Actually, America could never compete with other countries in the cost of production, but in the past, there was little competition. We had a vir-tual monopoly in selling farm produce, automobiles, steel, television sets, you name it. Other countries simply didn't have the know-how or the cap-ital or the natural resources to compete, and cost of production was an issue only between American competitors rather than with foreign com-petitors. Therefore, we were only too willing to share our know-how with other nations to help bolster their economies, never considering the long-range effects.

The first country to dent America's economic superiority was, of course, Japan, who after World War II began putting considerable talent and drive into the economy rather than the military. Not only could Japan put out a less expensive automobile, by the 1970s it was putting out higher quality cars, and American automakers went into a thirty-year nosedive that they have yet to recover from. America had lost its corner on the auto industry, and the electronics industry—televisions, cameras, stereos—was soon to follow.

Today, most of what Americans buy is foreign made, with China playing a major economic role. The toys we play with, the clothes we wear, the electronic gadgets we covet, the vehicles we drive, and increas-ingly more of the food we eat are imported. Our ratio of exports to imports is radically out of whack, and with America becoming more and more a consumer rather than producer nation, we have lost thousands upon thousands of jobs to the producing countries.

But why can't we compete in the global marketplace? The answer is simple. Workers in China and India and Chile and Mexico work for dirt-poor wages compared to U.S. workers. They make a fraction of what U.S. employees earn and have a correspondingly lower standard of living. China, where the standard of living is supposedly improving dramatically for millions of Chinese in their new capitalist economy, now boasts that many can afford a color television set and a modern refrigerator. Buying a car is still a dream for the future, as is owning a home.

In addition, many third-world countries don't have American-like labor laws that limit the hours and days that employees can work, that disallow child labor, and that require safe and sanitary working conditions for employees. Furthermore, most industries aren't regulated by American-like environmental standards, which are costly but protect our country and citizens from a great deal of air and water pollution.

In many ways, the industrial conditions in countries that are becoming players in the global economic game are similar to those in the U.S. in the early 1900s, where employees worked twelve-to fourteen-hour days six to seven days a week in dreadful conditions, children working alongside adults, all working for pitifully low wages, with benefits such as medical and disability insurance, sick leave days, vacation time, and pregnancy leave unheard of. No one in his right mind would want or expect Americans ever to return to the dismal working conditions and wretched way of life that might bring our production costs more in line with third-world countries. We would in effect become a third-world country ourselves.

Finally, America no longer has the edge in quality over other nations. Other countries have caught up with us in technology and industrial/ agricultural expertise, much of which we have provided them over the years, and are using what we have taught them, along with what they have learned on their own, to turn out excellent quality products. There is little today that we have to sell to other countries that they can't manufacture or produce just as well at home, and less expensively. It is no wonder that we import far more than we export, and that ratio will continue to get worse.

With the tremendous loss of American jobs over the past years and our growing reliance, albeit of our own will, on foreign products, one would think that America's economy would be in the throes of a dramatic downturn. However, most economic indicators don't point in that direction. Currently, America is enjoying low unemployment, low inflation, a rebounding stock market, positive economic growth, and a housing boom. Oil prices have been disturbingly high, but that at least is prodding the government into talking seriously about ending our reliance on foreign oil and developing alternative energy sources.

If there has been one constant in American economic history, it is the fact that changes are inevitable, and we have always been able to respond to those changes and create new opportunities. Who would have imagined one hundred and fifty years ago that agriculture, which comprised over 90% of the American economy then, would represent 2% of our economy today? And in just the past fifty years, we have gone primarily from a heavy industry to a light industry economy, with, for example, the steel industry collapsing and the computer industry emerging.

Can America's economy continue reinventing itself in the wake of tremendous foreign competition? Current economic indicators suggest that we can, but many experts feel that the greatest effects of the new global economy are on the horizon, and no one knows how far the exodus of American jobs and industries to other countries will go. On the positive side, imported products result in the least expensive goods for American consumers, and many companies that have their products manufactured overseas, such as Wal-Mart, are successful for that very reason. Further, as many nations of the world become more economically interdependent, including America, there is a greater chance for worldwide stability, as a safe and stable world provides the best economic climate for all nations. Finally, if history is any indicator, anyone who would predict a long economic decline for America must believe that American ingenuity is just a myth.

QUESTIONS FOR DISCUSSION

1. What is being compared in the Crooks essay?

2. What is Crooks's thesis, and how does he support it?

3. What are the major areas of comparison in the essay?

4. What conclusion does Crooks reach in his ending? What does the last sentence mean?

5. What, if any, effect might the changing world economy Crooks writes about have on the possible occupation or occupations you are preparing for, and why?

TRANSITION ACTIVITY 4.10

Fill in the following paragraphs with transitional words to tie sentences and paragraphs together. Fill in each blank with a word or phrase from the list of transitions that makes the most appropriate connection. Then reread your latest draft and see where you might add a transitional word or phrase to show a relationship between thoughts or different paragraphs, or to begin your concluding paragraph.

EXAMPLES   <u>Before</u> buying a new typewriter, shop around for a used one.

<u>Then</u> look for reasonably priced typing paper.

Computer Labs

Writing papers in a college computer lab can be very convenient. _____, you need to follow a few basic steps to have the greatest success. _____, you need to learn how to use the word processing program on the computers so that you can type your papers effectively. _____, you should learn how to add and delete words, move the cursor around, run the spell check, move sentences or paragraphs to different places, save your work, and print your paper. _____, it is important to know how to change the size and font of your letters and how to change your line spacing from single to double spacing or vice versa.

_____, you should always use a floppy disk or compact disc to save your work. You may not always finish a paper at the lab, but if you save your writing on a disc, you can take it home and work on it if you have a computer. _____, saving your papers on a disc allows you to go back and rework a previous paper and _____ keep a record of all your writings for a class.

_____, you need to save your work on your disc at frequent intervals while you type. Computers in a lab tend to have more problems than a home computer because they are all tied to the same system and get a lot of student use. _____, it is not uncommon for a computer program to "freeze" while you are typing a paper, meaning that the computer won't allow you to continue. _____, if you haven't saved your writing to that point on a disc, you will lose everything you have typed, which can be very frustrating. _____, if you have saved your writing regularly on your disc as you typed, you will not lose anything that you have saved before the computer freezes.

_____, you need to follow a few basic steps to have the most success typing your papers in a college computer lab. _____, if you follow these steps, you will not only be able to complete and print your papers successfully, you will enjoy the experience.

SENTENCE REVISION

For most writers, sentence revision is an important part of the writing process. You revise sentences to help readers understand your ideas better and to find the best wording possible. To accomplish this, you might change a word or two in one sentence, move a phrase in another, and completely reword a third.

In this section, you continue to hone your skills by revising typical first-draft sentences. Then you apply what you learn to revising the latest draft of your comparison paper.

Wording Problems Review

An important part of draft revision is improving the wording of individual sentences. Not only are you making your sentences more readable, you are also clarifying your thoughts for your readers and yourself.

REVISION REVIEW ACTIVITY 4.11

The following first-draft sentences have problems with wordiness, awkward phrasing, weak word choices, and vagueness. Rewrite each sentence to make it smoother, clearer, and more concise. Then read the latest draft of your comparison paper for possible sentence revisions.

EXAMPLE   When I work this summer at a job, I'm going to save my money for a car that is used.

REVISED   When I work this summer, I'm going to save my money for a used car.

1. I try to spend as much quality time as I can with my nieces and nephews as a group or on a one-to-one basis.

2. I hope that I can impact my nieces' and nephews' lives in a positive way, and when they grow up, they can remember that I will always be there for them when they need me.

3. We are a very close family, which means our family gatherings are so much fun and interesting also.

4. If you left one piece of trash anywhere on the high school grounds, the security guys would write you up for that and give you detention just for that.

5. When children meet new kids, they want to be friends with them, and sometimes they fight.

6. Not too much time had passed when I got another phone call from my daughter's teacher about the same problem, that my daughter talked a lot in class, and that she didn't pay attention in class.

7. I told the teacher that I felt she was discriminating against my son because he was Puerto Rican, but I also told her that I was not going to let her get away with it, and that if it didn't stop and she didn't start treating all children as equals, I was going to talk to the principal first.

8. One of the biggest problems that I can't stand is seeing my house all dirty.

9. I try to finish all my chores when I get home from school, even though I have a lot of help from my husband, who helps me make dinner, but I have to finish the rest by myself.

10. One of the biggest things that I would like to have is more time on my hands for me to enjoy my house, other than cleaning the house and having to go right to bed.

11. I enjoy a peaceful evening with my family, and not having a lot of stress to worry about, like problems at work.

12. Our players had a great football game, but our football coaches thought the total opposite of that.

Sentence Variety

Writers who use a variety of sentence structures express themselves most effectively and produce the most readable writing. The more structural options you use, the better equipped you are to express yourself, and the more readers can appreciate your writing.

Relative Clauses

A sentence structure that many writers find useful is the complex sentence with a *relative clause*. A relative clause begins with a relative pronoun—*who, whom, whose, which,* or *that*—that modifies the word preceding it.

EXAMPLES   The man <u>who borrowed your lawn mower</u> moved to Alaska.

Here on the table are the books <u>that you left at my house.</u>

The math problem <u>that Joan had trouble with</u> is puzzling everyone.

The men <u>who own the fruit stand</u> are selling some beautiful nectarines.

That blue Mazda is the car <u>that I'd like to own someday.</u>

Ralph picked the watermelon <u>that was the largest and ripest.</u>

The woman <u>whose money you found</u> lives in Paris.

Hanna's umbrella, <u>which she bought for $30,</u> has a hole in it.

The students <u>who did well on the geology final</u> all studied together.

As you can see, the underlined clauses beginning with *who, which, that,* and *whose* describe or identify the word directly before them. Here is how the relative pronouns are used.

WHO   used with *people.* The child <u>who</u> ate the gooseberries got sick.

WHOM   used with *people.* The plumber <u>whom</u> you sent to my house was expensive.

WHOSE   used with *people.* The girl <u>whose</u> book was lost is in the library.

WHOSE   used with *things.* The textbook <u>whose</u> cover is torn was sold at half price.

THAT   used with *people.* The family <u>that</u> lives next door moved.

          used with *things.* The magazine <u>that</u> you subscribe to is terrific.

WHICH   used with *things.* The L Street route, <u>which</u> is lined with trees, is very direct.

RELATIVE CLAUSE ACTIVITY 4.12

Complete the following complex sentences with your own words:

EXAMPLE   The man who lives behind us *mows his lawn at night.*

The alligator that _____

She was the actress who _____

The only students who _____

Your new toaster, which _____

That new teacher whom you _____

The rock group that _____

I like a hamburger that _____

Please return my stamp collection, which_____

The kind of dog that _____

The movie star whose _____

I really prefer a doctor who _____

RELATIVE CLAUSE ACTIVITY 4.13

Combine each of the following pairs of sentences to form a single sentence with a relative clause beginning with *who, whom, whose, which,* or *that.* Delete unnecessary words when you combine sentences. Separate the relative clause in the new sentence with commas when the person or thing it modifies is *named:* John Brown, who is a golfing instructor, attends college at night. The Barkley Tower, which stands in the middle of Heathcliff College, is three hundred feet tall. The man who is a golfing instructor attends college at night. The tower that stands in the middle of Heathcliff College is three hundred feet tall. Never use commas with relative clauses beginning with *that.*

EXAMPLE   Maria Gomez works at Bank of America. She lives down the street from me.

EXAMPLE   Maria Gomez, who works at Bank of America, lives down the street from me.

REVISED (OPTION)   Maria Gomez, who lives down the street from me, works at Bank of America.

1. The boy sat behind me in Algebra. He dropped the class after two weeks.

2. You took the woman's seat on the bus. She is very mad.

3. The Kings River flooded its banks yesterday. It is often dry this time of year.

4. The foreign students are from Laos and Cambodia. I met them at the student union yesterday.

5. Glen and Elvira are good students. They will do very well in graduate school.

6. *The Congo* by Michael Crichton was an intriguing book. I couldn't put it down.

7. I found a man's wallet at the supermarket yesterday. He gave me a $25 reward.

8. I tried to buy concert tickets from a scalper. They would have cost me $100 apiece.

9. Melissa Guthridge contributes to numerous charities for children. She is very generous with her money.

10. The Bay Bridge is over five miles long. It is the longest bridge in the western United States.

REVISION ACTIVITY 4.14

Read the latest draft of your comparison paper and revise sentences to vary your sentence structures, to replace any overused joining words (such as *and, but, so,* or *because*), to combine short sentences or divide overly long ones, or to combine pairs of sentences by inserting relative clauses.

FINAL EDITING

The last step in the writing process is to give your latest draft a final proofreading for errors. If you are using a computer, print out the draft rather than reading it on the screen. You will often find errors on the printed page that you would overlook otherwise.

PROOFREADING GUIDELINES

When you proofread your latest draft, make sure to cover the following areas, and pay particular attention to your personal error tendencies.

1. Make sure you have a period at the end of each sentence. Check for run-on sentences that need periods (or joining words) and for sentence fragments that should be attached to the sentences they belong with. (See the upcoming review sections on "Run-on Sentences" and "Fragments.")

2. Check word endings to make sure you have an *s* on plural words and an *ed* on regular past tense verbs and that your subjects and verbs agree. (Review the section on "Subject-Verb Agreement" in Unit Three.)

3. Check your spelling carefully, including homophones such as there/their/they're, know/no, its/it's, your/you're, and threw/through.

4. Check your internal punctuation, including comma usage in words in a series, in compound sentences, after introductory groups of words, and to set off relative clauses, "interrupters," and ending phrases. (See the upcoming section on "Comma Usage.") Make sure you use apostrophes in contractions and possessive words (John's dog, the pencil's eraser, the legislature's schedule) and quotation marks around direct quotations. (See the section on "Possessives" under "Spelling" in the Appendix.)

5. Check your use of subject pronouns (Martha and I; my mother, father, and I; Gretchen and she; the Joneses and they), and make sure all pronouns agree with their antecedents. (See the upcoming section on "Pronoun-Antecedent Agreement.")

PROOFREADING ACTIVITY 4.15

In small groups, proofread the following student draft for errors and make the necessary corrections. Next, proofread your latest draft for errors following the revision guidelines presented, and make corrections. (Your instructor may have you cover the upcoming sections on "Punctuation" and "Correct Usage" before proofreading.) Finally, write or print out your final draft to share with classmates and your instructor.

Space Vessels

STUDENT SAMPLE DRAFT   There is only one type of space vessel that we as a planet use that is the space shuttle. That is the one everyone knows about and has seen. Rite now they are working on a new one that they call the X-33. Which looks a lot like a plane rather than a space shuttle.

The old shuttle was more of a bullet shape with wings; its engines made a lot of unwanted pollution as a by-product of its engines working. However, the X-33's engines instead of polluting the air, make water, which gives the astronauts plenty of water. Which is a big help because they don't have to put any water on bored, making the ship lighter.

The old shuttle only had one way to take off and that was strait up, but the X-33 does not it can take off just like a plane making it much more practical than having to build a launch pad, not to mention those one-time usable booster rockets that costs about $400,000,000 to build.

The X-33 can also go faster and farther than the old shuttle could go. It also has a fully automatic venting system, which the shuttle does not the system will automatically suck any smoke or tocsin out into space it also reuses the air in the shuttle.

The X-33 also has new thermal plates that are able to stand reentry at least two time instead of one. So overall, the X-33 is a better ship for us all together. Which makes me think that we will see a lot more of space after it is finished in 2010.

JOURNAL ENTRY FIFTEEN

In your journal, relate one particular error tendency that you still have, the progress you have made in correcting it, and what you still need to do to eliminate the error in future writing.

SENTENCE PROBLEMS

The most common sentence problems—run-on sentences and fragments— have been introduced in earlier units. However, for students who have recurring problems, they will be reviewed in this section and throughout the text. You seldom eliminate a longtime error tendency after a brief lesson or two, but by working on it throughout the text, you can make great progress.

RUN-ON SENTENCE REVIEW ACTIVITY 4.16

The following passage contains some run-on sentences. Rewrite the passage and correct the run-on sentences by separating complete sentences or joining them with coordinate or subordinate conjunctions. Separate longer sentences and join shorter, related sentences.

EXAMPLE   The teachers were upset. They had received no raise for three years they decided not to return to school in the fall without a decent contract.

REVISED   The teachers were upset. They had received no raise for three years, so they decided not to return to school in the fall without a decent contract.

In the 2004 November election, the Republicans held their majority in the House of Representatives and gained a majority in the Senate. The Republicans now have control of both houses of the legislature and the presidency. Both parties want to be in this dominant political position, it seldom happens. Often in off-year national elections when the presidency isn't contested, the party of the president loses legislative seats this year was noticeably different. President Bush campaigned in many states for the Republican legislative candidates his presence seemed to make a difference. When a president has a low approval rating at mid term, he can be a liability to his party's candidates running for the House and Senate. However, Bush's popularity gave candidates a boost, and in states where he campaigned, most of the Republican legislative candidates won. Interestingly, the President's campaigning had little impact on governors' races these contests often turn on a state's economic issues rather than national issues, so the President's impact is minimal.

Fragments

As you learned in Unit Three, fragments are caused by separating a clause from the sentence it belongs with or by leaving out words that would complete the sentence.

EXAMPLE   I'm very tired this morning. Because I only got three hours of sleep last night.

CORRECTED   I'm very tired this morning because I only got three hours of sleep last night. (because *fragment is joined to sentence it belongs with*)

EXAMPLE   Walking to school this morning in the driving rain.

CORRECTED   I was miserable walking to school this morning in the driving rain. (*words added to form complete sentences*)

Fragments are most commonly created through punctuation errors and can be remedied by eliminating the period that separates them from the sentence they belong with.

FRAGMENT REVIEW ACTIVITY 4.17

Each of the following groups of sentences contains one fragment. Correct the fragment by adding it to the sentence that it belongs with.

EXAMPLE   Joe was late for work. Since others were also late. Joe had no problem.

REVISED   Joe was late for work. Since others were also late, Joe had no problem.

1. The food in the college cafeteria has gotten better. Since the school privatized the operation.

2. Instead of a school-run cafeteria with your usual food. The cafeteria is now a food court with a number of different vendors selling food.

3. Today you can get practically any kind of food you want. For example, Mexican, Chinese, Japanese, or Italian.

4. The cafeteria also looks much different today. At least a dozen food booths around the walls of the cafeteria, with seating in the middle.

5. The cafeteria is more crowded than ever. Especially between noon and 2:00 p.m.

6. Although I can't eat there very often. I've always enjoyed my food when I've gone.

7. The cafeteria has taken away a lot of lunch business from the fast food restaurants in the area. Because it has a number of fast food choices itself.

8. The purpose of changing the cafeteria was to keep more students on campus for lunch by offering a variety of good food. Which seems to be working out well.

PUNCTUATION

In earlier units the three most common uses for commas were introduced: within series of words, before conjunctions in compound sentences, and after introductory groups of words. In this section, you learn three new uses for commas: to set off relative clauses (which were introduced earlier in this unit), interrupters, and ending phrases.

Comma Usage

Add the following rules for comma usage to those you learned in previous units, including a more detailed presentation on punctuating relative clause:

1. *Relative clauses:* To punctuate relative clauses correctly, follow these basic rules:

   a. If the word modified by a *who* or *which* clause is clearly named or identified, the clause is set off by commas.

   Mary Garcia, <u>who owns the dress shop on G Street</u>, is my neighbor. (Mary Garcia *clearly names the person.)*

   The Golden Gate Bridge, <u>which spans San Francisco Bay</u>, is painted annually. (Golden Gate Bridge *clearly names the bridge.)*

   The new fish market on Oliver Avenue, <u>which opened its doors last Friday</u>, specializes in shellfish. (New fish market on Oliver Avenue *clearly identifies the market.)*

   Matt Golden, <u>who drives a milk truck</u>, married Emma Blue, <u>who lives on his route</u>. (Matt Golden *and* Emma Blue *clearly name the people.)*

   b. If a *who* or *which* clause is needed to identify clearly the word it modifies, don't set it off with commas.

   The men <u>who work for my aunt</u> live in Trenton. (Who work for my aunt *identifies the men.)*

The directions <u>which you gave us</u> were easy to follow. (Which you gave us *identifies the directions.*)

I'd like to meet the woman <u>who painted that strange picture.</u> (Who painted that strange picture *identifies the woman.*)

   c. Never use commas with relative clauses beginning with *that.*

The students <u>that sit in back of the room</u> are very talkative.

I'd like to see the watermelon <u>that weighs over fifty pounds.</u>

2. *Interrupters:* Set off incidental words and phrases that require reading pauses in a sentence.

<u>By the way</u>, what time are you going to class today?

I am interested, <u>of course</u>, in getting a good grade and in learning a lot about physics.

<u>Fortunately,</u> I did a lot of scuba diving before diving off the coast of Australia.

My father, <u>as you might know</u>, works with your father at the Lockheed Aircraft plant.

3. *Ending phrases:* To indicate a reading pause, insert a comma before an ending group of words that begins with an *-ing* word or the word *especially* or *particularly.*

Leticia sped through the multiple-choice half of her physics test, <u>knowing</u> that the thought problems in the second half would take a lot of time.

Jonathan walked home disappointedly from the Department of Motor Vehicles, <u>wondering</u> if he would ever pass his driving test.

Washington, D.C., is beautiful in the spring, <u>especially</u> when the cherry blossoms are in bloom.

Shop at Martin's Boutique for floral arrangements, <u>particularly</u> if you like silk flowers.

COMMA ACTIVITY 4.18

Place commas in the following sentences according to all the rules you have learned. Some sentences won't require commas. When you finish, proofread your latest draft for correct comma placement.

EXAMPLE   In the early morning hours Mary prowls the house and waits for dawn to break.

REVISED   In the early morning hours, Mary prowls the house and waits for dawn to break. *(comma after introductory phrase)*

1. John and Henrietta decided to jog to school and back three times a week.

2. John Helen and Henrietta decided to jog to school and they later decided to jog back home as well.

3. Before you try the cornflakes in the cupboard check the packaging date on the box and see how old they are.

4. Samantha really enjoys playing strange characters in plays because the parts are so different from her personality.

5. After Gladys fixed the radiator hose on her Honda the fan belt and the smaller radiator hose broke.

6. Working on his stamp collection and watching old *Cisco Kid* reruns on TV are Albert's pastimes and he ignores everything else around him for weeks at a time.

7. For the week-long field trip to Death Valley we'll need picks and shovels tents and cots food and water and heavy jackets.

8. Harvey left third base at the crack of the bat and raced for home plate well ahead of the ball.

9. From the looks of that cut on your head and your bruised knees you'd better see a doctor and do it fast!

10. Louise and Mavis invited Teddie and Rumford to the Lucky Horseshoe Casino and then didn't show up.

11. If I had a dime for every time you had an excuse for being late for work I could retire early and live like a king.

12. Allyson thought about attending Mumsford College and even sent in an application but at the last minute she decided to attend a business college.

13. Rex Garcia who was born in Santa Fe, New Mexico is now the mayor of his hometown.

14. When I returned to my apartment I found Marian Weber an old high school friend waiting for me outside.

15. I wanted to sit in a floor seat at the Green Day concert but since all floor seat tickets are sold I'll settle for a balcony seat which costs $15.

16. My uncle by the way knows your family well.

17. I'm not interested in going to the debate especially since it doesn't start until 10:00 p.m.

18. Pao didn't worry about the language entrance exam knowing he could take it again before school started.

19. You'll have no trouble finding the library which is the only round building on campus.

20. Incidentally do you know who our new neighbors are?

CORRECT USAGE

Standard English follows basic rules of grammar that govern the way we write and talk. Such rules make it possible for people to communicate effectively anywhere in the world where English is spoken. Knowledge of these rules and their practical application to writing and speaking is essential to our functioning effectively within the world of educated people.

In this section you are introduced to a new area of grammar—pronoun-antecedent agreement. Understanding and applying rules of agreement are fundamental to writing correctly.

Pronoun-Antecedent Agreement

Pronouns replace words that don't need repeating in a sentence or paragraph. To use pronouns most effectively, follow these basic conventions:

1. Replace a word with a pronoun instead of repeating the word unnecessarily.

   AWKWARD   The building lost the building's roof in the tornado.

   BETTER   The building lost its roof in the tornado.

   AWKWARD   Betty was going to be late for class, so Betty called her teacher.

   BETTER   Betty was going to be late for class, so she called her teacher.

2. A pronoun agrees in number and gender with the word it replaces: its *antecedent*. For example, if an antecedent is singular and female (Betty), the pronouns replacing it must be singular and female (she, her, hers). In the following examples, the antecedent is underlined twice; the pronoun replacing it is underlined once.

   EXAMPLES   A <u>student</u> in dental assisting must take twelve units of science if <u>she</u> wants to get a degree. *(The antecedent* student *is singular, so the pronoun* she *referring to* student *is also singular.)*

   <u>One</u> of the boys is missing <u>his</u> watch. *(The antecedent* one *is singular, so the pronoun* his *referring to* one *is also singular.)*

   <u>Women</u> should never downgrade <u>their</u> abilities. *(The antecedent* women *is plural, so the pronoun* their *referring to* women *is also plural.)*

<u>Jays</u> are beautiful birds. <u>They</u> are a brilliant blue color in winter. *(The antecedent* jays *is plural, so the pronoun* they *referring to* jays *is also plural, even if it is in a different sentence.)*

3. The following pronoun forms agree with the following antecedents:

   a. singular female antecedent (woman, Barbara): she, her, hers, herself

   b. singular male antecedent (man, Roscoe): he, him, his, himself

   c. singular genderless antecedent (book, desk): it, its, itself

   d. singular male/female antecedent (a person, a student, one): he or she, his or her, himself or herself

   e. plural female antecedent (girls, women): they, them, their, theirs, themselves

   f. plural male antecedent (boys, men): they, them, their, theirs, themselves

   g. plural genderless antecedent (trees, boxes): they, them, their, theirs, themselves

   h. others + yourself (John and I, the class and I): we, our, ours, ourselves

   i. person spoken to ("Mary," "Felix"): you, your, yours, yourself

   j. yourself: I, me, my, mine, myself

The following sentences show a variety of pronoun-antecedent agreement situations (the pronoun is underlined, and an arrow is drawn to the antecedent).

Rita lost <u>her</u> wallet, and <u>she</u> had twelve credit cards in it.

A twenty-dollar bill is lying on the kitchen table, and <u>it</u> had been there for a week.

Jack, Jonathan, and Sylvester all took <u>their</u> SAT tests last Saturday.

Marian and I always take <u>our</u> dirty clothes to the dormitory laundry service.

Clyde doesn't believe that <u>he</u> can maintain <u>his</u> current 3.4 GPA.

Thelma, <u>you</u> look stunning in <u>your</u> pink taffeta dress.

The students all took <u>their</u> compasses with <u>them</u> on the backpacking trip.

A student should always lock <u>his or her</u> car when it's in the parking lot.

PRONOUN-ANTECEDENT ACTIVITY 4.19

Substitute an appropriate pronoun for each word that is repeated unnecessarily in the following sentences, making sure that the pronoun agrees with its antecedent.

EXAMPLE   Mary brought Mary's baby brother with Mary to class Monday.

REVISED   Mary brought her baby brother with her to class Monday.

1. That building should have been torn down years ago. That building is a terrible fire hazard.

2. Gretchen used to weigh over 190 pounds, but now Gretchen is down to 130.

3. Marian and I used to shop at Macy's, but Marian and I don't shop there anymore.

4. The teachers at the high school are getting old, and the teachers seem bored with the teachers' jobs. A lot of the teachers should retire.

5. That blister on your heel looks sore, and that blister is going to get worse if you don't put medication on that blister.

6. Thelma should do Thelma a favor and get some sleep for a change.

7. John and I don't consider John and me close friends, but John and I do share a lot of interests.

8. My English book got my English book's cover torn off of my English book. Now my English book's pages are starting to come unbound.

9. The new movie playing at the Bijou is frightening. The new movie involves deranged killers on the loose on a college campus, and the college campus looks a lot like Hillcrest Community College.

10. Small earthquakes hit the valley a number of times last month, and although the small earthquakes caused little damage, the small earthquakes kept all of the neighbors on edge. Some of the neighbors are thinking about moving.

Indefinite Pronouns

Indefinite pronouns can cause agreement problems. They are always considered *singular* and therefore always require *singular* pronoun references:

anybody	everybody	nothing
anyone	everyone	one
each	everything	somebody
either	nobody	someone
every	no one	something

The following examples of pronoun-antecedent agreement involve indefinite pronouns. This is the most troublesome agreement situation because the incorrect plural pronoun references don't *sound* wrong to many people. Here are the correct and incorrect forms:

EXAMPLES

INCORRECT	Everyone should bring <u>their</u> books to the room.
CORRECT	Everyone should bring <u>his</u> or <u>her</u> books to the room.
INCORRECT	Each person should finish <u>their</u> homework before taking a break.
CORRECT	Each person should finish <u>his</u> or <u>her</u> homework before taking a break.
INCORRECT	No one did <u>their</u> best in the marathon because of the oppressive heat.
CORRECT	No one did <u>his</u> or <u>her</u> best in the marathon because of the oppressive heat.
INCORRECT	Somebody must have completed <u>their</u> art project before the contest deadline.
CORRECT	Somebody must have completed <u>his</u> or <u>her</u> art project before the contest deadline.

PRONOUN-ANTECEDENT ACTIVITY 4.20

Fill in the blanks in the following sentences with pronouns that agree with their antecedents. Underline the antecedent for each pronoun. When you finish, proofread your latest draft for pronoun-antecedent agreement.

EXAMPLE   The <u>mind</u> can snap if too much stress is placed on *it*.

1. The opossum hangs upside down beside _____ mate.

2. The man who won the canned hams should bring _____ car to the alley.

3. Each of the women works for _____ room and board.

4. A woman from the Bronx left _____ purse in a Manhattan theatre.

5. One of the trucks lost _____ brakes. _____ careened downhill.

6. Those bags she carries weigh a ton, and _____ are huge.

7. Pronouns should always agree in number with _____ antecedents.

8. A person should never press _____ luck.

9. Every one of the politicians made a promise that _____ couldn't keep.

10. The geraniums are losing _____ flowers very early.

11. John told me that it didn't matter to his instructors if _____ came to class late if _____ homework was completed and _____ maintained an A average on all quizzes.

12. One of the male monkeys in the middle cage kept spitting on _____ sister whom _____ shared a swing with.

JOURNAL ENTRY SIXTEEN

From this unit, relate in your journal what you learned about writing comparative papers—including prewriting, drafting, revising, and editing—that may help you with future writing.

WRITING REVIEW

In the "Writing Review," you apply what you have learned throughout the unit to a second writing assignment. To write your paper, follow the process provided, which summarizes the steps presented in this unit.

WRITING PROCESS

1. Write a paper for your classmates comparing two similar subjects: American and Japanese cars, renting or buying a home, leasing or buying an automobile, getting married or living together, attending a four-year or community college, American and foreign students, walking or jogging for fitness, dormitory or apartment living, two similar majors (for example, business and business administration), high school and college, high school and college students, two computer programs, college and professional basketball. Answer the following questions to help you decide on your topic:

   a. What topic am I interested in and knowledgeable about?

   b. What topic might be interesting to some of my classmates?

   c. What would my purpose be in writing about this topic?

   d. What conclusion might I draw based on the comparison?

STUDENT SAMPLE   I think I'll do some kind of comparison with students. I could compare high school and college students, but the differences seem too obvious. I could compare different types of college students on campus—athletes, aggies, student council members, computer geeks—but I think I'd end up stereotyping groups since I don't know that much about them.

I have met a number of foreign students from Southeast Asia at school and have gotten to know some of them fairly well. They have a different perspective on going to college than most American students I know. I could compare foreign students and American students, or more specifically Asian students and American students. I think I'll give it a try.

Since most American students don't mix much with foreign students, and vice versa, I think my best reading audience would be college students in general. I'm not sure what my purpose would be yet.

2. In what important areas are you going to compare your two subjects?

Follow these suggestions:

    a. Come up with four or five factors to compare your subjects on.

    b. Decide in what order you want to compare these factors in your paper.

    c. Evaluate your two subjects in each area before writing.

    d. Decide on your purpose, if you haven't done so.

STUDENT SAMPLE

Comparing Asian and American Students

    1. attitude toward going to college

    2. reasons for attending

    3. difficulties faced

    4. pressure to succeed

    PURPOSE   Help classmates understand their Asian peers on campus better

3. Write the first draft of your comparison paper following these suggestions:

    a. Include a beginning, middle, and ending to your paper. Introduce your topic in the beginning, make your comparisons in the middle, and draw your conclusion for readers in the ending.

    b. Keep the reading audience—your classmates—in mind as you write, and tell them things that many of them may not already know. (In other words, don't just repeat what would be common knowledge for most students.)

    c. Draw a reasonable conclusion for readers in the final paragraph(s) based on your comparison.

American and Asian Students

STUDENT SAMPLE DRAFT

America may be the great "melting pot," but at this college, not much "melting" has taken place yet with the newest wave of foreign students, most typically Southeast Asians. These students are easily distinguished from their American counterparts, both by the way they stick together on campus and by their relative seriousness. They seem to have a determination that is often lacking in American students.

I've gotten to know a few Asian students, not very well, but at least enough to get beyond "How ya doin'?" One thing I've learned is that they don't take college for granted like Americans. In their countries, like Cambodia, Laos, and Vietnam, college was restricted to the well-to-do, so the opportunity for a college education is a great thing for them. While most Americans take college for granted, many foreign students consider it a rare opportunity that shouldn't be wasted.

Many foreign students are attending college for different reasons than American students. They have come to America with hope but little else. Many are living in overcrowded apartments, their parents eeking out a living the best they can. These students realize that their passport out of poverty is a college degree, so they are highly motivated to succeed. Many American students come from relatively comfortable backgrounds, and they feel no urgency to change their living conditions or improve their lives. They want to eventually graduate, but in the meantime, life isn't so bad.

Foreign students are also going through tremendous transitions that American students can't relate to. While they are going to school, they are at the same time learning a new language, adjusting to a different culture, and trying to fit into a foreign society. It is little wonder that they stick together on campus and seem to be quiet and shy.

As my friend Latana said (in broken English), "You're never quite sure how Americans feel about you, so you feel uncomfortable a lot. You don't talk much because you feel you talk very poorly and are afraid of sounding stupid." On the other hand, American students have no such transitions to make. As Latana said, "Foreign students have to learn how to walk and run at the same time. American students have been walking all their lives."

A final difference between American and foreign students is the pressure they feel. With Asian students, according to math professor Dr. Lum Cho, there is first the traditional fear of failing in college and "losing face," causing the family disgrace. Second, there is pressure to succeed and help the family, who is counting on you. Third, there is pressure not to "blow" a great opportunity for an education, perhaps the only opportunity you will have. Most American students feel no such pressures, and without the pressures, they are more relaxed and carefree about school.

The more I get to know a few Asian students on campus, the more I like them. They are bright, funny, and very nice. And now that I've gotten beyond "How ya doin,'" I can begin to understand their seriousness, their determination, their shyness, and their sense of isolation in a strange land. They don't have a lot in common with the typical American students of today who take education for granted. They probably have a lot in common with the children of earlier Irish, Italian, and German immigrants who were sent to college with their families' hopes. In a way I envy them. For foreign students, the American dream is still exciting and alive.

4. When you finish your first draft, set it aside for a while before evaluating it. Then read the draft and apply the following revision guidelines. When you are ready, write your second draft, including all revisions for content, organization, and wording improvement.

   a. Evaluate the strength of your opening. Do you introduce your topic in an interesting way? Do readers understand what you are comparing and why? Would they want to read further?

   b. Evaluate the effectiveness of your comparison. Have you compared your subjects in all important areas? Can readers clearly see the differences (and similarities) between subjects? Have you used appropriate details and examples to help readers understand each point of comparison? Have you organized your comparison to help readers follow it clearly?

   c. Evaluate the strength of your conclusion. Does it follow logically from the comparisons you have made? If appropriate, have you given readers the best possible advice for making a decision? Is your conclusion unqualified (same recommendation for everyone) or qualified (optional recommendations based on differences among readers)?

   d. Check your paragraphing to see if readers can move smoothly through your opening, middle, and conclusion. Do you present your points of comparison in different paragraphs? Are your sentences and paragraphs tied together with appropriate transitional wording? Do you have any overly long paragraphs that need dividing or short paragraphs that need combining or developing further?

   e. Read each sentence carefully to see if you can improve its smoothness, clarity, or conciseness. Also check to see if you have over-relied on certain sentence structures or joining words, and make revisions to improve sentence variety. Finally, check the lengths of sentences and, when appropriate, combine pairs or groups of very short sentences or divide overly long ones.

5. When you have completed all revisions, proofread your paper for any remaining errors by following these guidelines:

   a. Make sure you have a period at the end of each sentence. Check your paper carefully for run-on sentences that need punctuating or for sentence fragments that need attaching to the sentences they belong with.

b. Check word endings to make sure you have an *s* on all plural words and an *ed* on regular past tense verbs and that your present tense verbs agree with their subjects.

c. Check your spelling carefully, including your use of homonyms such as there/their/they're, know/no, your/you're, threw/through, it's/its, and right/write.

d. Check internal punctuation. Have you inserted commas in series of words, before coordinate conjunctions in compound sentences, after introductory groups of words, and to set off relative clauses, interrupters, and ending phrases? Have you used apostrophes (') in contractions and possessive words, and quotation marks (" ") with direct quotations?

e. Have you used correct subject-pronoun forms with compound subjects? (John and I, my mother and I, Rudy and she, the Joneses and they.) Do your pronouns agree in number and gender with their antecedents? (Everyone invited his or her mother to the graduation. The Smiths brought their children with them to the party.)

6. When you are ready, write or print out the final draft of your comparison paper and share it with classmates and your instructor.

Writing about Problems and Solutions

Problem solving is an everyday task for most people. Class is about to begin and you can't find a parking place anywhere near your building. Where do you park? You have a cart-full of groceries and realize you don't have your credit card and have just a couple dollars on you. What do you tell the checker? You've run out of gas miles from any service station and you need to be at a meeting at work in a half hour. How do you get to work? Your garbage cans are overflowing and due to a holiday, the garbage pickup won't be for another week. How do you relieve your garbage problem?

Problems confront us all of the time, some of them ongoing (not enough money, not enough time), and some of them unforeseen (unplanned pregnancy, layoffs at work, classes canceled). Effective problem solving is an important part of dealing with life and whatever it sends our way.

Writing about problems and solutions has a number of values. First, it requires serious analysis of the problem: exactly what is the problem; what are its causes; what are its effects; how, if possible, can it be solved or reduced; and what will happen if it isn't solved or if it grows worse? Second, in writing problem/solution papers, you learn new organizational schemes, which are different from previous papers. Third, writing about problems and solutions can benefit the writer, who may find a new solution to a per-plexing problem, and the readers, who may face similar problems and benefit from the writer's analysis.

Problem solving is also a group activity, and solutions to difficult problems are often found by teams of people: engineers, scientists, boards of trustees, student councils, family councils, social workers. It makes sense that many minds working on the same problem will generate the most ideas, and often the best solutions come from combining ideas from different sources. During the prewriting process, you will do some problem solving in groups.

PREWRITING

For your unit writing assignment, you should write about a problem that affects you personally, but that also may affect other people. For example, if you are working full-time and going to school, finding time to do everything you need to may be a problem for you, but also for many other students. If the escalating cost of textbooks is eating up most of your school budget, you can bet it's affecting other students. And if you are in a relationship that is fraught with problems, you probably aren't alone.

Your first prewriting task is to decide on a problem to write about, one that you would like to eliminate from your life. Once you have selected a problem, you will do a problem analysis: how did it start, what are its causes, how is it affecting you, how may it be affecting others, how might it be solved? Next, you will consider a general organizational plan for your first draft. Then after considering the best reading audience for your paper and your purpose for writing, you should be ready to write your first draft.

Since problem solving is also a group activity, you will work in small groups to generate a number of problems to consider, and later you will bring your problem to the group to get opinions on possible solutions. Sometimes we feel that our problems are unique and that we are alone with them, but that is seldom the case. Working in groups helps us realize that.

TOPIC SELECTION

By this time, you may already have thought of a problem that is weighing on you that you may want to write about. However, sometimes the first problem that comes to mind may be the most immediate and short-lived: not having the money to buy tickets for an upcoming concert, having nothing to wear to Saturday's wedding, or having to share your car with your brother to a couple of weeks. Such problems are vexing, but they are relatively minor and soon pass.

For your writing assignment, choose a lingering problem that if not resolved, will continue to trouble you: not being able to find a part-time job; continually fighting with your spouse or girlfriend/boyfriend; not being able to control your drinking (or someone else's drinking); being without a major or career interest after two years of college. If you are facing a particularly difficult problem, no doubt others in the class have had or continue to have a similar problem.

TOPIC SELECTION ACTIVITY 5.1

In small groups, brainstorm to come up with a number of problems for writing consideration: personal problems, family problems, school-related problems, relationship problems, health problems, community problems, environmental problems, etc.

When you brainstorm, share with the group whatever ideas come to your mind without considering their relative importance. The purpose of brainstorming is to get the most ideas possible on the table. Through this process, you will undoubtedly uncover some excellent potential writing topics.

TOPIC SELECTION GUIDELINES

After considering the problems generated in your group's brainstorming session, and other problems you have thought of, you should be ready to decide on a problem to write about. In selecting a topic, consider these guidelines:

1. Select a topic that is a thorny problem for you: a problem that is affecting your well-being in some manner, and that can't continue as it is.

2. Select a problem that other people may also be facing or have faced—the people who would ideally form your reading audience.

3. Select a problem that you don't already have a ready solution for. One purpose of this assignment is to seek solutions where none is readily apparent.

4. Select a problem that you are comfortable writing about. If the problem is so personal and sensitive that you wouldn't want to share it with others, don't write about it.

5. Select a problem that no other students (or few students) are writing on. Your instructor may guide topic selection to avoid duplication.

TOPIC SELECTION ACTIVITY 5.2

Select the problem that will be the topic for your upcoming paper.

STUDENT SAMPLE My girlfriend is pregnant; I found out about a week ago. It's a tough situation because we haven't been getting along that great for a while. I was working out of the area for a month, and then she called and I found out. She wants to get married, and I've said okay. But this isn't how I wanted to get married. And I don't know if I really love her, at least the way I did earlier. But the pregnancy's my fault. It's my responsibility, and I'd feel like a jerk not marrying her. She's a good person, there's nothing wrong with her. It's me—I found myself looking at other girls when I was away. I didn't think about her much. Maybe she's got doubts like me. It's a real problem.

STUDENT SAMPLE The parking problem on campus is terrible. When I come in for my 9:00 class, I can't find a parking place anywhere. If I drive around and around waiting for someone to leave, I get really late for my class. If I park a half mile away on the street, I'm also late, and I worry about my car getting sideswiped by passing traffic or broken into. The school should have enough parking so all students can find reasonable parking. This is a real problem for me and a lot of other students. And our teachers get upset when we're late for class. One won't even let me in class if I'm like 10 minutes late.

PROBLEM ANALYSIS

Before writing about your problem, take some time to analyze the situation. Answer the following questions to help you investigate the problem, and to generate some ideas for your first draft:

1. What exactly is the problem? Try expressing it in one clear sentence.

   I'm late for class because there isn't adequate parking on campus at 9:00 a.m.

2. How did the problem get started, and what caused it?

   The size of the enrollment keeps going up, and more and more classes are offered. But the parking areas are the same as when the enrollment was quite a bit smaller. Off-campus parking is minimal and not that safe for the cars.

3. What effect(s) does the problem have on you?

   I'm often late for class. My teacher gets mad at me, and sometimes won't let me in class. I worry about my car when I park away from campus. I have to rush to school after I drop my daughter off at day-care, but there's still no parking, even fifteen or twenty minutes before class. By the time I get to class, I'm always stressed.

4. What effect(s), if any, does the problem have on others?

   Other students face the same problem, and they complain like I do. Some come an hour earlier just to get a space, but a lot of us can't do that. It affects teachers too because they don't like students coming late all the time.

5. What are possible solutions to the problem?

I think it's clear that the school needs more parking for students on campus. But I haven't looked into it to know if that's possible or where we'd park or anything. I haven't talked to anyone or tried to do anything about it. I wouldn't know where to start. Maybe there are other solutions I haven't thought of.

FINDING SOLUTIONS

Solving difficult problems is seldom simple. Sometimes unresolved problems between a parent and child, a husband and wife, employees and management, or two neighboring countries can go on for years and poison relationships. Some problems have plagued our country for decades. Over the past twenty years, America's "war on drugs" has failed in large part to solve the country's significant drug problem. Experts can't even agree on the main causes of the problem or the best ways to eliminate them.

In seeking solutions to a problem, the following suggestions will help you consider different possibilities and evaluate their chances for success:

1. What exactly does it mean to "solve" the problem? What do you want to accomplish through its being solved? For example, the college parking problem may be considered solved when all students attending 9:00 a.m. classes can find on-campus parking and do not have to walk farther than ten minutes to class.

2. What are the roots or causes of the problem? It may be impossible to solve a problem if you don't have a clear understanding of its causes. For example, experts believe that America's drug problem has a number of complex causes, including poverty, organized crime, easy access, profit motive, drug importation, lack of programs for addicts, and perhaps even its illicit status. A problem with multiple causes is often more difficult to solve.

3. Consider possible solutions that could attack these causes and either eliminate or reduce their impact. For example, a major cause of America's drug problem is the desire for drugs among millions of Americans. Many experts believe that if this desire is not reduced—through education and positive lifestyle alternatives—the drug problem will never be solved.

4. Consider both short-term progress toward solving the problem and longer-term solutions. Success in the beginning may be improving a situation that will take a longer time to resolve. For example, professional baseball averted a strike in 2004 by each side making some

concessions that would move baseball toward greater revenue sharing and salary caps, but there is still much to be done to solve baseball's financial problems.

5. Come up with as many solutions as possible, including those that may seem implausible or rather drastic. Often your first ideas are the most obvious and traditional, but not necessarily the best. For example, your first idea on improving a campus parking situation may be to build more lots. However, the more novel ideas of having campus shuttles taking students to classes from off-campus parking areas, or building the campus's first multi-story parking garage, shouldn't be ruled out.

6. Consider compromises in finding a solution to a problem. Oftentimes, particularly in relationships, the solution to a problem involves two or more parties finding a middle ground, by each party giving up something to get something. Solutions are often not perfect, and in dealing with problems when others are involved, the best solution is often one that satisfies no one completely but improves the situation.

7. Consider how time will affect the problem and its ultimate solution. For example, sometimes people have to ride out a difficult situation for a time, knowing that their circumstances will change. You may have an absolute "roommate from hell," but when the semester is over, or when the six-month apartment lease is up, or when you get a job so you don't need a roommate to help with expenses, your roommate problem will go away. While the adage "don't run away from your problems" is often good advice, solutions that help take you out of a bad situation are worth considering.

8. Talk to other people about the problem. Seldom are problems unique to individuals. Usually you can find people who either have the same problem or have worked through it in the past. Effective problem solving often is a collective effort, so don't feel that you have to solve a problem by yourself.

SOLUTION ACTIVITY 5.3

In small groups, have each classmate present the problem he or she is going to write about. Taking into consideration the eight points presented on solving problems, brainstorm possible solutions to the problem. The purpose is for the group to generate a number of solution alternatives for each classmate to consider. Your group may come up with some ideas that you hadn't considered, or you may realize that your problem is going to be very difficult to solve, and will require step-by-step progress toward an ultimate solution.

AUDIENCE AND PURPOSE

Before writing the first draft of your problem/solution paper, consider the following:

1. What reading audience would I want to share my paper with? Who might benefit from reading about it?

   Any student who has morning classes has a parking problem, but I'd also like the teachers and administration and campus police to know it's their problem too. I'd like to write to all of them.

2. What would my purpose be in writing for a particular audience?

   To get something done about the current bad parking situation. To get things changed. I guess I'd have to come up with a definite plan or solution and say, "This is what needs to be done, and this is how it can be done," something like that.

AUDIENCE ACTIVITY 5.4

Decide on a particular reading audience that you would like to read your paper. It may be your classmates, a particular group of students within your class (women with children, students who work and go to school, students who take day and night classes), or a completely different group of readers. Select your reading audience based on your topic, who you think would benefit from reading your paper, and whom you would like to read it.

Next, decide on your purpose for writing to this audience. Why are you writing to them, and what do you want to accomplish?

JOURNAL ENTRY SEVENTEEN

In your journal, relate how the prewriting activities have helped prepare you to write your first draft. What, if anything, stands out as being most useful?

FIRST DRAFTS

Now that you have selected a topic for your problem/solution paper, analyzed the problem, its causes, and possible solutions, and considered your reading audience and writing purpose, you are ready to write the first draft. The following suggestions will help you get started.

DRAFTING GUIDELINES

1. As you write your first draft, consider using this basic organizational plan, which is easy for readers to follow.

a. Introduce the problem, why you are concerned about it, and why, if at all, your readers should be concerned.

b. Present the cause(s) of the problem. How did it start and develop?

c. Present the effect(s) of the problem on you, and if applicable, on others.

d. Present a single solution, alternative solution that should be tried, short-term and longer-term solutions, a compromise that could solve the problem, or anything else you have thought of to improve the situation. If you are dealing with a difficult problem, you may not be presenting a single, simple solution, but rather a more real-istic way of dealing with the problem in different ways. Or if the problem seems impossible to solve completely, you may discuss ways to improve the situation.

e. As you follow this plan, feel free to make changes in organization that better fit your particular topic and how you want to present it. For example, if it seems better to present the problem's effects on you before you get into its causes, reverse the order. Or if you feel it's important to let readers know in the beginning what your solu-tion is (so they will have it in mind as they read), present it.

2. Paragraph your paper as you move to its different parts: introduction (presenting the problem and your concern with it), causes of the problem, effects of the problem, possible solution(s).

3. Keep your readers and purpose in mind as you write. What are you trying to accomplish by writing about this particular problem? What do you want your readers to take from the paper?

DRAFTING ACTIVITY 5.5

Before writing your draft, read the following draft and in small groups, identify each of the following: what the problem is, its causes, its effects, and the writer's solution. In addition, discuss the writer's organizational plan and how effective it is.

Black Men and Public Spaces
Brent Staples

My first victim was a woman—white, well-dressed, probably in her early twenties. I came upon her late one evening on a deserted street in Hyde Park, a relatively affluent neighborhood in an otherwise mean, impover-ished section of Chicago. As I swung onto the avenue behind her, there seemed to be a discreet, uninflammatory distance between us. Not so. She cast back a worried glance. To her, the youngish black man—a broad six feet two inches with a beard and billowing hair, both hands shoved into the pockets of a bulky military jacket—seemed menacingly close. After a few more quick glimpses, she picked up her pace and was soon running in earnest. Within seconds she disappeared into a cross street.

That was more than a decade ago. I was 22 years old, a graduate student newly arrived at the University of Chicago. It was in the echo of that terrified woman's footfalls that I first began to know the unwieldy inheritance I'd come into—the ability to alter public space in ugly ways. It was clear that she thought herself the quarry of a mugger, rapist, or worse. Suffering a bout of insomnia, however, I was stalking sleep, not defenseless wayfarers. As a softy who is scarcely able to take a knife to a raw chicken—let alone hold it to a person's throat—I was surprised, embarrassed, and dismayed all at once. Her flight made me feel like an accomplice in tyranny. It also made it clear that I was indistinguishable from the muggers who occasionally seeped into the area from the surrounding ghetto. That first encounter, and those that followed, signified that a vast, unnerving gulf lay between nighttime pedestrians—particularly women—and me. And I soon gathered that being perceived as dangerous is a hazard in itself. I only needed to turn a corner into a dicey situation, or crowd some frightened, armed person in a foyer somewhere, or make an errant move after being pulled over by a policeman. Where fear and weapons meet—and they often do in urban America—there is always the possibility of death.

In that first year, my first away from my hometown, I was to become thoroughly familiar with the language of fear. At dark, shadowy intersections in Chicago, I could cross in front of a car stopped at a traffic light and elicit the *thunk, thunk, thunk, thunk* of the driver—black, white, male, or female—hammering down the door locks. On less traveled streets after dark, I grew accustomed to but never comfortable with people who crossed to the other side of the street rather than pass me. Then there were the standard unpleasantries with police, doormen, bouncers, cab drivers, and others whose business it is to screen out troublesome individuals *before* there is any nastiness.

I moved to New York nearly two years ago and I have remained an avid night walker. In central Manhattan, the near-constant crowd cover minimizes tense one-on-one street encounters. Elsewhere—visiting friends in SoHo, where sidewalks are narrow and tightly spaced buildings shut out the sky—things can get very taut indeed.

Black men have a firm place in New York mugging literature. Norman Podhoretz in his famed (or infamous) 1963 essay, "My Negro Problem—and Ours," recalls growing up in terror of black males; they "were tougher than we were, more ruthless," he writes—and as an adult on the Upper West Side of Manhattan, he continues, he cannot constrain his nervousness when he meets black men on certain streets. Similarly, a decade later, the essayist and novelist Edward Hoagland extols a New York where once "Negro bitterness bore down mainly on other Negroes." Where some see mere panhandlers, Hoagland sees "a mugger who is clearly screwing up his nerve to do more than just *ask* for money." But Hoagland has "the New Yorker's quick-hunch posture for broken-field maneuvering," and the bad guy swerves away.

I often witness that "hunch posture," from women after dark on the warrenlike streets of Brooklyn where I live. They seem to set their faces on neutral and, with their purse straps strung across their chests bandolier style, they forge ahead as though bracing themselves against being tackled. I understand, of course, that the danger they perceive is not a hallucination. Women are particularly vulnerable to street violence, and young black males are drastically overrepresented among the perpetrators of that violence. Yet these truths are no solace against the kind of alienation that comes of being ever the suspect, against being set apart, a fearsome entity with whom pedestrians avoid making eye contact.

It is not altogether clear to me how I reached the ripe old age of 22 without being conscious of the lethality nighttime pedestrians attributed to me. Perhaps it was because in Chester, Pennsylvania, the small, angry industrial town where I came of age in the 1960s, I was scarcely noticeable against a backdrop of gang warfare, street knifings, and murders. I grew up one of the good boys, had perhaps a half-dozen fist fights. In retrospect, my shyness of combat has clear sources.

Many things go into the making of a young thug. One of those things is the consummation of the male romance with the power to intimidate. An infant discovers that random flailings send the baby bottle flying out of the crib and crashing to the floor. Delighted, the joyful babe repeats those motions again and again, seeking to duplicate the feat. Just so, I recall the points at which some of my boyhood friends were finally seduced by the perception of themselves as tough guys. When a mark cowered and surrendered his money without resistance, myth and reality merged—and paid off. It is, after all, only manly to embrace the power to frighten and intimidate. We, as men, are not supposed to give an inch of our lane on the highway; we are to seize the fighter's edge in work and in play and even in love; we are to be valiant in the face of hostile forces.

Unfortunately, poor and powerless young men seem to take all this nonsense literally. As a boy, I saw countless tough guys locked away; I have since buried several, too. They were babies, really—a teenage cousin, a brother of 22, a childhood friend in his mid-twenties—all gone down in episodes of bravado played out in the streets. I came to doubt the virtues of intimidation early on. I chose, perhaps even unconsciously, to remain a shadow—timid, but a survivor.

The fearsomeness mistakenly attributed to me in public places often has a perilous flavor. The most frightening of these confusions occurred in the late 1970s and early 1980s when I worked as a journalist in Chicago. One day, rushing into the office of a magazine I was writing for with a deadline story in hand, I was mistaken for a burglar. The office manager called security and, with an ad hoc posse, pursued me through the labyrinthine halls, nearly to my editor's door. I had no way of proving who I was. I could only move briskly toward the company of someone who knew me.

Another time I was on assignment for a local paper and killing time before an interview. I entered a jewelry store on the city's affluent Near North Side. The proprietor excused herself and returned with an enormous red Doberman pinscher straining at the end of a leash. She stood, the dog extended toward me, silent to my questions, her eyes bulging nearly out of her head. I took a cursory look around, nodded, and bade her good night. Relatively speaking, however, I never fared as badly as another black male journalist. He went to nearby Waukegan, Illinois, a couple of summers ago to work on a story about a murderer who was born there. Mistaking the reporter for the killer, police hauled him from his car at gunpoint and but for his press credentials would probably have tried to book him. Such episodes are not uncommon. Black men trade tales like this all the time.

In "My Negro Problem—and Ours," Podhoretz writes that the hatred he feels for blacks makes itself known to him through a variety of avenues—one being his discomfort with that "special brand of paranoid touchiness" to which he says blacks are prone. No doubt he is speaking here of black men. In time, I learned to smother the rage I felt at so often being taken for a criminal. Not to do so would surely have led to madness—via that special "paranoid touchiness" that so annoyed Podhoretz at the time he wrote the essay.

I began to take precautions to make myself less threatening. I move about with care, particularly late in the evening. I give a wide berth to nervous people on subway platforms during the wee hours, particularly when I have exchanged business clothes for jeans. If I happen to be entering a building behind some people who appear skittish, I may walk by, letting them clear the lobby before I return, so as not to seem to be following them. I have been calm and extremely congenial on those rare occasions when I've been pulled over by the police.

And on late-evening constitutionals along streets less traveled by, I employ what has proved to be an excellent tension-reducing measure: I whistle melodies from Beethoven and Vivaldi and the more popular classical composers. Even steely New Yorkers hunching toward nighttime destinations seem to relax, and occasionally they even join in the tune. Virtually everybody seems to sense that a mugger wouldn't be warbling bright, sunny selections from Vivaldi's *Four Seasons*. It is my equivalent of the cowbell that hikers wear when they know they are in bear country.

DRAFTING ACTIVITY 5.6

Write the first draft of your problem/solution paper following the guidelines presented.

REVISIONS

When you write a first draft, you are probably thinking more about getting your ideas on paper than on how your reading audience will respond. Therefore, it is important to revise your draft with your readers in mind. The success of your writing depends on how it is received by readers, so it is useful to learn to read a draft as if through the eyes of others. It is also valuable to get feedback from readers to see what kind of an effect your draft is having.

REVISION GUIDELINES

When evaluating your first draft, consider these suggestions:

1. Evaluate the opening of your paper. Does it introduce your problem in some manner so that readers know what you are writing about? Do you present the problem in a way that creates reader interest? Is there anything you might add? Answer the question, "Based on my opening, what would inspire readers to want to read further?"

2. Evaluate the middle part of the paper: how well do you present the causes of the problem? How effectively do you show the effects that the problem has on you and on others? What might you add to help readers understand the problem better or make the paper more interesting?

3. Evaluate your conclusion. Do you present a realistic solution or possible solutions that deal with the problem's causes? Do you explain what this solution will do for you, and perhaps for others? The solution part of your paper is perhaps the most important since readers may discover something they hadn't considered.

4. Evaluate your paragraphing. Does it help readers move smoothly through the opening, middle, and ending of your paper? Have you used transitions (first, second, then, however, therefore, as you can see, for example, finally) to tie sentences and paragraphs together? Have you dealt with causes and effects in separate paragraphs, or introduced different causes or different effects in new paragraphs?

5. Evaluate the organization of your paper. Have you presented the different parts of your paper in the best order? Does a particular sentence or paragraph seem out of place where it is? What might you move to a different location where it would make more sense? (See the upcoming section on "Essay Organization.")

6. Read each sentence carefully to see if you can improve its clarity, smoothness, or conciseness. Many first draft sentences can be improved through the revision process. In addition, make revisions to

improve sentence variety, replace overused joining words, and combine pairs of short sentences. (See the upcoming section on "Sentence
Revision.")

7. Read the draft from your readers' perspective. Have you presented a
serious enough problem for readers to take an interest in? Have you
written in a way that readers will clearly understand the problem and
how it is affecting your life? Have you presented a solution or possible
solutions that truly address the problem and give readers something to
consider?

REVISION ACTIVITY 5.7

In small groups, evaluate the following student draft by applying the revision guidelines presented. Note suggestions for revision along with things
that the writer does well.

Next, make copies of your draft for your group to read, and critique
each student draft as you did the sample student draft to give each classmate some ideas for revision.

STUDENT DRAFT   My problem is that my boyfriend left me while I was still pregnant with
my son. I think about him all the time, especially when I look at my son.

I wish I could get over him, but my son looks so much like him that it
reminds me of all the time we spent together. However, I would not take
him back or let him near my son.

The biggest problem is the fact that I am so heart-broken because my
son will never know his father. One reason is because his father will most
likely never come back, and the second, I will never let him near my son.

I don't think he even cares about us anyway. I figure if he did, he
would have called me by now to see how we are doing. He hasn't called
me since the day he left, and I don't think he ever will. I keep hoping he
would, but it is only hope and wishes that won't come true any time soon.

The only solution to my problem is I have to let go. I know that it will
be hard at first, but with the help of my family and the love for my son, I
can get through this. I just need to ask God for help along the way. I guess
deep down in my heart I have always known what to do, but it was up to
me to do it. Now I will do what I have to do, which is move on with my
life, and with God's help, I will.

REVISION ACTIVITY 5.8

Evaluate your own draft a last time using the revision guidelines. (Your
instructor may first have you go over the upcoming sections on "Essay
Organization" and "Sentence Revision.") When you are ready, write your
second draft.

JOURNAL ENTRY EIGHTEEN

In your journal, record the improvements you made in your second draft. In what ways do you think the second draft is superior to the first?

ESSAY ORGANIZATION

The organization of any paper has something of an *organic* quality: It comes in part from the uniqueness of that particular paper based on your topic and what you want to accomplish. For example, while you have probably followed the organizational plan presented in this unit for a problem/solution paper—introduce the problem, present its causes, present its effects, present possible solutions—such a scheme may not be best for every problem/solution paper. As you write and reread your draft, you will develop a sense for what should come next, and what should follow that, based on your writing purpose and the most effective organization for achieving it.

As you read the first draft of your problem/solution paper to evaluate its organization, consider these questions:

1. Does it make sense to present my solution in the opening when I present the problem, or am I better off waiting until the end of the paper after I have presented everything else?

2. Might it be more effective to present the effects of the problem rather than presenting the causes first? Which is the most effective order based on my topic and what I want to achieve?

3. Assuming your problem has more than one cause and more than one effect, what is the most effective order for presenting the causes? For presenting the effects? What organization most effectively highlights the most important cause(s) and effect(s)?

ORGANIZATIONAL ACTIVITY 5.9

Read the following essay, "Taming the Anger Monster," and analyze its organization. In small groups, identify the problem the essay is presenting, its causes, its effects, and its solution. Evaluate the effectiveness of the essay's organization based on what you believe to be the author's purpose.

Taming the Anger Monster
Anne Davidson

Laura Houser remembers the day with embarrassment.

"My mother was visiting from Illinois," she says. "We'd gone out to lunch and done some shopping. On our way home, we stopped at an intersection. When the light changed, the guy ahead of us was looking at a map or something and didn't move right away. I leaned on my horn and automatically yelled—well, what I generally yell at people who make me wait. I didn't even think about what I was doing. One moment I was talking and laughing with my mother, and the next I was shouting curses at a stranger. Mom's jaw just dropped. She said, 'Well, I guess *you've* been living in the city too long.' That's when I realized that my anger was out of control." Laura has plenty of company. Here are a few examples plucked from the headlines of recent newspapers:

- Amtrak's Washington-New York train: When a woman begins to use her cell phone in a designated "quiet car," her seatmate grabs the phone and smashes it against the wall.

- Reading, Mass.: Arguing over rough play at their ten-year-old sons' hockey practice, two fathers begin throwing punches. One of the dads beats the other to death.

- Westport, Conn.: Two supermarket shoppers get into a fistfight over who should be first in a just-opened checkout line.

Reading these stories and countless others like them which happen daily, it's hard to escape the conclusion that we are one angry society. An entire vocabulary has grown up to describe situations of out-of-control fury: road rage, sideline rage, computer rage, biker rage, air rage. Bookstore shelves are filled with authors' advice on how to deal with our anger. Court-ordered anger management classes have become commonplace, and anger management workshops are advertised in local newspapers.

Human beings have always experienced anger, of course. But in earlier, more civil decades, public displays of anger were unusual to the point of being aberrant. Today, however, whether in petty or deadly forms, episodes of unrepressed rage have become part of our daily landscape.

What has happened to us? Are we that much angrier than we used to be? Have we lost all inhibitions about expressing our anger? Are we, as a society, literally losing our ability to control our tempers?

According to Sybil Evans, a conflict-resolution expert in New York City, there are three components to blame for our societal bad behavior: time, technology, and tension.

What's eating up our time? To begin with, Americans work longer hours and are rewarded with less vacation time than people in any other industrial society. Over an average year, for example, most British employees work 250 hours less than most Americans; most Germans work a full 500 hours less. And most Europeans are given four to six weeks vacation every year, compared to the average American's two weeks. To make matters worse, many Americans face long, stressful commutes at the beginning and end of each long workday.

Once we Americans finally get home from work, our busy day is rarely done. We are involved in community activities; our children participate in sports, school programs, and extracurricular activities; and our houses, yards and cars cry out for maintenance. To make matters worse, we are reluctant to use the little bit of leisure time we do have to catch up on our sleep. Compared with Americans of the nineteenth and early twentieth centuries, most of us are chronically sleep-deprived. While our ancestors typically slept nine-and-a-half hours a night, many of us feel lucky to get seven. We're critical of "lazy" people who sleep longer, and we associate naps with toddlerhood. (In doing so, we ignore the example of successful people including Winston Churchill, Albert Einstein, and Napoleon, all of whom were devoted to their afternoon naps.)

The bottom line: we are time-challenged and just plain tired—and tired people are cranky people. We're ready to blow—to snap at the slow-moving cashier, to tap the bumper of the slowpoke ahead of us, or to do something far worse.

Technology is also to blame for the bad behavior so widespread in our culture. Amazing gadgets were supposed to make our lives easier—but have they? Sure, technology has its positive aspects. It is a blessing, for instance, to have a cell phone on hand when your car breaks down far from home or to be able to "instant message" a friend on the other side of the globe. But the downsides are many. Cell phones, pagers, fax machines, handheld computers and the like have robbed many of us of what was once valuable downtime. Now we're *always* available to take that urgent call or act on that last-minute demand. Then there is the endless pressure of feeling we need to keep up with our gadgets' latest technological developments. For example, it's not sufficient to use your cell phone for phone calls. Now you must learn to use the phone for text messaging and downloading games. It's not enough to take still photos with your digital camera. You should know how to shoot ultra high-speed fast-action clips. It's not enough to have an enviable CD collection. You should be downloading new songs in MP3 format. The computers in your house should be connected by a wireless router, and online via high-speed DSL service. In other words, if it's been more than ten minutes since you've updated your technology, you're probably behind.

In fact, you're not only behind; you're a stupid loser. At least, that's how most of us end up feeling as we're confronted with more and more unexpected technologies: the do-it-yourself checkout at the supermarket, the telephone "help center" that offers a recorded series of messages, but no human help. And feeling like losers makes us frustrated and, you guessed it, angry. "It's not any one thing but lots of little things that make people feel like they don't have control of their lives," says Jane Middleton-Moz, an author and therapist. "A sense of helplessness is what triggers rage. It's why people end up kicking ATM machines."

Her example is not far-fetched. According to a survey of computer users in Great Britain, a quarter of those under age 25 admitted to having kicked or punched their computers on at least one occasion. Others confessed to yanking out cables in a rage, forcing the computer to crash. On this side of the Atlantic, a Wisconsin man, after repeated attempts to get his daughter's malfunctioning computer repaired, took it to the store where he had bought it, placed it in the foyer, and attacked it with a sledgehammer. Arrested and awaiting a court appearance, he told local reporters, "It feels good, in a way." He had put into action a fantasy many of us have had—that of taking out our feelings of rage on the machines that so frustrate us.

Tension, the third major culprit behind our epidemic of anger, is intimately connected with our lack of time and the pressures of technology. Merely our chronic exhaustion and our frustration in the face of a bewildering array of technologies would be enough to cause our stress levels to skyrocket, but we are dealing with much more. Our tension is often fueled by a reserve of anger that might be the result of a critical boss, marital discord, or (something that many of today's men and women experience, if few will admit it) a general sense of being stupid and inadequate in the face of the demands of modern life. And along with the challenges of everyday life, we now live with a widespread fear of such horrors as terrorist acts, global warming, and antibiotic-resistant diseases. Our sense of dread may be out of proportion to actual threats because of technology's ability to so constantly bombard us with worrisome information. Twenty-four-hours-a-day news stations bring a stream of horror into our living rooms. As we work on our computers, headlines and graphic images are never more than a mouse click away.

Add it all together—our feeling of never having enough time; the chronic aggravation caused by technology; and our endless, diffuse sense of stress—and we become time bombs waiting to explode. Our angry outbursts may be briefly satisfying, but afterwards we are left feeling—well, like jerks. Worse, flying off the handle is a self-perpetuating behavior. Brad Bushman, a psychology professor at Iowa State University, says, "Catharsis is worse than useless." Bushman's research has shown that when people vent their anger, they actually become more, not less, aggressive. "Many people think of anger as the psychological equivalent of the steam in a pressure cooker. It has to be released, or it will explode. That's not true. The people who react by hitting, kicking, screaming, and swearing just feel more angry."

Furthermore, the unharnessed venting of anger may actually do us physical harm. The vigorous expression of anger pumps adrenaline into our system and raises our blood pressure, setting the stage for heart attack and strokes. Frequently angry people have even been shown to have higher cholesterol levels than even-tempered individuals.

Unfortunately, the culprits behind much of our anger—lack of time, frustrating technology, and mega-levels of stress—are not likely to resolve themselves anytime soon. So what are we to do with the anger that arises as a result?

According to Carol Tavris, author of *Anger: The Misunderstood Emotion*, the keys to dealing with anger are common sense and patience. She points out that almost no situation is improved by an angry outburst. A traffic jam, a frozen computer, or a misplaced set of car keys are annoying. To act upon the angry feelings those situations provoke, however, is an exercise in futility. Shouting, fuming, or leaning on the car horn won't make traffic begin to flow, the screen unlock, or keys materialize.

Patience, on the other hand, is a highly practical virtue. People who take the time to cool down before responding to an anger-producing situation are far less likely to say or do something they will regret later. "It is as true of the body as of arrows," Tavris says, "that what goes up must come down. Any emotional arousal will simmer down if you just wait long enough." When you are stuck in traffic, in other words, turn on some soothing music, breathe deeply, and count to ten—or thirty or forty, if need be.

Anger-management therapist Doris Wild Helmering agrees. "Like any feeling, anger lasts only about three seconds," she says. "What keeps it going is your own negative thinking." As long as you focus on the idiot who cut you off on the expressway, you'll stay angry. But if you let the incident go, your anger will go with it. "Once you come to understand that you're driving your own anger with your thoughts," adds Helmering, "you can stop it."

Experts who have studied anger also encourage people to cultivate activities that effectively vent their anger. For some people, it's reading the newspaper or watching TV, while others need more active outlets, such as using a treadmill, taking a walk, hitting golf balls, or working out with a punching bag. People who succeed in calming their anger can also enjoy the satisfaction of having dealt positively with their frustrations.

For Laura Houser, the episode in the car with her mother was a wake-up call. "I saw myself through her eyes," she said, "and I realized I had become a chronically angry, impatient jerk. My response to stressful situations had become habitual—I automatically flew off the handle. Once I saw what I was doing, it really wasn't that hard to develop different habits. I simply decided I was going to treat other people the way I would want to be treated." The changes in Laura's life haven't benefited only her former victims. "I'm a calmer, happier person now," she reports. "I don't lie in bed at night fuming over stupid things other people have done and my own enraged responses." Laura has discovered the satisfaction of having a sense of control over her own behavior—which ultimately is all any of us can control.

ORGANIZATIONAL ACTIVITY 5.10

Read the following sample draft of a problem/solution paper and evaluate its organization. In small groups, discuss possible organizational changes that would make the paper more effective. Could some paragraphs be better located? Then read your latest draft and consider any organizational changes that would strengthen it.

SAMPLE DRAFT My sister's toddler is turning into a very spoiled baby. When I'm around other babies her age, which is nineteen months, I realize how differently she acts. Of course, she doesn't know any better because she is just a baby, so it's not her fault. However, if my sister and her husband don't start taking control and teaching her how to behave now, she's just going to get worse and she'll suffer for it when she gets into school and has to mind a teacher and get along with other kids.

To be honest, my sister and her husband get invited a little less frequently to family get-togethers because we all know Samantha will run wild and make it hard on everyone. It's particularly hard on the rest of us relatives because we really want to discipline her for her own good, but with her parents there, it's almost impossible to do. And it's like they're totally oblivious to the problem. They just laugh at everything she does or ask her not to do something and when she doesn't mind, they ignore it. Samantha also keeps getting bolder as she gets older, and she thinks she can do anything. Since she has no limits, the time will come when she puts herself in danger—for example running out into the street—and her parents can only blame themselves.

Samantha is a beautiful, happy baby who could be a real joy to be around. However, she's out of control. She goes where she wants, she does what she wants, and she doesn't mind her parents at all. When she stands in her high chair and they tell her to sit down, or when they tell her to come here, or when they tell her "Don't do this" or "Don't do that," she ignores them, or she gives them a little smile and just keeps on going. And when she finally doesn't get her way, she pitches a huge tantrum, throwing herself on the ground kicking and screaming. But her parents don't like to see her throw tantrums, so they usually give in.

The problem is that my sister and brother-in-law think everything she does is cute. They idolize her, and they can't get mad at her for anything. They also want her to be happy all the time, so she is really the one in control, leading them all over the house where she wants to go, or all over the park or all over the neighborhood. She's in control, and she knows it. And when it comes to sharing, forget it. If there's a cousin around or a baby of a friend, Samantha goes and takes anything the other baby is playing with, and if someone tries to take something from her, she screams bloody murder. She is totally into herself and her needs, and her parents have let her become that way.

Finally, whenever I baby-sit Samantha, or when other relatives help out, we need to start doing what her parents haven't done: letting her know that as a baby, she isn't in control. I love her and want her to be happy also, but I'm not afraid to discipline her, and neither are some of my aunts.

So we need to start being firmer when she's with us and her parents aren't around. If Samantha doesn't learn some self-control, she's going to be miserable as she gets a little older. Nobody likes a five-year-old brat, and she's not going to be popular with anyone—her fellow students or teachers. There's still hope, because she's only nineteen months old—but it's time to get her going in the right direction, with my sister's help or not.

There are some really good books out there about setting limits for babies, and the consequences if you don't, so a sly way to perhaps get them thinking is to mail them, anonymously, two or three of these books. That may make them mad, but perhaps they'd get the message, especially if they think any number of people could have sent the books, which is possible. I also think our family needs to lay some "tough love" on them and just not invite them to some traditional family get-together that everyone gets invited to.

My sister doesn't realize it, but she's hurting her daughter when she thinks she's being a good mother. I can't say anything to her, because first I'm the younger sister who knows nothing, and second, I have no kids of my own, so what do I know? My mom is sometimes just about as bad as my sister, so she won't tell her anything. Besides, I don't think talking to her would help anyway. I think they believe everything is just fine.

SENTENCE REVISION

All writers share the task of revising first-draft sentences. The goal of such revision is to craft sentences that flow smoothly and express your thoughts clearly. Like most writers, you will continue to improve your sentence revision skills as long as you write.

Wording Problems Review

The first step in revising first-draft sentences is learning to identify sentences that need some work. Basically, you are looking for sentences that appear vague, awkward, or wordy. If a sentence doesn't look or sound right to you, it probably needs revising. When you locate a problem sentence, experiment with different wording options until you find the best combination. Here is an example:

FIRST-DRAFT SENTENCE With sentence revision, you are working with both improving the clarity of a sentence's content and the wording through which to express that content best.

> **REVISED** With sentence revision, you are improving both your clarity of thought and the wording through which that thought is expressed.

> **REVISED** Through sentence revision, you are clarifying your thoughts and improving the way you express them.

FINAL REVISION   Through sentence revision, you clarify your thoughts and improve your wording.

Compare the first, second, third, and final drafts of the sentence. The first sentence struggles to get the writer's thoughts on paper; and the final draft expresses them clearly, smoothly, and concisely. Such revisions often occur over time throughout the drafting process.

SENTENCE REVISION ACTIVITY 5.11

For revision practice, rewrite the following paragraphs to make the sentences clearer, smoother, and more concise. When you finish, read your latest draft and revise sentences that could be improved.

At first, I felt sorry for my roommate because she was lonely. I did things with her, tried to cheer her up when she was depressed, and my clothes she could borrow anytime. Nothing seemed to help out the situation for long though because I'd come back to the dorm after class and there she'd be just staring at the ceiling or just crying for no reason on the bed. I couldn't be with her all the time. One night a dance was put on by the college and I met a guy who seemed really nice. We started going out, and my roommate was made very angry by that. She wouldn't talk to me or say anything to me when I came back from dates. It was like as if she was being betrayed for having a boyfriend.

On top of that, my clothes were now borrowed by her without asking, and she was even getting into my make-up. Finally, I'd had enough. Anxious to get out of that room, I asked the dorm adviser when another dorm room would become vacant. I moved out of that room and into a single room, and even though I had to pay more for it, having to pay the extra money was worth the freedom that I received from my old roommate. I hope some psychological counseling can be gotten by her both for her own good and before she drives another roommate crazy.

Sentence Variety Review

In the sections on sentence variety, you use different sentence structures to express yourself most effectively. Like many writers, you may sometimes overuse favored structures and joining words, which can become boring to readers. Working with different structures makes you more aware of your options and more comfortable in using them.

SENTENCE REVISION ACTIVITY 5.12

Revise the following paragraphs by combining sentences to form more effective and informative ones. Your revised paragraph should include a variety of simple, compound, and complex sentences, including some with relative clauses beginning with *who, which, whose,* or *that.*

When you finish, reread your latest draft to evaluate your sentence variety and use of joining words, and make revisions for improvement.

Obesity is a big concern for many Americans. We are the most overweight people in the world. We consume the most food per person.

There are different causes for obesity. The biggest factors are overeating and eating the wrong foods. Both of these factors can be overcome. Heredity can also be a factor in obesity. Children of obese parents don't have to become obese. The tendency toward obesity must be addressed in early childhood.

Overeating usually begins in childhood. Eating the wrong foods usually begins in childhood. These bad habits are not easily broken.

Parents often set a bad example. They eat junk food in front of their young children. Junk food includes hamburgers, french fries, soft drinks, onion rings, and rich desserts. These are all loaded with fat and sugar. Over-consumption of fat and sugar is a leading cause of obesity.

American restaurants add to the problem. They compete to see who can serve the largest portions. They do this to attract customers. Customers often seek the biggest meals for the price. Fast food restaurants are the biggest culprit. They "super size" their meals to give customers larger servings of french fries and soft drinks.

There is a disparity in America. The ideal American image is a slender, fit body. This is projected through advertising. The average American is overweight and unfit. This disparity leads to unhappiness and depression. It doesn't seem to change people's eating habits.

Other Structural Problems

Three specific sentence problems are covered in the "Sentence Revision" section of the Appendix: nonparallel construction, dangling modifiers, and misplaced modifiers. Your instructor may refer you to those sections if those types of problems occur in your writing.

JOURNAL ENTRY NINETEEN

In your journal, relate the kinds of sentence revisions that you make to improve your wording. What are the most common flaws in your first-draft sentences, and how do you eliminate them through revision?

FINAL EDITING

The last step in the writing process is to give your draft a final proofreading for errors. Rather than scanning your draft for grammatical, spelling, and punctuation errors simultaneously, try concentrating on one area at a time. That way you are least likely to overlook a particular kind of error.

PROOFREADING GUIDELINES

When proofreading your draft, make sure to cover the following areas:

1. *Sentence endings:* Make sure you have a period at the end of each sentence, and correct any run-on sentences or sentence fragments. (If you have a particular problem with run-on sentences or fragments, see the upcoming review section.)

2. *Word endings:* Check to make sure plural words end in *s* or *es*, regular past tense verbs end in *ed*, and present tense verbs agree with their subjects. Also check for *er* and *est* endings on comparative and superlative adjectives. (See the upcoming section on "Comparative and Superlative Adjectives.")

3. *Spelling:* Check your spelling carefully, and look up any words you are uncertain of. Also check your use of homophones such as there/their/they're, your/you're, no/know, through/threw, and its/it's.

4. *Internal punctuation:* Check your use of commas with words in series, before conjunctions in compound sentences, after introductory groups of words, and to set off relative clauses, interrupters, and ending phrases beginning with *especially, particularly,* and *ing-ending* words. (See the upcoming section on "Comma Usage Review.") Check for apostrophes in contractions and possessives and for quotation marks around direct quotations. Finally, check your use of semicolons and colons. (See the upcoming section on "Punctuation.")

5. *Pronoun usage:* Check your subject pronoun usage (Marianne and I, my brother and he, we and they), and make sure that all pronouns agree with their antecedents. (See the upcoming section on "Pronoun-Antecedent Agreement Review.")

ONLINE ACTIVITY: PROOFREADING TIPS

Are you still having problems detecting errors in your drafts? For some online assistance, go to Purdue University's Resources for Writers: http://owl.english.purdue.edu/handouts/general/gl_proof2.html.

When you arrive, read the specific suggestions for proofreading your drafts effectively. Make note of the most useful suggestions, and apply them when you proofread your latest draft.

EDITING ACTIVITY 5.13

In small groups, proofread the following student draft for errors and make the necessary corrections.

STUDENT SAMPLE DRAFT

I've had obsticles threw out my life. One of my biggest problems that I've incurred was when I had my divorce. I know that it effected my life completely. As well as my children. I got married at an early age of 15. It seemed hard to become a grown up at such an early age.

I became a very young mother, at fifteen and wasn't able to enjoy my childhood. But that was no one's fault but mind. I tried to become a responsiable mother. I worked hard and I became a responsiable parent for my child.

I knew that it wasn't going to be easy. But with lots of help from my family I was able to be strong. My plans when I was young were to live a happy life. But I guess that I followed the footsteps of my parents. I don't blame my parents because I guess just like my relationship, their marriage wasn't meant to be.

I know that I tried to be a good wife to keep my relationship working. But when your husband don't cooperate it's impossiable to make anything happen. But we tried to work it out for nine years. We had our ups and downs but life just seemed to work out its own way. But I guess everything happens for the best. Because we have gone our own different ways.

We have remained friends for our kids sake. I've remarried know and I'm happily married, I have know found my true husband, he has made me very happy. God is know part of my life and I have put a lot of my love into my relationship.

EDITING ACTIVITY 5.14

Proofread your latest draft for errors following the guidelines presented earlier in this unit. Concentrate in particular on eliminating your personal error tendencies. (Your instructor may have you cover the upcoming punctuation and grammar sections before proofreading.)

When you have corrected all errors, write or print out the final draft of your paper to share with readers.

JOURNAL ENTRY TWENTY

In your journal, relate the progress you have made during the course on eliminating errors from your writing. In what areas have you made improvement, and how have your proofreading skills—your ability to identify existing errors—improved?

SENTENCE PROBLEMS

The following activity is for students who continue to have problems with run-on sentences and fragments. If you have such problems, do the activity before proofreading your draft.

RUN-ON AND FRAGMENT REVIEW ACTIVITY 5.15

The following passage contains run-on sentences and fragments. Rewrite the passage and correct errors by changing or adding punctuation, or by adding joining words to combine sentences.

EXAMPLE   The service at the restaurant was terrible. Because there was one waitress for ten tables. People got frustrated, they left without ordering.

REVISED   The service at the restaurant was terrible because there was one waitress for ten tables. People got frustrated, and they left without ordering.

This was the last semester that Charlotte would carpool. Because she had too many bad experiences. She had gotten in a car pool at the beginning of the semester with three other girls who lived nearby. When Ela drove, she was always five to ten minutes late, she always had elaborate excuses. Marsela, on the other hand, was always ten minutes early, tooting her horn and waking up the neighborhood. The third girl was totally unpredictable, she relied on her brother to pick her up. One day she was on time, the next day early, and the next day late, sometimes she wouldn't come at all. Since Charlotte was the only one with first-period classes, the others weren't concerned about the time. Next semester Charlotte will take a bus to school. Even though the bus stop is a mile from her house.

CORRECT USAGE

The following section introduces a new grammatical area that you should find useful: comparative and superlative adjectives. In addition, pronoun-antecedent agreement is reviewed.

Comparative and Superlative Adjectives

Writers frequently use adjectives to compare things: people, cars, colleges, movies, jobs, cities, or religions. They may use adjectives to compare the size of four brothers, the speed of two sports cars, the cost of tuition at a number of colleges, the endings of Steven Spielberg movies, the difficulty of different jobs, the crime rate in different cities, or the creation myths in different religions. Adjectives that are used in comparisons take particular forms which follow grammatical rules.

An adjective may be used to describe a single person or thing, to compare two people or things, or to compare one person or thing to many others. Here are examples of these three uses for adjectives and the three forms the adjectives take:

Descriptive   Sally is <u>short</u>. (Short *describes Sally*.)

Comparative   Sally is <u>shorter</u> than Sue. (Shorter *compares the height of Sally to that of Sue*.)

Superlative   Sally is the <u>shortest</u> person in her family. (Shortest *compares the height of Sally to that of all others in her family*.)

Notice that with the one-syllable adjective *short*, the *er* ending is added for comparing two things, and the *est* ending is added for comparing more than two things. Here are three more examples of the uses for adjectives with a longer descriptive word:

Descriptive   Sally is <u>considerate</u>. (Considerate *describes Sally*.)

Comparative   Sally is <u>more considerate</u> than Sue. (More considerate *compares Sally to Sue*.)

Superlative   Sally is the <u>most considerate</u> person in the class. (Most considerate *compares Sally to all of her classmates*.)

Notice that with longer adjectives (two syllables or more), a *more* is added before the adjective for comparing two things, and a *most* is added before the adjective for comparing more than two things.

Now that you have a general idea of the forms that adjectives take, the following rules for making comparisons with adjectives should help you use them correctly in your writing.

Comparative Form (Comparing Two Things):

1. Add *er* to *one-syllable adjectives*.

   I am <u>shorter</u> than you are.

   Sam is <u>smarter</u> than Phil.

   Mercury lights are <u>brighter</u> than florescent lights.

2. Add *more* in front of adjectives with *two or more syllables*.

   I am <u>more depressed</u> than you are.

   Sam is <u>more graceful</u> than Phil.

   Mercury lights are <u>more effective</u> than florescent lights.

3. Exception: Add *er* to two-syllable words ending in *y* or *ow* (drop the *y* and add *ier*).

   I am <u>lonelier</u> than you are.

   Sam is <u>sillier</u> than Phil.

Mercury lights are <u>prettier</u> than fluorescent lights.

The river is <u>shallower</u> today than last week.

4. The word *than* often comes after an adjective in sentences comparing two things. (See all of the examples from items 1, 2, and 3.)

5. Never use both *more* and an *er* ending with an adjective.

Wrong	You are <u>more smarter</u> than I am.
Right	You are <u>smarter</u> than I am.
Wrong	You are <u>more beautifuler</u> than ever.
Right	You are <u>more beautiful</u> than ever.

Superlative Form (Comparing Three or More Things):

1. Add *est* to *one-syllable adjectives*.

   I am the <u>shortest</u> person in my family.

   Sam is the <u>smartest</u> elephant in the zoo.

   Mercury lights are the <u>brightest</u> lights for tennis courts.

2. Add *most* in front of adjectives with *two or more syllables*.

   I am the <u>most dependable</u> person in the family.

   Sam is the <u>most curious</u> elephant in the zoo.

   Mercury lights are the <u>most expensive</u> lights on the market.

3. Exception: Add *est* to two-syllable words ending in *y* or *ow* (drop the *y* and add *iest*).

   I am the <u>rowdiest</u> person in my family.

   Sam is the <u>heaviest</u> elephant in the zoo.

   Mercury lights give off the <u>loveliest</u> glow of any outdoor lights.

   That is the <u>shallowest</u> that I've ever seen Lake Placid.

4. The word *the* often comes before the adjective in sentences comparing three or more things. (See all of the examples in items 1, 2, and 3.)

5. Never use both *most* and an *est* ending with an adjective.

Wrong	You are the <u>most smartest</u> person I know.
Right	You are the <u>smartest</u> person I know.
Wrong	Francine is the <u>most remarkablest</u> artist in the school.
Right	Francine is the <u>most remarkable</u> artist in the school.

ADJECTIVE ACTIVITY 5.16

Each of the following sentences compares two things. Fill in the correct *comparative* form of each adjective in parentheses. Count the number of syllables the adjective has, add *er* to one-syllable adjectives and two-syllable adjectives ending in *y* or *ow*, and add *more* in front of other adjectives of two syllables or more.

EXAMPLES   (quick) You are a *quicker* runner this year than last.

(beautiful) The nearby hills are *more beautiful* in the spring than in the summer.

1. (interesting) The first day of school was _____ than I thought it would be.

2. (friendly) The teachers were _____ than I imagined.

3. (fascinating) The lectures were _____ than my high school lectures.

4. (short) The classes were also _____ than usual, since it was the first day.

5. (fast) The whole day went by _____ than I expected.

6. (tedious) I thought college would be _____ than it was.

7. (enthusiastic) Now I am _____ than ever about coming back tomorrow.

8. (long) However, tomorrow's classes will be much _____ than today's.

9. (difficult) The homework will definitely be _____ than today's.

10. (typical) Tomorrow will be _____ of a regular college day than today was.

ADJECTIVE ACTIVITY 5.17

Each of the following sentences compares three or more things. Fill in the correct *superlative* form of each adjective in parentheses. Count the number of syllables the adjective has; add *est* to one-syllable adjectives and two-syllable adjectives ending in *y* or *ow*, and add *most* in front of other adjectives with two syllables or more.

EXAMPLES   (quick) I felt the *quickest* today in track practice that I've ever felt.

(unusual) The antique knife display in the library is the *most unusual* display of the year.

1. (interesting) The first day of school was the _____ of the week.

2. (friendly) I met some of the _____ teachers I have ever encountered.

3. (fascinating) The lectures were the _____ I have ever taken.

4. (short) The classes were also the _____ I have ever attended.

5. (fast) It was the _____ day of school I've been through.

6. (tedious) I thought college would be the _____ part of my education.

7. (enthusiastic) Now I am the _____ I've ever been about going to school.

8. (long) Although the classes tomorrow will be the _____ I've had, I should still enjoy them.

9. (difficult) Although the homework will be the _____ I've done, I don't think I'll mind it.

10. (typical) Students say that the second week of college is the _____ week to judge school by, so I hope it goes as well as the first.

ADJECTIVE ACTIVITY 5.18

Fill in each of the following blanks with an appropriate comparative or superlative adjective, following the rules presented. Include both one-syllable and multi-syllable adjectives.

EXAMPLES   In winter the days grow *shorter* while in summer they grow *longer*.

That is the *most expensive* purse I've ever bought.

1. The clarinet is _____ to play than the saxophone.

2. The oboe is the _____ woodwind instrument to play.

3. The oboe has the _____ sound of any woodwind.

4. The cornet is somewhat _____ than the trumpet.

5. The tuba is the _____ brass instrument.

6. The conductor grew _____ every time the band got out of tempo.

7. When a woodwind squeaks, it is one of the _____ sounds there is.

8. A French horn can produce the _____ sound of any brass instrument.

9. Percussion instruments are often the _____ to play.

10. The snare drum is _____ to play than the timpani.

11. Some people are _____ to see a marching band than others.

12. Some band members are _____ to march in a parade than others.

13. The piccolo is the _____ instrument in the band.

14. In addition, the piccolo makes the _____ sound.

15. Some people find it _____ to attend an orchestra concert than a band review.

Pronoun-Antecedent Agreement Review

As you recall from the previous unit, pronouns must agree in number and gender with their antecedents:

John visited <u>his</u> grandparents in Florida by <u>himself</u>.

Melissa and I took <u>our</u> final a day early because <u>we</u> had to work the next day.

The boat tore <u>its</u> hull on some rocks, and <u>it</u> began sinking rapidly.

Writers sometimes have problems when an *indefinite pronoun* is the antecedent: each, one, everyone, someone, no one, somebody, everybody. Indefinite pronouns are singular and require singular pronoun references:

Everyone brought <u>his</u> or <u>her</u> blue book to the history final.

One of the boys lost <u>his</u> wallet at the baseball game.

Each of the mothers took <u>her</u> turn working at the school bake sale.

Nobody wants <u>his</u> or <u>her</u> name slandered by gossip.

PRONOUN-ANTECEDENT ACTIVITY 5.19

For more practice with pronoun-antecedent agreement, fill in the blanks in the following sentences with pronouns that agree in number with their antecedents. Underline the antecedent for each pronoun.

EXAMPLE   <u>People</u> can usually be trusted if <u>they</u> are given responsibility.

1. The old shack lost _____ tin roof in the hurricane.

2. Each of the girls has a room to _____ in the bungalow.

3. Two men from New Zealand left _____ passports at the airport.

4. A student needs to set _____ priorities straight before _____ can do well in college.

5. Every one of the geraniums got _____ bloom at the same time.

6. Hawaii is a favorite vacation spot for Japanese tourists. _____ is _____ island home away from home, and _____ flock there by the thousands.

7. Humans are _____ own worst enemy in destroying _____ environment. _____ must reverse the destructive process _____ have initiated.

8. Maria did _____ math totally by _____ for the first time in _____ life, and _____ was very proud.

9. A person in need of financial help should consult an expert, and _____ should stay away from _____ well-meaning friends no better off than _____ is.

10. Each cadet was instructed to do _____ own locker inspection, and no one was to leave the barracks before _____ had finished _____ chores.

11. The watches that I bought from the catalog have all lost _____ plastic covers because _____ weren't properly attached to the faces.

12. Skateboards are being seen on college campuses again. _____ lost _____ appeal to students in the late seventies, but now _____ are back in vogue as a means of transportation.

13. Either Sarah or Brunhilda left _____ beaker in the chemistry lab.

14. The presents that you bought me for my birthday lost _____ charm when I heard you paid for _____ with my credit card.

15. The women who got the best bargains at the garage sale did _____ shopping before 7:00 a.m., and the rest of us were left with what _____ had picked over.

PUNCTUATION

This section introduces two new punctuation marks that writers find useful: semicolons and colons. It also includes a review of comma usage.

Semicolons and Colons

The semicolon (;) and colon (:) allow writers to vary their sentence structure and add flexibility to their writing. Semicolons and colons are used in the following ways:

1. *Semicolon:* joins two complete sentences that are related in meaning and that are relatively short (used as an alternative to separating sentences with a period or joining sentences with a conjunction).

   EXAMPLES   Marion should be at the checkout any minute; her ten-minute break is almost over.

Hank's health is his number one concern; in fact, nothing else seems important right now.

Melissa should never have tried to run a hard mile without warming up; she knows better.

2. *Colon:* (a) used after a *complete thought* to indicate that a series of items follows.

EXAMPLES   We need the following utensils for the picnic: knives, forks, spoons, spatulas, and a cheese grater.

Sandra has the characteristics of an outstanding athlete: intelligent, dedicated, coachable, goal oriented, and confident.

Note—A common misuse of the colon is after the words *"such as,"* *"like,"* and *"includes."*

WRONG   Tools we need to install the wall plug include: pliers, a screwdriver, and wire cutters.

RIGHT   Tools we need to install the wall plug include pliers, a screwdriver, and wire cutters.

RIGHT   We need the following tools to install the wall plug: pliers, a screwdriver, and wire cutters. (The colon now follows a complete thought.)

3. *Colon:* (b) used after a *complete thought* to highlight a single item that follows.

EXAMPLES   There's one virtue that Peter definitely lacks: patience.

The answer to Maria's financial problem is obvious: find a better job.

As a camp counselor, you've made one thing apparent: your concern for troubled children.

I've got something that you need: the keys to the house.

PUNCTUATION ACTIVITY 5.20

Add semicolons and colons to the following sentences where they are needed. Put a C in front of each correctly punctuated sentence.

EXAMPLE   You show a real aptitude for computer programming; you have a promising future.

1. ___ There's one class in college I've had trouble passing physiology.

2. ___ I know how to get from our dormitory to the downtown library I went there several times last semester.

3. ___ Everyone fails occasionally don't get discouraged.

4. ___ Freda replaced her computer's floppy disk system with a hard disk drive the new system is much faster and stores more information.

5. ___ Millicent has been taking aerobic dance four times a week for four years she started when she was forty-five years old.

6. ___ One attribute comes to mind when considering golfer Jack Nicklaus's years of unparalleled success mental toughness.

7. ___ The chain saw equipment in the garage should include two 16-inch Weber chain saws, a bag of extra chains, a gallon of gasoline, three cleaning rags, and four pints of chain saw oil.

8. ___ My aunt's cat Tiger is a fearless fighter her other cat Chubby prefers hiding behind the washing machine.

PUNCTUATION ACTIVITY 5.21

For practice, write five of your own sentences that require semicolons and five more that require colons, and punctuate them correctly. (Use the words *however* and *therefore* after the semicolons in at least two sentences, and write some sentences in which the colon is followed by a single word and others in which it is followed by a series.) When you finish, check your latest draft to see where you might use a semicolon or colon.

Comma Usage Review

The following review activity is for students who are still having some problems with comma usage.

COMMA REVIEW ACTIVITY 5.22

Following the comma usage rules presented in the text, insert commas where they are needed in the following essay:

My freshman year I really enjoyed the freedom that came with college. After having been in "prison" for four years of high school it felt great not having classes every hour of the day and even greater being able to miss a class now and then.

The problem was the "now and then" became more frequent as the semester went on. I mostly had large lecture classes and the teachers didn't take roll or worry about who was there and who wasn't. Therefore I started sleeping in more and more often and I often relied on the notes that friends would take in class.

My grades started slipping more and more but I was determined to make up for it all by doing well on my finals. The trouble was I had missed so much class and gotten so far behind that I tried to do about a month's studying in a few nights. I vowed to stay up all night studying before each final but it never worked out. I was hopelessly behind and I did terribly on my finals.

For the first semester I ended up with one C and the rest Ds and Fs. I was so ashamed that I lied to my parents and my friends. Basically I blew my first semester of college and I learned that the freedom of college was deceptive. In college they give you enough rope to hang yourself so that's what I did. If you don't learn to take the responsibility to go to class and put your free time to good use you'll end up in a hole. This semester I'm having to dig myself out including taking two classes over again. I'll also have to go to summer school if I want to end up with thirty units for the year. I'm going to class regularly taking my own notes and keeping up on my reading better. So far I'm doing okay but there are still twelve weeks to go. I hope I've learned my lesson especially since my parents are paying my tuition.

WRITING REVIEW

In the "Writing Review," you apply what you have learned throughout the unit to a second problem/solution paper. The following writing process summarizes the steps presented throughout the unit. While following the process, feel free to make changes in it that you have found helpful for writing other papers.

WRITING PROCESS

1. Select a problem to write about that affects most or all of the students in your class. It may be a school-related problem, a common type of personal or relationship problem, or a common work-related problem. Pick a problem that your classmates—your reading audience for the paper—will be interested in.

2. Before writing about your problem, take some time to analyze the situation. Answer the following questions to help you investigate the problem, and to generate some ideas for your first draft:

   a. What exactly is the problem? Try expressing it in one clear sentence.

   b. How did the problem get started, and what caused it?

   c. What effect(s) does the problem have on you?

   d. What effect(s), if any, does the problem have on others?

   e. What are possible solutions to the problem?

3. In seeking solutions to your problem, use the following suggestions:

   a. What exactly does it mean to "solve" the problem? What do you want to accomplish through its being solved?

   b. What are the roots or causes of the problem? It may be impossible to solve a problem if you don't have a clear understanding of its causes.

   c. Consider possible solutions that could attack these causes and either eliminate or reduce their impact.

   d. Consider both short-term progress toward solving the problem and longer-term solutions. Success in the beginning may be improving a situation that will take a longer time to resolve.

   e. Come up with as many solutions as possible, including those that may seem implausible or rather drastic. Often your first ideas are the most obvious and traditional, but not necessarily the best.

   f. Consider compromises in finding a solution to a problem. Oftentimes, particularly in relationships, the solution to a problem involves two or more parties finding a middle ground, by each party giving up something to get something. Solutions are often not perfect, and in dealing with problems with others involved, the best solution is often one that satisfies no one completely.

   g. Consider how time will affect the problem and its ultimate solution. For example, sometimes people have to ride out a difficult situation for a time, knowing that their circumstances will change. Solutions that help take you out of a bad situation are worth considering.

   h. Talk to other people about the problem. Seldom are problems unique to individuals. Usually you can find people who either have the same problem or have worked through it in the past. Effective problem solving often is a collective effort, so don't feel that you have to solve a problem by yourself.

4. Determine your purpose for writing to your classmates about this problem. What do you want to accomplish? What do you want your classmates to learn or understand?

5. Write the first draft of your paper following these guidelines:

   a. As you write your first draft, use this basic organizational plan, which is easy for readers to follow.

      1. Introduce the problem, why you are concerned about it, and why, if at all, your readers should be concerned.

      2. Present the cause(s) of the problem. How did it start and develop?

      3. Present the effect(s) of the problem on you, and if applicable, on others.

4. Present a single solution, alternative solutions that should be tried, short-term and longer-term solutions, a compromise that could solve the problem, or anything else you have come up with to improve the situation. If you are dealing with a difficult problem, you may not be presenting a single, simple solution, but rather a more realistic way of dealing with the problem in different ways. Or if the problem may seem impossible to solve completely, you may be discussing ways to improve the situation.

b. As you follow this plan, feel free to make changes in organization that better fit your particular topic and how you want to present it. For example, if it seems better to present the problem's effects on you before you get into its causes, reverse the order. Or if you feel it's important to let readers know in the beginning what your solution is (so they will have it in mind as they read), present it.

c. Paragraph your paper as you move to its different parts: introduction (presenting problem and your concern with it), causes of problem, effects of problem, possible solution(s).

d. Keep your readers and purpose in mind as you write. What are you trying to accomplish by writing about this particular problem? What do you want your readers to take from the paper?

My Problem as a Newlywed

STUDENT SAMPLE DRAFT The first years of our marriage, my husband and I were like travelers, going from here to there and there to here. My husband would come down and pick me up in Mexico and we'd come to the United States. Once I would get tired of being in the United States, I'd just tell him, "I want to go back to Mexico," and he would take me back. He would drop me off and return to the United States. He did this many times and never complained for the first years of our marriage.

However, things did not stay like this because he eventually got tired. He told me he was not going to be picking me up and taking me back whenever I felt like it. I remember the last time he picked me up from Mexico. Everything was smooth as usual. Once we arrived in Texas, everything was fine until I again grew tired of being here and wanted to go back to my family. I began telling him one evening when he got home from work that I wanted to go back again.

I still remember how calmly he responded and his exact words. He said, "Ok, if you want to go back to Mexico, then go. I think that by now you know the route and are able to go alone because I'm not going to take you back and go get you whenever you feel like it anymore. Go ahead and leave and stay as long as you wish. Enjoy your stay and be happy, and when you decide to return, you know the way back. I just hope that by the time you decide to return you don't find the house occupied."

Even though he said this, I still left because I didn't believe he was serious. A month went by and then another, and I noticed he was becoming more distant and not calling as often. I still believed he would come for Christmas like he always did, but he didn't come. Then I thought he was waiting for New Year's, but still nothing. Finally I called him and told him how upset I was, and again he reminded me of what he had said. I still waited until February but when I realized he was serious, I knew I had to go back to him on my own.

This is the way I finally realized that I would have to start my married life here in the United States even if I didn't want to. It was very difficult for me to become accustomed to the new traditions and a new culture, but I realized that my life is here. I suffered a lot because I didn't and still don't have family members in this country. Even now I sometimes get sad and lonely, but I have maintained good communication with my sisters in Mexico.

Even though a part of me will always want to go back, I cannot because my husband and daughter are here, and I belong with them as their wife and mother. I had to grow up and realize that my place is with my husband and daughter, no matter how much I miss the rest of my family. I am also lucky that my husband was patient with me for many years and let me return to Mexico. And he was happy that I finally came back on my own for good.

6. When you finish your first draft, set it aside for a while, and then reread and evaluate your paper for possible revisions, following these guidelines:

   a. Evaluate the opening of your paper. Does it introduce your problem in some manner so that readers know what you are writing about? Do you present the problem in a way that creates reader interest? Is there anything you might add? Answer the question, "Based on my opening, what would inspire readers to want to read further?"

   b. Evaluate the middle part of the paper: How well do you present the causes of the problem? How effectively do you show the effects that the problem has on you and on others? What might you add to help readers understand the problem better or make the paper more interesting?

   c. Evaluate your conclusion. Do you present a realistic solution or possible solutions that deal with the problem's causes? Do you explain what this solution will do for you, and perhaps for others? The solution part of your paper is perhaps the most important since readers may discover something they hadn't considered.

   d. Evaluate your paragraphing. Does it help readers move smoothly through the opening, middle, and ending of your paper? Have you used transitions (first, second, then, however, therefore, as you can see, for example, finally) to tie sentences and paragraphs together? Have you dealt with causes and effects in separate paragraphs, or introduced different causes or different effects in new paragraphs?

e. Evaluate the organization of your paper. Have you presented the different parts of your paper in the best order? Does a particular sentence or paragraph seem out of place where it is? What might you move to a different location where it would make more sense? (Review the section on "Essay Organization" earlier in this unit.)

f. Read each sentence carefully to see if you can improve its clarity, smoothness, or conciseness. Many first draft sentences can be improved through the revision process. In addition, make revisions to improve sentence variety, replace overused joining words, and combine pairs of short sentences. (Review the section on "Sentence Revision" earlier in this unit.)

g. Read the draft from your readers' perspective. Have you presented a serious enough problem for readers to take an interest in? Have you written in a way that readers will clearly understand the problem and how it is affecting your life? Have you presented a solution or possible solutions that truly address the problem and give readers something to consider?

7. Write the second draft of your paper, including all revisions you have noted to improve it.

8. When you have completed your latest draft, proofread it for errors following these guidelines, and make the necessary corrections:

a. *Sentence endings:* Make sure you have a period at the end of each sentence, and correct any run-on sentences or sentence fragments.

b. *Word endings:* Check to make sure plural words end in *s* or *es*, regular past tense verbs end in *ed*, and present tense verbs agree with their subjects. Also check for *er* and *est* endings on comparative and superlative adjectives.

c. *Spelling:* Check your spelling carefully, and look up any words you are uncertain of. Also check your use of homonyms such as there/their/they're, your/you're, no/know, through/threw, and its/it's.

d. *Internal punctuation:* Check your use of commas with words in series, before conjunctions in compound sentences, after introductory groups of words, and to set off relative clauses, interrupters, and ending phrases beginning with *especially, particularly,* and *ing-ending* words. Check for apostrophes in contractions and possessives and for quotation marks around direct quotations. Finally, check your use of semicolons and colons.

  e. *Pronoun usage:* Check your subject pronoun usage (Marianne and I, my brother and he, we and they), and make sure that all pronouns agree with their antecedents. (See the section on "Pronoun-Antecedent Agreement Review" earlier in this unit.)

9. Write the final error-free draft of your paper to share with classmates and your instructor.

Writing about Issues

Writers write for a variety of reasons: to inform, educate, analyze, problem solve, and entertain. Another common reason for writing is to influence readers' thoughts or actions, particularly on issues important to the writer. When you write to influence readers, you want them to understand and support your position, which may mean changing their minds or getting them to take seriously something they hadn't considered before.

People frequently write about issues in newspaper editorials, "letters to the editor," work-related communications, and letters to individuals or groups of people. A writer may try to convince readers to vote for a particular candidate, to help reverse the firing of the city's philharmonic orchestra conductor, to vote against the city bond measure requiring a tax increase, to support a city-wide curfew for minors, to oppose a tuition increase at the local college, or to contribute money to build a performing arts building at the college. A common purpose for writing about issues is to move people to action they would not otherwise take.

Your audience for issue-oriented writing is a challenging one-people who either don't agree with you or don't have a strong opinion. You obviously don't have to convince people who already agree with you on the issue, so your challenge is either to change other people's minds or to get them thinking about an issue they may know or care little about. Audience awareness is a crucial part of writing effectively about issues, and there is an interesting psychological component to consider: what makes people change their opinions?

Writing about issues comes at the end of the text so that you can draw upon all that you have learned through previous writing experiences. The skills you have developed in writing about personal experiences, supporting an opinion convincingly, making comparisons and drawing reasonable conclusions, analyzing problems, organizing your thoughts, and wording your papers clearly will all contribute to how effectively you are able to write about issues.

PREWRITING

Writing about issues requires addressing topics that people have different opinions on. If most people agree on something, such as ten-year-olds not being allowed to drive, there is little to write about. However, if there was a legislative bill in your state to raise the legal driving age to eighteen, or to lower the legal drinking age to eighteen, people would have different viewpoints, and much would be written on the issue.

You may already have definite opinions on some important issues. You may, for example, favor gun control, disagree with capital punishment, condone legalized abortion, support gay rights, support rent control, disagree with legalizing marijuana, or support an increase in the speed limit on freeways. Often the biggest challenge in writing effectively on a particular issue is to support your viewpoint in ways that convince skeptical readers of its validity and good sense.

In analyzing your opinion on an issue, you may discover that it is based more on emotion than reason, or on beliefs you hold but have never questioned. You may even find that the viewpoint isn't really yours, but that of parents or friends whose opinion you've adopted. None of this means that you should abandon your viewpoint on a particular issue, but you may need to examine it critically before writing.

Next, while it is easy to write for readers who agree with you, those aren't the people who need convincing. Instead, you must engage readers who disagree with you or have no opinion in ways that keep them reading and thinking. Sometimes just getting a reader to question his or her viewpoint, or to think about an issue in a different way, is a real breakthrough. People seldom change their minds on important issues overnight, but you may plant a seed that at least makes them question their thinking.

TOPIC SELECTION

For your writing assignment, you will select an issue that you and others feel is important enough to write about. One that people have different opinions on. When writing your paper, you will take a position on the issue and "make a case" for your viewpoint in a way that you feel will influence readers. The purpose of writing about a particular issue is to change people's minds, to move them to action, to cause them to think differently, or to get them thinking seriously about something they hadn't considered. Different readers will react differently to what you write based on their personal viewpoint, their level of interest, and their knowledge of the issue.

To select an issue to write about, consider the following:

1. Select a *controversial* topic—one that people have different positions on. It may be a local controversy—something related to your school or community—or a state, national, or international concern. It could be in the area of education, politics, sports, music, health, fashion, family, criminal justice, etc.

2. Select a topic that you are knowledgeable about. You need to know enough about the issue, based on your experience, reading, and other sources, to write about it effectively. You may also want to talk to others to get ideas or examples for your paper, to better understand opposing viewpoints, to test your own belief and reasoning, or to learn more about the issue.

3. Select an issue that you are interested in, that you feel is important, and that you feel other people should know more about.

4. Select a topic that is specific enough to develop in a 400–500 word paper. For example, gun control is a general topic that you might write a book on. Therefore, you might narrow that topic to something specific like "Banning Assault Weapons," "Gun Control and the Fifth Amendment," "Minnesota's Handgun Control Initiative," or "Guns in the Home: Protection or Liability?"

TOPIC SELECTION ACTIVITY 6.1

In small groups, brainstorm to come up with a number of issues that students may be interested in and want to write about. Consider issues in different areas: local school-related issues, local community issues, state issues, education issues, political issues, sports/athletic issues, health issues, exercise/fitness issues, music issues, fashion issues, family issues, legal issues, ethnic/racial issues, etc. Make a list of any issues that come to mind, neither evaluating nor discarding any issue. The purpose is to generate a number of potential topics areas and to find out what people are interested in.

TOPIC SELECTION ACTIVITY 6.2

Following the suggestions presented on page 187, select an issue to write about. Take your time thinking about different topics, and consider issues that affect (or may affect) you and people you know. Consider issues that you may know more about than most of your classmates. Your instructor may want to approve your topic to ensure that a variety of issues is covered by the class.

STUDENT SAMPLE ISSUE CONSIDERATION

What's controversial these days? There's a bill in the state legislature to increase community college tuition by 15% next year. That could hurt some students. In the local paper this morning it said the city council is debating whether to spend a couple hundred thousand dollars to "beautify" the downtown area, and some people think it's a waste of money; others think it's a good idea. On campus, there's a controversy on whether condom vending machines should be installed in the bathrooms.

There's the instant replay debate in professional football. What about steroid use? Does anyone disagree that it's bad? What about beer being sold in eating places at four-year colleges? Is that an issue anymore? On our campus there's some concern over whether campus police should be allowed to carry guns. I don't know what I want to write about yet.

After more thinking, none of those topics really moved me. Then I remembered the rumor that the college newspaper may be shut down after this year. I checked it out and it's true. The school is planning on dropping the paper after next semester because, from what I've heard, it's hard to get students to enroll in the class or to get an instructor to teach it on a regular basis. I may want to write about that. It's going to be controversial, at least with some students.

POSSIBLE ISSUE FOR PAPER

Shutting down the college newspaper

PREWRITING CONSIDERATIONS

Before writing your first draft, consider the following prewriting plan:

1. Decide on a tentative *thesis* for the paper: the position you want to take on the issue and support in your paper. Consider your thesis carefully, for it will influence everything that you write.

THESIS STATEMENT EXAMPLES

TOPIC: GUN CONTROL   Banning assault weapons does not go far enough in curbing violence in America.

TOPIC: COLLEGE CAFETERIA   To improve the quality of food and reduce prices, the college cafeteria operation should be privatized.

TOPIC: GARBAGE PICKUP	The city's proposal to increase the garbage pickup in Rockport from once to twice a week should be supported.
TOPIC: IRAQI WAR	U.S. military intervention in Iraq was a big mistake.
TOPIC: DORMITORY CURFEW	Since college students are adults, there should be no curfew for students living in the dormitories.

2. Decide on your reading audience: the people that should read about this issue and your position on it. Who are the people that are most important to influence, and how can you best reach them—a letter to the editor in the college paper? The city paper? Letters to the college board of trustees? Personal letters to key individuals?

EXAMPLE   **TOPIC: DORMITORY CURFEW**   My audience would be the dormitory director, the dean of students, the college president, the board of trustees, and the student council, all of whom have a role in setting school policy. I would send my letter to all of them.

3. Decide on your writing purpose: what you hope to accomplish with your readers. Do you want to change their minds? Change their behavior? Encourage them to support your position on the issue? Take a particular action?

EXAMPLE   **TOPIC: DORMITORY CURFEW**   I want them to take an action: do away with the obsolete dormitory curfew that I guess few colleges in the country still have.

4. Generate a list of possible supporting points for your thesis position: reasons you believe the way you do. Readers will evaluate your position based primarily on the effectiveness of your supporting points.

EXAMPLE   **TOPIC: DORMITORY CURFEW**   Reasons why the curfew should be discontinued:

a. Students are adults.

b. No other college in the area has a dormitory curfew.

c. Current curfew doesn't work anyway.

d. Many students won't live in dorms due to curfew.

e. Discrimination against dormitory students.

f. Curfew distracts from serious dorm problems.

5. Think of a few *opposing* arguments to your position on the issue: reasons why some readers might disagree with you. Also, consider how might you counter or refute those arguments in your paper. Sometimes readers are more influenced by how you discredit their arguments than how you present your own.

EXAMPLE   TOPIC: DORMITORY CURFEW   Reasons some people favor the curfew:

   a. Parents' concern for students' safety.

   b. Curfew reduces potential for bad behavior (late night drinking, vandalism, fights, etc.).

   c. Some students in dorms favor the curfew so students won't come in late and wake people up.

6. Besides what you already know about your topic, what else might you need to know to write the best possible paper? Talk with people who can provide the best information. You may want to talk to individuals who have opposing viewpoints to understand their thinking.

PREWRITING ACTIVITY 6.3

Following the suggestions just presented, do an informal prewriting outline for your topic that includes the following:

1. Topic:

   Dropping the school newspaper

2. Thesis (position statement):

   The school newspaper is too important to students to be dropped.

3. Audience:

   The school board, who is considering eliminating the paper, and also the students, whose support is needed to keep the paper

4. Purpose:

   Convince the school board not to drop the paper, and convince students to get involved.

5. Supporting points for thesis:

   a. Student enjoyment in reading paper

   b. Only source of outside news for most students

   c. Main source of information for college activities

   d. Source of debates and discussion

   e. Tradition of the college

6. Arguments against your position:

   a. Budget problems at the college

   b. Having trouble staffing paper with students

   c. Faculty advisor problems

7. Countering arguments:

   a. Newspaper is a tiny part of school budget—not a big savings.

   b. Newspaper could generate more income through more sales of advertising space.

   c. Many small schools have some trouble with staffing, but they don't get rid of their papers.

   d. Recruit journalism students like college recruits athletes.

   e. Make faculty advisor regular full-time faculty member rather than part-time person.

8. Things to find out before writing:

   a. Talk with some students on the newspaper staff to see if they have any good ideas for saving the paper.

   b. Talk with faculty advisor to get budget figures for the newspaper.

PREWRITING ACTIVITY 6.4

With a partner, present your topic and what you plan to do with it. Evaluate topics and plans, ask questions, discuss other positions on the issue, and make suggestions that might help your partner prepare for writing.

JOURNAL ENTRY TWENTY-ONE

After having done prewriting work for several papers throughout the course, relate in your journal what you find to be the most effective prewriting process for you. In other words, what things do you prefer doing to help you write a first draft?

FIRST DRAFTS

Now that you have selected an issue and have done some prewriting, you are ready to write the first draft. The following suggestions will help you get started:

DRAFTING GUIDELINES

1. Open the paper by introducing your topic and presenting your thesis: your position on the issue. Begin the paper in a way that will motivate readers to continue. Let them know why they should take an interest in the topic.

2. In the middle paragraphs, present and develop your supporting points, and also present and counter one or two opposing arguments. It is important to cast some doubt in your readers' minds about their beliefs as well as to support your own.

3. Keep your readers in mind as you write. Since you are trying to influence them, you don't want to alienate or offend them, which may occur if your tone seems very angry, or if you imply that their beliefs are inferior to yours. In addition, consider what you need to remember about your particular audience.

   For example, if you are writing to a board of trustees, these are people who probably care about the college and the students, who are college graduates themselves, but who aren't involved enough in the day-to-day operation to know exactly what's going on. They probably aren't the enemy, but they may need educating on an issue.

4. In the conclusion, make your purpose clear to readers. Why did you write to them? What do you want them to do or think? How can you conclude your paper to best accomplish your purpose?

PREWRITING ACTIVITY 6.5

Before writing your first draft, meet in small groups to discuss how best to influence people who don't agree with you on something. Answer the following questions to help you think of ways that people are influenced. Make a list of things that you might do in a paper to influence readers.

1. When you really want something from someone (have someone do a particular favor for you, have someone help you with something), how do you best accomplish your purpose? How might that knowledge help you write your paper?

2. How can someone get you to change your mind about something of importance? How might this knowledge help you write your paper?

3. If you were going to talk to a group of high school seniors on the importance of practicing safe sex and avoiding pregnancies, what might be the best way to get them to take you seriously? How might this knowledge help you write your paper?

4. What would be the best "psychology" to use on a six-year-old to convince her to get a flu shot that she is unwilling to get? How might this knowledge help you write your paper?

5. You have a neighbor who belongs to the National Rifle Association and owns a number of guns. What do you think would be the best approach to get him to support legislation banning the ownership of handguns? How might this knowledge help you write your paper?

6. Divide your group, half in support of legalized abortion, half against (you may have to take a position you don't agree with), and have a discussion. Listen carefully to the reasons the group members with the opposing position believe as they do, and try to understand their viewpoint. How might trying to understand the thinking and feelings of readers with opposing viewpoints help you write your paper?

DRAFTING ACTIVITY 6.6

Read the following essay, "Ban the Things. Ban Them All" by Molly Ivins, to get some ideas on openings, middle paragraph development, and conclusions, and to see how she dealt with her reading audience: people opposed or reluctant to banning guns. Identify her supporting points and the opposition arguments that she counters.

Then write the first draft of your persuasive paper keeping in mind the guidelines presented.

Ban the Things. Ban Them All
Molly Ivins

Guns. Everywhere guns.

Let me start this discussion by pointing out that I am not anti-gun. I'm pro-knife. Consider the merits of the knife.

In the first place, you have to catch up with someone to stab him. A general substitution of knives for guns would promote physical fitness. We'd turn into a whole nation of great runners. Plus, knives don't ricochet. And people are seldom killed while cleaning their knives.

As a civil libertarian, I of course support the Second Amendment. And I believe it means exactly what it says: "A well-regulated militia being necessary to the security of a free state, the right of the people to keep and bear arms shall not be infringed." Fourteen-year-old boys are not part of a well-regulated militia. Members of wacky religious cults are not part of a well-regulated militia. Permitting unregulated citizens to have guns is destroying the security of this free state.

I am intrigued by the arguments of those who claim to follow the judicial doctrine of original intent. How do they know it was the dearest wish of Thomas Jefferson's heart that teenage drug dealers should cruise the cities of this nation perforating their fellow citizens with assault rifles? Channeling?

There is more hooey spread about the Second Amendment. It says quite clearly that guns are for those who form part of a well-regulated militia, i.e., the armed forces including the National Guard. The reasons for keeping them away from everyone else get clearer by the day.

The comparison most often used is that of the automobile, another lethal object that is regularly used to wreak great carnage. Obviously, this society is full of people who haven't got enough common sense to use an automobile properly. But we haven't outlawed cars yet.

We do, however, license them and their owners, restrict their use to presumably sane and sober adults and keep track of who sells them to whom. At a minimum, we should do the same with guns.

In truth, there is no rational argument for guns in this society. This is no longer a frontier nation in which people hunt their own food. It is a crowded, overwhelmingly urban country in which letting people have access to guns is a continuing disaster. Those who want guns—whether for target shooting, hunting, or potting rattlesnakes (get a hoe)—should be subjected to the same restrictions placed on gun owners in England, a nation in which liberty has survived nicely without an armed populace.

The argument that "guns don't kill people" is patent nonsense. Anyone who has ever worked in a cop shop knows how many family arguments end in murder because there was a gun in the house. Did the gun kill someone? No. But if there had been no gun, no one would have died. At least not without a good footrace first. Guns do kill. Unlike cars, that is all they do.

Michael Crichton makes an interesting argument about technology in his thriller *Jurassic Park*. He points out that power without discipline is making this society into wreckage. By the time someone who studies the martial arts becomes a master—literally able to kill with bare hands—that person has also undergone years of training and discipline. But any fool can pick up a gun and kill with it.

"A well-regulated militia" surely implies both long training and long discipline. That is the least, the very least, that should be required of those who are permitted to have guns, because a gun is literally the power to kill. For years, I used to enjoy taunting my gun-nut friends about their psychosexual hang-ups—always in a spirit of good cheer, you understand. But letting the noisy minority in the National Rifle Association force us to allow this carnage to continue is just plain insane.

I do think gun nuts have a power hang-up. I don't know what is missing in their psyches that they need to feel they have the power to kill. But no sane society would allow this to continue.

Ban the damn things. Ban them all.

You want protection? Get a dog.

REVISIONS

While you should always revise with your readers in mind, it is particularly important to revise issue-oriented papers with the question in mind, "How will my readers respond to this?" For example, you may write a paper supporting euthanasia that people who agree with you would love but that your reading audience would find unconvincing. If such a draft isn't skillfully revised, it may miss its target audience: people whose minds you are trying to change.

REVISION GUIDELINES

When evaluating your first draft for possible revisions, consider these suggestions:

1. *Evaluate the opening of your paper.* Does it introduce your topic clearly and present your thesis so readers know your position on the issue? Is it interesting enough to keep readers engaged who may have a different opinion from yours? Do readers know why they should be interested in this issue?

2. *Evaluate your middle paragraphs.* Do you present some strong supportive points and develop each point effectively? (Read the upcoming section on "Paragraph Development" before revising your draft.) In addition, do you present and refute one or two opposing arguments to get readers to reconsider their own beliefs?

3. *Evaluate your conclusion.* Is it a strong part of your paper that leaves readers with something to think about? Does it clearly reveal your purpose so readers know why you have written to them? Do they understand what you would like them to think or do?

4. *Evaluate your paragraphing.* Does it help readers move smoothly through the opening, middle, and ending of your paper? Have you used transitions (first, second, then, however, therefore, as you can see, for example) to tie sentences and paragraphs together? Have you developed your supportive points in different paragraphs?

5. *Read each sentence carefully to see if you can improve its clarity, smoothness, or conciseness.* In addition, make revisions to improve sentence variety, replace overused joining words, and combine pairs of short sentences. (See the upcoming section on "Sentence Revision Review" in this unit.)

6. *Read the draft from your readers' perspective.* Does it sound like it was written by a reasonable person who respects his or her readers although they may disagree? Was it written by a person whose viewpoint is based on a thorough knowledge of the issue?

REVISION ACTIVITY 6.7

In small groups, evaluate the following student draft by applying the revision guidelines just presented. Make note of what is done well in the essay and what might be improved through revision.

With a partner, exchange drafts and evaluate each other's draft similarly, taking into account the audience that he or she is writing for.

Keeping the School Newspaper
(written for school board)

It is hard to believe the school board is thinking about dropping the newspaper. It's been around since the school began. It's as much a part of the school as the football team, the band, the student council or anything else.

I know a lot of students who read the school paper. In fact, that is the only paper they ever read, so they would be losing their one newspaper source. I know the paper isn't exactly the *New York Times*, but it serves a purpose. It keeps students interested in what's going on around school. We don't have much involvement in activities and government as it is. Without a newspaper keeping us in touch with sports, activities, meetings, and rallies, there would be even less involvement.

The newspaper also brings in some news of the outside world—things that are happening in education, some world events, things that are happening in state politics. As I said, it's not like major news coverage, but for me and other students, it is the only news we read regularly.

The paper also gives students a chance to express their viewpoints. I like reading letters to the editor and student editorials, and sometimes students do get involved in issues and take sides—for example, when they were considering changing the name of the college. There was some real student involvement, and a lot of it came out of the coverage the paper gave the issue. Students don't get involved in many issues at the college. Without the paper, they wouldn't know any issues to get involved in.

The paper also gives some people a chance for a little attention. It's fun getting your name or picture in the paper. I don't know any student who doesn't like that. A lot of students get their pictures and opinions in when they ask a weekly question like "How do you feel about the new early semester calendar?" That's one of my favorite weekly regulars in the paper, and a lot of others too.

The paper also provides some journalism training for a lot of students. Without a paper, where would the journalism majors go? That would wipe out a program, and our enrollment would drop.

Finally, the paper can't be a big expense. It doesn't look as though it's expensively done up. What's the big cost to justify dropping the program? Why don't you look for other things to cut that are less important? Why don't you look for ways to save the paper? I'd really miss the paper. It's important to the school. What's a school without a newspaper? Even my old junior high still runs a weekly newspaper. And this college can't?

REVISION ACTIVITY 6.8

After working through the upcoming section on "Paragraph Development," and considering your partner's evaluation suggestions and your personal evaluation, write the next draft of your paper following the guidelines presented.

JOURNAL ENTRY TWENTY-TWO

In your journal, relate the most typical kinds of revisions you make during the drafting process. What do you tend to change, add, or delete in a draft as you revise? To what extent does your second draft of a paper differ from your first draft, and in what ways?

PARAGRAPH DEVELOPMENT

Effective paragraph development in an issue-oriented paper is important to accomplishing your purpose. Within your paragraphs, you answer skeptical readers' questions such as, How do you know that? How can you prove that? Why is that the case? or Why does that matter?

Providing Evidence

An important part of paragraph development in writing about issues is providing evidence that what you are saying is true or reasonable. Here are some examples of statements that need some supportive evidence to convince readers of their validity:

EXAMPLES   Handgun control laws are working well in New Hampshire. (Give examples of how they are working well.)

Most people on welfare could be working. (Provide evidence. How do you know that is the case?)

The college bookstore is overcharging students for textbooks. (How can you prove that? Give examples.)

Yosemite Falls is a scenic wonderland. (How can the reader tell? Provide convincing details.)

The college newspaper budget is a fraction of the total school budget. (To convince readers, compare the cost of the newspaper to the school's budget and show the percentage of cost.)

For many students, a sixty dollar annual parking fee at the college can be a hardship. (How can readers be convinced? Provide examples of students affected by the fee.)

To make your supportive points most convincing to readers, follow these guidelines:

1. Provide evidence for all points in support of your thesis: your position on the issue.

EXAMPLE THESIS   Community college transfer students are better risks for success at four-year schools than incoming freshmen.

SUPPORTING POINTS

a. Transfer students are more mature. (How are they "more mature"? How does being "more mature" help with success?)

b. Transfer students have already made the transition to college. (What does that mean? How does it affect success?)

c. Transfer students have already proven that they can handle college work. (How have they proven that? Give examples.)

d. Transfer students are by and large more serious about college. (How can that be proved? What evidence is there to support that claim?)

2. Provide evidence for any statement that readers wouldn't necessarily accept as true.

EXAMPLES   America is an ethnically diverse country. (No evidence needed—an obvious true statement that readers would agree with.)

Today's immigrants create problems that earlier immigrants didn't. (Evidence is needed to support the statement. What kinds of problems? What proof do you have? What examples can you give?)

America would be better off if it closed its borders to immigrants. (Evidence is needed to support the statement. Why should we close our borders? How would we be better off? What proof do you have?)

3. For a particular supporting point, provide the most effective type of evidence to convince readers of its truth or reasonableness: facts, examples, details, statistics, explanations, or reasons.

EXAMPLES   Meredith Quiring is guilty of extorting money from her ailing grandmother. (Provide *facts* that support the claim.)

America's trade relationship with Japan is deteriorating. (Provide *examples* to support the claim.)

A standard car leasing agreement is too complicated. (Provide *details* that reveal its complicated nature.)

Our school district has a problem with unfunded liabilities. (Provide an *explanation* of what "unfunded liabilities" means, and then explain the problem.)

Children of divorced parents are more likely to divorce than children whose parents stay together. (Provide *statistics* to prove the alleged fact.)

Clayton would make a better governor than McWilliams. (Provide the *reasons* Clayton would be a superior governor.)

ONLINE ACTIVITY: PROVIDING EVIDENCE

For more suggestions on providing evidence to support your main points, go to the University of North Carolina Writing Center: http://www.unc.edu/depts/wcweb/handouts/argument.html. Within the "Argument" presentation, scroll down and read the "Evidence" section. In addition, read the two sections on "Counterargument" and "Audience" at the same website, which also provide some good points to consider when revising your paper.

PARAGRAPH ACTIVITY 6.9

Read the following essay, "College Lectures: Is Anybody Listening?" by David Daniels, and determine the issue he is writing about and the essay's *thesis*: his position on the issue. In addition, note the types of examples, evidence, and details Daniels uses to make his points.

College Lectures: Is Anybody Listening?
David Daniels

A former teacher of mine, Robert A. Fowkes of New York University, likes to tell the story of a class he took in Old Welsh while studying in Germany during the 1930s. On the first day the professor strode up to the podium, shuffled his notes, coughed, and began, "*Guten Tag, Meine Damen und Herren*" ("Good day, ladies and gentlemen"). Fowkes glanced around uneasily. He was the only student in the course.

Toward the middle of the semester, Fowkes fell ill and missed a class. When he returned, the professor nodded vaguely and, to Fowkes's astonishment, began to deliver not the next lecture in the sequence but the one after. Had he, in fact, lectured to an empty hall in the absence of his solitary student? Fowkes thought it perfectly possible.

Today, American colleges and universities (originally modeled on German ones) are under strong attack from many quarters. Teachers, it is charged, are not doing a good job of teaching, and students are not doing a good job of learning. American businesses and industries suffer from unenterprising, uncreative executives educated not to think for themselves but to mouth outdated truisms the rest of the world has long discarded. College graduates lack both basic skills and general culture. Studies are conducted and reports are issued on the status of higher education, but any changes that result either are largely cosmetic or make a bad situation worse.

One aspect of American education too seldom challenged is the lecture system. Professors continue to lecture and students to take notes much as they did in the thirteenth century, when books were so scarce and expensive that few students could own them. The time is long overdue for us to abandon the lecture system and turn to methods that really work.

To understand the inadequacy of the present system, it is enough to follow a single imaginary first-year student—let's call her Mary—through a term of lectures on, say, introductory psychology (although any other subject would do as well). She arrives on the first day and looks around the huge lecture hall, taken a little aback to see how large the class is. Once the hundred or more students enrolled in the course discover that the professor never takes attendance (how can he?—calling the role would take far too much time), the class shrinks to a less imposing size.

Some days Mary sits in the front row, from where she can watch the professor read from a stack of yellowed notes that seem nearly as old as he is. She is bored by the lectures, and so are most of the other students, to judge by the way they are nodding off or doodling in their notebooks. Gradually she realizes the professor is as bored as his audience. At the end of each lecture he asks, "Are there any questions?" in a tone of voice that makes it plain he would much rather there weren't. He needn't worry—the students are as relieved as he is that the class is over.

Mary knows very well she should read an assignment before every lecture. However, as the professor gives no quizzes and asks no questions, she soon realizes she needn't prepare. At the end of the term she catches up by skimming her notes and memorizing a list of facts and dates. After the final exam, she promptly forgets much of what she has memorized. Some of her fellow students, disappointed at the impersonality of it all, drop out of college altogether. Others, like Mary, stick it out, grow resigned to the system and await better days when, as juniors and seniors, they will attend smaller classes and at last get the kind of personal attention real learning requires.

I admit this picture is overdrawn—most universities supplement lecture courses with discussion groups, usually led by graduate students; and some classes, such as first-year English, are always relatively small. Nevertheless, far too many courses rely principally or entirely on lectures, an arrangement much loved by faculty and administrators but scarcely designed to benefit the students.

One problem with lectures is that listening intelligently is hard work. Reading the same material in a textbook is a more efficient way to learn because students can proceed as slowly as they need to until the subject matter becomes clear to them. Even simply paying attention is very difficult; people can listen at a rate of four hundred to six hundred words a minute, while the most impassioned professor talks at scarcely a third of that speed. This time lag between speech and comprehension leads to daydreaming. Many students believe years of watching television have sabotaged their attention span, but their real problem is that listening attentively is much harder than they think.

Worse still, attending lectures is passive learning, at least for inexperienced listeners. Active learning, in which students write essays or perform experiments and then have their work evaluated by an instructor, is far more beneficial for those who have not yet fully learned how to learn. While it's true that techniques of active listening, such as trying to anticipate the speaker's next point or taking notes selectively, can enhance the value of a lecture, few students possess such skills at the beginning of their college careers. More commonly, students try to write everything down and even bring tape recorders to class in a clumsy effort to capture every word.

Students need to question their professors and to have their ideas taken seriously. Only then will they develop the analytical skills required to think intelligently and creatively. Most students learn best by engaging in frequent and even heated debate, not by scribbling down a professor's often unsatisfactory summary of complicated issues. They need small discussion classes that demand the common labors of teacher and students rather than classes in which one person, however learned, propounds his or her own ideas.

The lecture system ultimately harms professors as well. It reduces feedback to a minimum, so that the lecturer can neither judge how well students understand the material nor benefit from their questions or comments. Questions that require the speaker to clarify obscure points and comments that challenge sloppily constructed arguments are indispensable to scholarship. Without them, the liveliest mind can atrophy. Undergraduates may not be able to make telling contributions very often, but lecturing insulates a professor even from the beginner's naïve question that could have triggered a fruitful line of thought.

If lectures make so little sense, why have they been allowed to continue? Administrators love them, of course. They can cram far more students into a lecture hall than into a discussion class, and for many administrators that is almost the end of the story. But the truth is that faculty members, and even students, conspire with them to keep the lecture system alive and well. Lectures are easier on everyone than debates. Professors can pretend to teach by lecturing just as students can pretend to learn by attending lectures, with no one the wiser, including the participants. Moreover, if lectures afford some students an opportunity to sit back and let the professor run the show, they offer some professors an irresistible forum for showing off. In a classroom where everyone contributes, students are less able to hide and professors are less tempted to engage in intellectual exhibitionism.

Smaller classes in which students are required to involve themselves in discussion put an end to students' passivity. Students become actively involved when forced to question their own ideas as well as their instructor's. Their listening skills improve dramatically in the excitement of intellectual give-and-take with their instructors and fellow students. Such interchanges help professors do their job better because they allow them to discover who knows what—before final exams, not after. When exams are given in this type of course, they can require analysis and synthesis from the students, not empty memorization. Classes like this require energy, imagination, and commitment from professors, all of which can be exhausting. But they compel students to share responsibility for their own intellectual growth.

Lectures will never entirely disappear from the university scene both because they seem to be economically necessary and because they spring from a long tradition in a setting that values tradition for its own sake. But the lectures too frequently come at the wrong end of the students' educational careers—during the first two years, when they most need close, even individual, instruction. If lecture classes were restricted to junior and senior undergraduates and to graduate students, who are less in need of scholarly nurturing and more able to prepare work on their own, they would be far less destructive of students' interests and enthusiasms than the present system. After all, students must learn to listen before they can listen to learn.

REVISION ACTIVITY 6.10

The following paper contains a number of questionable statements that aren't supported by evidence. In small groups, read the draft and underline statements that most readers wouldn't accept without evidence. In addition, decide what kind(s) of evidence might be provided.

Next, read your draft to find supporting statements that you may provide little or no evidence for. Underline each statement and provide evidence (examples, facts, explanations, details, reasons) in the next draft that will convince readers of its credibility.

Welfare Fraud

If you see someone driving around in a Cadillac, he may be a hardworking American who's made his money honestly. On the other hand, he may be a welfare recipient who receives taxpayers' money for doing nothing. Working Americans are getting ripped off by welfare cheaters, and it's time to dismantle the welfare system.

Most able-bodied men and women are on welfare because they are too lazy to work. The government literally pays them for being lazy. Most of these people are making more money sitting home doing nothing than they would make if they had a job. Something is wrong with a system that rewards laziness more than hard work.

What's more, they are producing another generation of welfare addicts: their children. They learn from their parents how to play the welfare game, and then they teach their own children through example. The vicious cycle goes on and on.

The system is further abused by government officials who get kickbacks from the welfare industry. By continuing to pass welfare legislation, they get a little welfare of their own from the welfare bureaucrats whose jobs are dependent on the system's survival. It's no wonder that few people on Capitol Hill question the tremendous abuses that pervade the welfare system.

I'm calling on all Americans to write their congressman and demand that legislation be implemented to dismantle our present welfare system. For every person it helps legitimately, there are ten people who take advantage of it. We need to get these welfare cheaters off their sofas and into jobs. Most of America's problems—crime, deteriorating cities, deteriorating families, drug use—are the results of our welfare system.

PARAGRAPHING REVIEW

By this time in the course, you should have a good understanding of basic paragraphing and its importance in helping you organize your ideas and convey them effectively to readers. This final review activity is for students who could benefit from some additional practice in paragraphing papers.

PARAGRAPHING ACTIVITY 6.11

Divide the following essay into paragraphs by placing the paragraph symbol (¶) in front of each new paragraph. Change paragraphs each time the writer moves to a different aspect of his topic. Then evaluate the paragraphing of your latest draft, and make any changes that would make the paragraphing more effective for readers.

Teaching Hours for Faculty Nurses

One semester the faculty nurses at the college had their teaching days extended at the hospital. They couldn't understand why they were having to teach more hours for the same hospital laboratory classes they had been teaching for years, and they were being paid no additional money. Some of the faculty nurses contacted the teachers union to find out what their rights were. They discovered through the union representative contract language that forbid the college from creating a new practice when it came to assigning classes and hours that had not been negotiated with the union. No such negotiations had taken place, so the union representative said that it appeared that the college had violated the contract and that the nursing faculty had a right to file a grievance. In all, ten nursing faculty had been affected by the change in hours, and they all agreed to file a class action grievance against the college for violating their contractual rights. The first step in the process produced a revelation as to why the faculty's class hours had been changed. There is a college requirement that ten minutes of break time must occur after every ninety minutes of class. However, with the nursing program, no such breaks can take place because the students must be on the hospital floor with their patients, and the instructor must be present to supervise the students. Students must break individually when they need to use the rest room, but otherwise, the lab class goes straight through until there's a lunch break. The break time that is never taken had always been counted as regular class time by the college, but the college had changed its practice and was now discounting the break time that isn't taken, thus requiring faculty nurses to add more hours to their classes. Of course, the faculty nurses were very upset by this recalculation by the college that essentially was giving neither them nor the students credit for the work time that took place in lieu of the breaks which never occurred. It seemed unfair to both the faculty and the students, so the grievance forged ahead. When it got to the office of the college president, she requested a meeting with the faculty nurses and the union representative to see whether the situation could be resolved short of going to an arbitration hearing. The nurses carefully and patiently explained how lab hours were taught in the hospital and how neither students nor faculty could take breaks and leave the patients they were responsible for unattended. They explained that they had not been taking the ten-minute breaks for the past fifteen years, and that the time had always counted as a part of the teaching day for faculty and students. The union representative pointed out that he believed there was a clear violation of the contract forbidding new practices without union agreement, and that a return to the regular practice of scheduling faculty nursing classes was an appropriate resolution. Fortunately the college president had formerly been an administrator in the allied health division of another college, so she understood the unique clinical situations that hospital lab classes were taught under. She accepted the nursing faculty's contention that they and the students had to work through the designated break times, and that it was a necessary practice if the college was to maintain its hospital classes for nursing students. Therefore, the president agreed that the schedule of teaching hours for nursing faculty would revert to the way they had been calculated in the past. When the president investigated who it was that decided on recalculating the break time and adding teaching hours to the nursing faculty's schedule, there was much buck passing among administrators, and no administrators would admit that it was their original idea, as if they were carrying out an edict from some phantom force. The faculty nurses went back to their regular teaching hours, happy that they had contacted the union and stuck up for their rights, but leery that something similar might happen again. They were hopeful that the college president would take some action against the person who had unilaterally tried to increase their work load, who had to be either the director of nursing or the dean of the allied health division, both of whom were keeping their distance from the faculty.

SENTENCE REVISION REVIEW

This final review section gives you more practice revising first-draft sentences to improve their wording and structural variety. Sentence revision is a critical part of the writing process, and your revising skills will continue to grow as long as you write.

Wording Problems

To help you improve first-draft sentences, here is a summary of the different kinds of sentence problems that writers often revise:

1. *Wordiness:* Sentences often contain more words than necessary to express a writer's thoughts. These sentences contain repeated words and phrases or unnecessarily complicated wording to make simple statements. To revise wordy sentences, eliminate unnecessary words and replace complicated phrases with simpler ones.

   WORDY SENTENCE   We were out in the rays of the sun for six hours of daylight, but we didn't burn due to the fact that we wore a sunscreen that kept us from burning.

   REVISED   We were out in the sun for six hours, but we didn't burn because we wore a sunscreen.

2. *Awkward phrasing:* First-draft sentences often contain awkward wording that occurs when a writer first tries out his or her thoughts on paper. If a sentence sounds odd to a writer, it will probably give a reader problems. To correct awkward wording, find a better way to express the thought. Changing a word or two may make the difference, or you may have to revise the entire sentence.

   AWKWARD WORDY   There is a square cement floor with trees and bushes
   SENTENCE   that are around the cement.

   REVISED   Oak trees and a few bushes surround the cement patio.

3. *Poor word choices:* First-draft sentences sometimes contain words that don't say quite what the writer wants. You can often tell when you've used a word in a first draft that doesn't sound right, but you can't think of a better choice. On returning to a draft after a few hours or

days, the poorer word choices stand out even more, and often, better choices will come to you. To correct poor word choices, replace them with more appropriate words.

POOR WORD	The clown made the boy full of fear instead of enjoying him.
REVISED	The clown frightened the boy instead of entertaining him.

4. *Concrete language:*

Vague, general wording should be replaced by concrete language that *shows* the reader what the writer sees, hears, and feels.

VAGUE WORDING	The boy works one part of the year.
REVISED	My ten-year-old neighbor, Jim Jones, works all summer at his father's feed store.

SENTENCE REVISION ACTIVITY 6.12

The following paragraph needs revising for sentence improvement. Rewrite the paragraph, making each sentence as clear and smooth as possible.

There are many different sports that I like such as baseball, basketball, and football, but there is one sport that is my favorite, and that is baseball. Baseball is the one sport that I like to watch because I can watch it on television or when there is a family member that plays, like my brother. I watch my brother play in college, and it's not boring to watch, and I would rather go to a baseball game than go to a movie. My favorite baseball team is the Dodgers because I think that their uniforms are bad with the color combination. If I had a chance to be born again, I would have wanted my parents to have me play baseball as a youngster.

Sentence Variety

Here is a summary of what you have learned about sentence variety in your writing:

1. Writers sometimes have a tendency to overuse certain sentence structures and joining words, which can lead to monotonous prose.

2. Check your first-draft sentences to see whether you have relied too heavily on a particular structure, for example, simple sentences (one subject, one verb) or compound sentences joined primarily by *and, but,* or *so.*

3. Vary sentence structures to include a combination of simple, compound, and complex sentences, and vary joining words by using many of the following: and, but, so, for, yet, or, when, before, after, while, as, until, since, although, unless, if, because, who, whose, which, that.

4. Writers sometimes tend to string pairs or groups of short sentences together, or to write overly long, involved sentences.

5. Check your first draft to find short sentences that could be effectively combined or overly long sentences that could be divided by inserting periods and eliminating some joining words.

SENTENCE VARIETY ACTIVITY 6.13

Revise sentences in the following paragraph in different ways: combine sentences with joining words and eliminate unnecessary words; group similar words; and divide overly long sentences by inserting periods and deleting joining words. Vary your sentence structures and joining words, and don't try to squeeze too many ideas uncomfortably into a single sentence.

EXAMPLE   Melba likes to listen to her stereo. Thad likes to listen to his. They both enjoy using their headphones. They are brother and sister.

COMBINED   Melba and Thad, <u>who are brother and sister</u>, enjoy listening to their stereos and using their headphones.

The cold air in Chicago was hard to describe. It was blowing off of Lake Michigan. It was late afternoon. The cold wind cut through coats and sweaters. It pierced the bone. There was no way to escape it. Thousands of people were leaving work. They came out into the cold. They were stunned momentarily by the wind. These people had lived and worked in Chicago for years. They hadn't felt a wind like this. It brought in record low temperatures. The wind was difficult to walk into. It was blowing south off the Lake. I had to walk toward the lake to my car. I literally could not stand straight up. The wind would blow me backwards. I had to lean far forward. I walked at a forty-five degree angle to the sidewalk. No one was talking. Hats were flying everywhere. Couples huddled together for warmth. Policemen stayed in their cars. I finally reached my car. I could barely open the door because of the wind. I finally got in. My whole body was shaking. I turned on the radio. I heard that the wind chill factor was ten degrees below zero. That amazed me. I'd never heard of such a low temperature. It was only November.

FINAL EDITING

By this time in the course, you may need little guidance in proofreading your drafts and correcting errors. You may have even worked out your own error detection process. Undoubtedly, you are aware of your personal error tendencies and conscientiously scrutinize your drafts in those areas.

For those of you relying on the proofreading guidelines in the text, a final summary is provided. In the future, you need to internalize such guidelines to use them for any writing you may do.

PROOFREADING GUIDELINES

1. Check to make sure you have a period at the end of each sentence, and correct any run-on sentences, comma splices, or sentence fragments.

2. Check your word endings to make sure that plural words end in *s* or *es,* regular past tense verbs end in *ed,* one-syllable comparative and superlative adjectives end in *er* and *est,* respectively, and present tense verbs with singular subjects end in *s.*

3. Check your spelling carefully, looking up any words you are uncertain of. Also check your use of homophones such as there/their/they're, know/no, its/it's, your/you're, and threw/through.

4. Check your comma usage in words in series and compound sentences, after introductory groups of words, and to set off relative clauses, interrupters, and ending phrases beginning with *especially, particularly,* and *ing*-ending words. Also check your use of apostrophes, quotation marks, semicolons, and colons.

5. Check pronoun usage to make sure you are using the correct subject pronouns in compound subjects and that all pronouns agree in number and gender with their antecedents.

EDITING ACTIVITY 6.14

In small groups, proofread the following student draft and correct any errors you find.

When you finish, proofread your latest draft following the guidelines presented. Correct any remaining errors, and then write or print out your final draft and share it with your classmates and instructor.

Abortion

STUDENT SAMPLE DRAFT I am writing about one of the most important problems in our society, legalized abortion. This problem is very controversial for many reasons and many people believe that abortion is a good solution to a woman or a couples problems. Other believe that if a woman has an abortion it is a crime.

Today abortion is legal in the United States however, I think abortion should be made illegal because I do believe it is a crime. The killing of a fetus is the taking of a human life weather it is in the mothers womb or not it is a live human being, and no one has the right to take its life but God.

If a woman doesn't want to have a baby, she should take precautions before having sex. For example, she has available many birth control measures, pills, shots, condoms, or other devices that prevent pregnancy. The better way to prevent pregnancy is don't have sex at all, this could help lower the abortion rate in our country greatly.

This problem of abortion is worse among adolescents because they do not have enough information about birth control and abortion. Sometimes the adolescent has little or no communication with her parents, for these reasons, they become pregnant when they are teenagers later they decide to abort because they this it is the best solution for their lifes. They prefer abortion to taking responsiability for a baby.

Abortion is a big problem in the United States and a crime in my opinion. Women have different options than abortion, for example, they can study and enroll in programs that can help them with the baby such as free day care and continuation school, or they can give the baby up for adoption, many couples are looking to adopt babies. In my opinion women in the United States should take these different options before having an abortion, abortion should be made illegal and the law should be changed.

JOURNAL ENTRY TWENTY-THREE

In your journal, relate how your proofreading and error correction has improved during the course. What do you do better now than you used to? What if anything do you need to continue working on? What have you found most valuable in helping you eliminate errors from your writing?

SENTENCE PROBLEMS REVIEW

The following review activity is for students who still have some problems with run-on sentences, comma splices, or fragments. Punctuating sentences correctly is fundamental to effective writing, so if run-ons or fragments still persist in your writing, keep working on the problem whenever you write.

PROOFREADING ACTIVITY 6.15

Proofread the following paragraphs for run-on sentences and sentence fragments. Separate run-ons and comma splices with periods or join the sentences to form compound or complex sentences. Attach fragments to the sentences they belong with or add words to form complete sentences.

Community College Vs. Four-Year Colleges

Community colleges have both advantages and disadvantages compared to four-year schools. One advantage of community colleges is their cost. Throughout the country, community college tuition is less expensive than for four-year colleges, ranging from $300 to $600 per year. Most community college students also live at home, saving on the cost of room and board. Four-year colleges, on the other hand, range in tuition from $1,500 a year for some state-operated colleges to $15,000–$25,000 a year for private schools on top of that, most four-year college students live away from home. Spending $5,000–$8,000 per year on room and board. It is not surprising that many students choose to spend two years at a community college. Before transferring to a more expensive four-year school.

On the whole, community colleges are not as difficult as four-year colleges. Studies show that GPAs for community college transfer students drop in their third year while those of four-year college students do not. Surveys also indicate that most community college transfer students find their four-year college courses more difficult and time-consuming than community college courses. Therefore, it appears that community colleges may not prepare students as well as four-year colleges do, some community college students may find themselves at a disadvantage when they transfer.

Community colleges also don't have the activities that four-year colleges do. Since community colleges are by and large "commuter" schools. With students living at home, participation in campus activities is much lower than at four-year schools with their live-in dormitory populations. Participation in school government and on-campus clubs is limited student attendance at football and basketball games often numbers a hundred or fewer. Community college students on the whole miss out on the excitement and social involvement that can be an important part of the college experience.

CORRECT USAGE REVIEW

The first five units covered grammar usage situations in which writers sometimes make errors: past tense verbs, subject-verb agreement, subject pronoun usage, pronoun-antecedent agreement, and comparative and superlative adjectives. This section provides a final proofreading activity to help you recognize and correct such errors in your writing.

PROOFREADING ACTIVITY 6.16

Proofread the following paragraphs for grammar errors involving subject-verb agreement, subject pronouns, pronoun-antecedent agreement, or superlative and comparative adjectives. Make the necessary corrections.

The thing I like least about the apartments I live in are the topless dumpsters sitting in front of the west bank of apartments. First, it creates a bad smell. In the summer when it is full of garbage and used diapers, a putrid odor sweeps across the apartments when the afternoon breeze come up. Second, it is too small to accommodate a week's supply of trash. The garbage that gets piled up on top fall out, and dogs and the wind scatter them all over the driveway and lawn. By Friday before pickup time, the place is a littered mess.

The most worst problem are the flies. The garbage in the open dumpsters attract thousands of flies in warm weather, and they take up residence at the apartments. If you are outside, you constantly have to swat them off your face and body. They also find his or her way indoors, congregating in the kitchen while you eat and attacking your face while you sleep at night. From May to September, you can always hear flies buzzing somewhere in the apartment. They are the terriblest health problem at the apartments.

Obviously, the apartments need new dumpsters, ones that is covered to keep the flies away and the stench in, and ones that is large enough to hold a week's worth of garbage. It should also be moved to the east side of the apartments so that the breeze will carry the odor away from the buildings. If the owner isn't willing to pay a little more for decent covered dumpsters, I think the health department should be called. Some of the neighbors and me are prepared to do just that.

PUNCTUATION REVIEW

This final section provides a proofreading activity covering everything you have learned about using commas, apostrophes, quotation marks, semicolons, and colons in your writing.

PROOFREADING ACTIVITY 6.17

Proofread the following paragraphs for punctuation omissions, and insert commas, apostrophes, quotation marks, semicolons, and colons where they are needed.

The Inequity of College Grants

When I walk through the business services office at school I often notice a line of students getting their grant checks for the month. I don't begrudge them their checks because I know they need the money but when I see them Im reminded that I applied for every local and state grant I could and I didn't qualify for anything.

Because I get no financial aid I have to work at least thirty hours a week to help pay for my college and living expenses. I work at least four hours a day during the week and ten hours on weekends. With the colleges expenses so high, something needs to be done for lower-middle-income students like myself who are caught in between too "well off" for aid but too poor to survive without working long hours. I often ask myself why are people in my situation not given help?

As an example my mother and fathers combined income is $25,000. That may sound pretty good, but when there are four kids in the family house payments and the usual bills theres not much left for college expenses. My parents can't come close to paying for my tuition books fees and living expenses yet because of their salary bracket I didn't qualify for any grants. To stay in school I have to make at least $500 a month.

Having to work long hours I'm at a real disadvantage. Most students on grants don't work a lot and many students from middle and upper-income families don't work at all. While I'm working thirty hours a week they can be putting those hours into studying. I never feel there's enough hours in the day to get my reading and studying done.

Another problem is I usually end up taking only the 12-unit minimum per semester to maintain a full-time students status I don't have time for more classes. This means I'll have to put in an extra semester or year of college to graduate or go to summer school every summer which is even more expensive than regular semesters. I also have to cram all of my classes into the morning hours so I can be at work by one o'clock on weekdays limiting my choice of courses and instructors.

The most aggravating thing is I know I could do so much better in school. When I was at home and going to high school my grades were good because I only worked a few hours a week. Now I feel like I have two full-time jobs and I don't have the time or energy to do my best in school. I end up settling for C's when I know I could be getting A's and B's. If I decide one day to apply for graduate school my grades are going to be a problem.

However I know I'm not in this alone. There are a lot of students caught in the same dilemma who tell me I have the same problems that you have. It just doesn't seem fair that going to college has to be made so much more difficult for some students than for others. In America everyone has the right to a college education but having the right and being given a fair opportunity to succeed are two different things. With some financial aid and a reduced work load I know I could succeed.

In the future I don't realistically see college expenses going down. Therefore I feel that for students like myself the salary limit for grant qualification should be raised. Im not saying I should have the full grant status that poorer students have but I feel that I should be entitled to at least a partial grant. Why couldnt someone in my position receive a half or quarter grant rather than being shut out completely? And why has the salary qualification level remained the same the last four years when the cost of college has gone up tremendously? One thing should be raised automatically with increased college expenses: the ceiling on grants.

JOURNAL ENTRY TWENTY-FOUR

In your journal, provide your opinion on the small group activities you have done throughout the course. How do you feel about the small group work in general, and why? What kinds of group activities in particular did you find most useful? What recommendations, if any, would you make for improving the small group activities?

WRITING REVIEW

In the "Writing Review," you apply what you have learned throughout the unit to a second issue-oriented paper. The following writing process summarizes the steps presented throughout the unit. Follow the process as presented or a more individualized process that works best for you.

WRITING PROCESS

1. Write about an issue that you would like to see people take action on: a situation that needs changing. Follow these suggestions:

   a. Pick an issue that is important—something that you would definitely like to see changed.

   b. Decide on your thesis for the paper: the position you will take on the issue.

   c. Decide on your reading audience—the people that can help change the situation—and on your purpose: what you want them to do to help change it.

2. To help plan your paper, do the following prewriting work:

   a. List some supporting points for your thesis: reasons that why you are taking this position on the issue. Then decide what kind of evidence (facts, examples, details, explanations, personal experiences) you might use to substantiate each point.

   b. List one or two opposing arguments—reasons people might disagree with you—and decide how you might refute those arguments in your paper.

STUDENT SAMPLE   Something that I think needs changing is the college's practice of over-scheduling courses each semester and then canceling course sections that get lower enrollments. I've had three or four classes canceled, which really messed up my schedule a couple of semesters.

| TOPIC | The college's over-scheduling of courses |
| THESIS | When the college over-schedules and then cancels courses, students get hurt. |

READING AUDIENCE   Students, administrators, admissions department

PURPOSE   Convince the school to stop the practice and offer only those classes that have a good chance of making enrollment.

Support points for thesis:

- My own experience with canceled courses. (Provide example from last semester.)

- Students believe their schedules are set. (Explain why.)

- Students have to change their entire schedules. (Give examples.)

- Students often can't get into other classes. (Explain why.)

- Classes often aren't canceled until the second or third week. (Explain effects on students in canceled classes.)

- Practice can jeopardize students' full-time status. (Explain negative effects.)

Opposing points to refute:

- Cost-effective for school to maintain only high enrollment classes. (Refute: What's good for school is bad for students in this case. Offer fewer courses to begin with and put them in prime times for maximum enrollment.)

- Can schedule faculty most effectively this way. (Refute: College is here for the students, not for the convenience of teachers.)

3. When you complete your prewriting, write the first draft of your paper following these suggestions:

   a. In the opening, introduce your topic and thesis in a way that will engage your readers' interest or concern.

   b. In the middle paragraphs, present and develop your supporting points, and present and refute one or two opposing arguments.

   c. In the conclusion, make your purpose clear and provide whatever final thoughts you feel would best accomplish your purpose.

   d. Keep your readers in mind, and write in a way that you feel will produce the desired response.

Scheduling Woes

STUDENT SAMPLE DRAFT   Last semester I was lucky enough to enroll in all five classes that I needed for general education requirements. All the course sections I had in my schedule were still open when I registered. I didn't have to worry about back-up classes since I figured my schedule was set.

By the end of the second week of the semester, three of my five classes had been canceled, due to a lack of the "necessary" enrollment. Then I was forced, along with many other students, to scrounge around for other classes, which was frustrating and difficult. I ended up getting into only two other courses, neither of which I would have taken by choice. Clearly, there's something wrong with the scheduling practice at the college, and students are suffering.

For the second semester now, the college has scheduled significantly more sections of general ed courses than have been "made." It appears the school, or deans, or whoever makes the enrollment decisions waits to see which sections reach the magic minimum of twenty enrollees, and then cancels all those with fewer than twenty. Students caught in the smaller classes are then compelled to seek out other sections or courses, with no guarantees that they'll be allowed in.

To make matters worse, sometimes smaller sections are "carried" through the second week in hopes of late enrollments, leaving students desperately seeking classes in the third week of the semester. Some instructors have a policy of not accepting any students after the second week of the semester, and the students are often treated as if they have no business trying to get into classes late.

The effects of sections being canceled are obvious. First, students are lulled into believing that their schedules are set for the semester, so they don't worry about "double enrolling" in additional courses to cover themselves, a practice the college frowns on. Second, they are left, often for two weeks into the semester, with the uncertainty and anxiety of not knowing which of their classes will "make" and which will be canceled. Third, once classes are canceled, students are left with the responsibility of finding other classes to fill their schedules, and the college guarantees them nothing. Finally, and most damaging, they often end up taking classes they didn't want or need, and taking fewer classes than they had planned, which could jeopardize their grant eligibility and lengthen their stay at the college.

I'm sure the college has its reasons for over-scheduling sections of courses. It can see which sections fill and then cancel the smaller sections that are more costly. It can also list the instructors for most sections as "staff" and then place teachers in sections where there are the best enrollments. And the college knows that with many small sections being canceled, the enrollment in the sections that "make" will only get better. In short, the administrators are doing what's best financially for the college at the expense of the students.

The college's current practice of over-scheduling sections of courses is very unfair to students. The number of sections offered any semester should reflect the number of classes that realistically should fill with at least twenty students. That number can be pretty well determined by checking the number of sections of a course that "made" the same semester of the previous year. A two- or three-year study, taking college enrollment fluctuations into account, might provide an even more accurate indicator. The excuse that the college can't really predict how many sections to offer in any given semester just doesn't wash.

Last semester, according to the college admission's office, twenty-four sections of general ed pattern courses were canceled due to small enrollment. That is a scandalously high number. I think anyone could understand four or five sections needing to be canceled or added, based on enrollment fluctuations, but twenty-four canceled sections indicates a clearly intended practice of over-scheduling and canceling classes, strictly for the financial benefit and convenience of the school and at the expense of the students.

This practice needs to be stopped immediately, and I am asking the administration to meet with a student committee before next semester's schedule is published. We want to ensure that all of the classes scheduled, based on current overall enrollment, have a realistic chance of reaching minimum enrollment figures. When that occurs, students' registration schedules will accurately reflect their load for the semester, students won't be forced to scrounge for classes after the semester begins, and students will have a better chance of getting the classes and the units they need. After all, the college is here for the students, and not the other way around.

4. Set your draft aside for a while, and then evaluate it for possible revisions. Follow these guidelines:

   a. Evaluate the strength of your opening. Are your topic and thesis clearly presented? Does your reader have a good idea why you are writing?

   b. Evaluate your middle paragraphs. Do you have some strong supportive points for your thesis? Do you provide evidence to substantiate each point? Have you effectively refuted an opposing argument or two that your reader may have?

   c. Evaluate the strength of your conclusion. Will the readers clearly understand your purpose? Have you told them what needs to be done? Do you conclude in a way that will elicit a positive response from them?

   d. Revise sentences to make them clearer, smoother, and more concise and to vary sentence structures and joining words.

   e. Read the draft from your readers' perspective, and make any final changes that you feel will make the person more responsive to your message.

5. Proofread your latest draft for errors following these guidelines:

   a. Make sure that each sentence ends with a period and that you correct any run-on sentences, comma splices, or fragments.

   b. Check word endings to make sure that plural words end in *s* or *es*, regular past tense verbs end in *ed*, present tense verbs agree with their subjects, and comparative and superlative adjectives have appropriate *er* and *est* endings.

   c. Check your spelling carefully, including your use of homophones such as there/their/they're, your/you're, know/no, its/it's, and through/threw.

   d. Check your internal punctuation: commas, apostrophes in contractions and possessives, quotation marks around direct quotations, and semicolons and colons, if needed.

   e. Check your pronoun usage: correct subject pronouns in compound subjects (Joan and I, my mom and she, we and they) and pronouns that agree with their antecedents (A person should do *his or her* best in life. Mal and I did *our* projects by *ourselves*.)

6. Write the final draft of your paper and share it with the person it is intended for and your instructor.

Appendix

This appendix contains a number of writing activities that individual students may find useful. As your instructor becomes familiar with your writing needs, he or she may assign specific activities from the Appendix on a diagnostic basis. For example, if you struggle with irregular verb tenses, dangling modifiers, or punctuation of possessive words, you will find help in the Appendix.

The Appendix is intended to be used as an ongoing supplement to the rest of the text. The material has not been relegated to the Appendix because it is less important, but because all students will not use it similarly. For example, one student may find the "Spelling" section valuable while another may have no need for it. Putting such writing elements in the Appendix makes them available to students without overloading the units and distracting students from the writing process.

SENTENCE REVISION

Sentence revision is a task shared by all writers. This section will help you write and revise sentences more effectively by broadening your sentence repertoire and making you aware of common structural problems.

COMBINING SENTENCES

The best way to eliminate of short, monotonous sentences in a draft is to combine pairs or groups of sentences to form more informative and interesting ones. Here are ways to combine short sentences:

1. Eliminate unnecessary words that are duplicated in the sentences.

2. Move descriptive words in front of the word they describe.

3. Join similar sentence parts with an *and, or,* or *but.*

Here are examples of groups of short sentences that have been combined in the revised versions following the methods just described.

EXAMPLES

DRAFT   Joanie is a student. She is a very good one.

REVISED   Joanie is a very good student.

DRAFT   Fernando bought a shirt. It was red. It was long-sleeved.

REVISED   Fernando bought a red, long-sleeved shirt.

DRAFT   Alan went to the barbecue. Felicia went with him.

REVISED   Alan and Felicia went to the barbecue together.

COMBINING ACTIVITY 1

Each pair or group of short sentences below can be combined to form one improved sentence. Combine the sentences into single sentences by eliminating and moving words around and by joining similar words or groups of words with *and, or,* or *but.*

EXAMPLE   Gwen went to school. Maria went to school. They went with Bob.

REVISED   Gwen and Maria went to school with Bob.

1. The frog leaped onto the log. He plopped into the water. He disappeared.

2. Harry was tired. He was thirsty. He wasn't hungry.

3. Ellie got a B on her term paper. She got the same grade on her algebra test. She flunked her pop quiz in German.

4. Your X-rays could be in the drawer. They could be on the shelf. They could be almost anywhere in the house.

5. The kitten was fat. It was fluffy. It was playing with a grasshopper. The grasshopper was badly injured.

6. Marge finally got a letter. It was from her parole officer. She was relieved.

7. The week was long. It was boring. It was almost over. Julian was very happy.

8. Susan's clothes were plain. They were cheap. They were also stylish. They were also in good taste.

9. The car spun toward the wall. It crashed. It burst into flames. The driver wasn't injured. He was lucky.

10. That puppy is very cute. It is black and white. It has droopy ears. It is in the pet store window. It isn't for sale.

A second way to combine shorter sentences is to join two complete sentences with *coordinate conjunctions* to form *compound sentences*.

These are the most commonly used coordinate conjunctions:

and   but   or   for   yet   so

The following are examples of two first-draft sentences joined by coordinate conjunctions to form single compound sentences. Notice that different conjunctions show different relationships between the two sentences they join. The conjunctions are underlined.

EXAMPLE	The Rolling Stones were popular in the 1960s. They are still popular today.
REVISED	The Rolling Stones were popular in the 1960s, <u>and</u> they are still popular today. (And *joins the information together.*)
EXAMPLE	Divorce statistics are rising. Couples are marrying in record numbers.
REVISED	Divorce statistics are rising, <u>but</u> couples are marrying in record numbers. (But *shows a contrast; something happened* despite *something else.*)
EXAMPLE	Rita may go to a movie tonight. She may stay home and read a mystery novel.

REVISED	Rita may go to a movie tonight, <u>or</u> she may stay home and read a mystery novel. (Or *shows a choice; alternatives are available.*)
EXAMPLE	James makes his own shirts. He enjoys sewing.
REVISED	James makes his own shirts, <u>for</u> he enjoys sewing. (For *means* because; *something occurs because of something else.*)
EXAMPLE	Working and going to school is difficult. Many students do both.
REVISED	Working and going to school is difficult, <u>yet</u> many students do both. (Yet is *similar to* but; *it shows a contrast.*)
EXAMPLE	The air is moist and cold. We'd better bundle up for the parade.
REVISED	The air is moist and cold, <u>so</u> we'd better bundle up for the parade. (So *is like* therefore; *one thing leads to another.*)

As you can see, different conjunctions serve different purposes. Being able to use a variety of conjunctions at appropriate times makes your writing more effective.

COMBINING ACTIVITY 2

Combine the following pairs of shorter sentences with conjunctions to form compound sentences. Use the conjunction that best joins each sentence pair: *and, but, or, for, yet, so.* Put a comma before the conjunction.

EXAMPLE	The weather is miserable today. It should be better tomorrow.
REVISED	The weather is miserable today, but it should be better tomorrow.

1. Jogging is a popular exercise. Some doctors don't recommend it.

2. You can take typing this semester. You can take it next semester.

3. Ms. Avery is an unpopular teacher. She lectures too fast.

4. Jodie didn't like the foreign movie. It was praised by the critics.

5. The smells from the cafeteria were wonderful. The food was disappointing.

6. Rain collected in jars on the back porch. We used the water to test for acid rain.

7. Freddie may be at the Pizza Palace. He may be at the roller derby with Lucinda.

8. Lupe joined the swim team. She wanted the exercise and the units.

9. Sam tried to return the defective smoke alarm. The store was closed.

10. Alicia couldn't study for the essay test. She got a good night's sleep instead.

A third way to combine sentences is to join two complete sentences with words called *subordinate conjunctions* to form *complex sentences*. Subordinate conjunctions may be placed between the two sentences or at the beginning of the first sentence. The following subordinate conjunctions are most commonly used in complex sentences:

after	if	whenever
although	since	where
as	unless	whereas
because	until	wherever
before	when	while

The following examples show two first-draft sentences joined by subordinate conjunctions to form complex sentences. Notice the different relationships that the subordinate conjunctions show and their use at the beginning or in the middle of the complex sentence. The subordinate conjunctions are underlined.

EXAMPLE   You are going to be late for biology class. You should contact your teacher.

REVISED   Since you are going to be late for biology class, you should contact your teacher.

EXAMPLE   Fred's friends took him home. They went out for pizza.

REVISED   After Fred's friends took him home, they went out for pizza.

EXAMPLE   I'm cleaning up your mess. You are watching television!

REVISED   I'm cleaning up your mess while you are watching television!

EXAMPLE   You have worked very hard. You have gained everyone's respect.

REVISED   Because you have worked very hard, you have gained everyone's respect.

EXAMPLE   George wants to pass the geography test. He will have to identify six mountain ranges.

Revised	If George wants to pass the geography test, he will have to identify six mountain ranges.
Example	Joanna refuses to exercise. She would like to be in shape.
Revised	Joanna refuses to exercise although she would like to be in shape.

As you can see, subordinate conjunctions can show different relationships: time (*when, as, after, while*), cause and effect (*since, because, if, unless*), place (*where, wherever*), or contrast (*although, even though, whereas*). You may use them at the beginning or in the middle of a complex sentence depending on what you want to emphasize. Using complex sentences adds variety to your writing and helps you express a wide range of relationships between ideas.

COMBINING ACTIVITY 3

Join the following pairs of shorter sentences with appropriate subordinate conjunctions to form complex sentences. You will begin some sentences with subordinate conjunctions and use others between sentences. When you begin a sentence with a subordinate conjunction, put a comma between the two sentences you are combining. (Some sentence pairs won't go together well until they are combined with a subordinate conjunction.)

Example	The party was over. Ruby drove around until dawn.
Revised	After the party was over, Ruby drove around until dawn.
Example	The dog limped along the road. It had a thorn in its paw.
Revised	The dog limped along the road because it had a thorn in its paw.

1. You leave for school tomorrow. Please pick me up at the corner.

2. Jim dropped his gymnastics class. He had a time conflict.

3. The economy improves greatly. The unemployment rate will climb.

4. Gina spent a lot of time reading romances. She still did well in school.

5. You believe everything Harley says. You are very naive.

6. I told you before. I'll be glad to water your ferns this weekend.

7. Ms. Howard is a fascinating teacher. She uses slides, movies, and field trips in her anthropology class.

8. The electricity is off in the apartments. Everyone is buying candles.

9. The shower door was broken. Manuel moved into the dormitory.

10. You've had experience with electrical work. Don't try to change that outlet.

COMBINING ACTIVITY 4

Rewrite the following passage. Combine sentences by adding joining words, moving words and phrases around, and eliminating unnecessary words. Combine the fourteen sample sentences into a few well-crafted ones.

EXAMPLE	Nona moved into her apartment today. She paid her rent a week ago. She was living alone. She was looking for a roommate to share expenses.
REVISED	Nona moved into her apartment today, but she paid her rent a week ago. Although she was living alone, she was looking for a roommate to share expenses.

Corrine collects records from the fifties and sixties. She has over one thousand 45 rpm discs. Her brother is a disc jockey. She buys duplicate records from his station cheaply. She enjoys the music of the eighties. She prefers the sound of early rock 'n' roll. She has every record Buddy Holly ever recorded. He was her favorite singer. She'll invite her friends over. They'll listen to old songs for hours. She's heard them hundreds of times. She never gets tired of them. She never considers her collection complete. She'll spend the weekend looking for records by Bo Diddley and Danny and the Juniors.

COMBINING ACTIVITY 5

Combine the following sentences to form single sentences using the combining methods you have learned.

EXAMPLE	The bed is below the picture. It has a walnut headboard. It is a single bed.
REVISED	The single bed with the walnut headboard is below the picture.
EXAMPLE	Jane got to the museum early. She still had to wait in line for an hour.
REVISED	Jane got to the museum early, but she still had to wait in line for an hour.
EXAMPLE	Sam had a good time at the drag races. He thought they would be boring.

REVISED	Sam had a good time at the drag races, although he thought they would be boring.

1. Marta worked in a commercial laundry. She worked the night shift.

2. Her best friend's name was Gloria. She also worked the night shift.

3. Marta loaded towels into a large dryer. The towels came from the washing machines. She started the machine. Gloria did the same things. They worked together.

4. The dryer would finally stop. The girls unloaded it. They put the partially dry towels in a second dryer. It dried by hot air.

5. Sometimes the dryer made a racket. That was when the load was unbalanced. The girls had to stop it.

6. The floor boss would hear the noise. He would come over to their station. He would scold them for getting behind.

7. The towels were very heavy to handle. The girls got tired. Their backs got sore. They got very hot.

8. One cycle of towels would dry. Another bin of towels would be waiting for them. There was never any rest.

9. The work was very hard. Marta and Gloria lasted for six months.

10. They finally quit their job. They found a better job. They began working at the college. They worked in the admission's office. They registered late students.

COMBINING ACTIVITY 6

Combine the following sentences to form single sentences using the combining methods you have learned. Here is an example of each method:

DRAFT	The desk is in the corner. It is walnut. It is for studying. It is twelve years old.
REVISED	The walnut study desk in the corner is twelve years old. *(repeated words eliminated, modifying words moved in front of word they describe)*
DRAFT	I never had problems with my hearing. Lately I don't hear the television well.
REVISED	I never had problems with my hearing, but lately I don't hear the television well. *(compound sentence formed by using coordinate conjunction but to join sentences)*

Draft	She is really tired of school. She'll stick it out for her last semester.
Revised	Although she is really tired of school, she'll stick it out for her last semester. *(complex sentence formed by adding subordinate conjunction* although *to join sentence)*
Draft	Josephine finally went to an acupuncturist. She was bothered by nagging headaches.
Revised	Bothered by nagging headaches, Josephine finally went to an acupuncturist. *(introductory phrase used in place of second sentence and unnecessary words eliminated)*

1. Obesity is a big concern for many Americans. We are the most overweight people in the world. We consume the most food per person.

2. There are different causes for obesity. The biggest factors are overeating and eating the wrong foods. Both of these factors can be overcome.

3. Heredity can be a factor in obesity. Children of obese parents don't have to become obese. The tendency toward obesity must be addressed in early childhood.

4. Obese children usually become obese adults. That is not difficult to understand. It occurs in most instances.

5. Overeating usually begins in childhood. Eating the wrong foods usually begins in childhood. These bad habits are not easily broken.

6. Parents often set a bad example. They eat junk food in front of their young children. Junk food includes hamburgers, french fries, soft drinks, onion rings, and rich desserts. These are all loaded with fat and sugar. Overconsumption of fat and sugar is a leading cause of obesity.

7. American restaurants add to the problem. They compete to see who can serve the largest portions. They do this to attract customers. Customers often seek the biggest meals for the price.

8. Fast food restaurants are the biggest culprit. They "super size" their meals to give customers larger servings of french fries and soft drinks. They do this for an additional fifty cents or so. People think they're getting a bargain. They go for the bigger servings.

9. Families used to eat at home most of the time. They would get better-balanced meals including regular vegetables. Now they eat out regularly. They dine frequently on junk food.

10. The ideal American image is a slender, fit body. The average American is overweight and unfit. This disparity leads to unhappiness and depression. It doesn't seem to change people's eating habits.

SENTENCE PROBLEMS

Three structural problems that may occasionally creep into your sentences are *nonparallel constructions, dangling modifiers,* and *misplaced modifiers.*

This section will help you identify and eliminate such problems in your writing.

Nonparallel Construction

One sentence problem that leads to awkward and confusing wording is *nonparallel construction.* It is not uncommon for a writer to join two or more groups of words together in a sentence. For the sentence to be clear, these groups of words need to be very similar, or *parallel,* in structure. Here is an example of a sentence with parallel construction. The groups of words joined together are underlined.

EXAMPLE   Last night we <u>ate outside,</u> <u>sat by the river,</u> and <u>listened to the frogs.</u>

The underlined groups of words are parallel because they follow the same structure: past tense verb followed by modifying words. Now read the same sentence with some problems with parallelism.

EXAMPLE   Last night we ate outside, by the river sat, and listening to the frogs.

This sentence is very awkward. In the second group of words, the order of the past tense verb and the modifying words is changed, and in the last group, the verb has the wrong ending. The resulting sentence would bother any reader.

Here are other examples of sentences with nonparallel constructions followed by revised corrected versions.

EXAMPLE   Joleen is tall, slender, and brown hair. (Brown hair *isn't parallel with* tall *and* slender.)

REVISED   Joleen is tall and slender and has brown hair.

EXAMPLE   I leaped across the creek, landed on the bank, and back in the water did slip. (Back in the water did slip *is not parallel with the first two parts.*)

REVISED   I leaped across the creek, landed on the bank, and slipped back into the water.

EXAMPLE   Swimming, jogging, and a tennis game are good forms of exercise. (A tennis game *is not parallel with* swimming *and* jogging.)

REVISED   Swimming, jogging, and tennis are good forms of exercise.

EXAMPLE   The MG is metallic blue, has four speeds, and racy. (*Racy isn't parallel with the other parts.*)

REVISED   The MG is metallic blue, has four speeds, and is racy.

REVISION ACTIVITY 7

The following sentences have problems with parallel construction. Rewrite each sentence and improve the wording by correcting the nonparallel part of the sentence.

EXAMPLE   John looked out the window, scanned in all directions, and no one.

REVISED   John looked out the window, scanned in all directions, and saw no one.

1. I enjoy skating, reading, to swim, and the sport of hockey.

2. Claude is short, stout, intelligent, brown eyes, and generosity.

3. We walked through the field, finding hundreds of acorns, and bring them home in baskets.

4. You may check out the periodical or in the library you may read it.

5. Doing dishes, cleaning her room, homework, to babysit her brother, and the flossing of her teeth were chores Eileen avoided.

6. Mildred walked into the class, does one hundred push-ups, and out the door.

7. You can chew gum in Kaser's class, but gum chewing in Bowie's class you can't do, and no gum in Borafka's class.

8. Not only is college harder than high school but also greater is the cost and more is the difficulty.

9. The news about the earthquake was terrible, the reports being shockingly graphic, the death count is tragically high, and more bodies being uncovered still.

10. Georgia is willing to organize activities for her sorority but no more tutoring pledges for their finals, and not willing to chair the pledge meetings.

Misplaced and Dangling Modifiers

Two common wording problems that can confuse readers involve *misplaced* and *dangling modifiers*. While the misplaced modifying phrase is located in an awkward position in a sentence, a dangling modifying phrase has nothing in the sentence to modify.

Follow these suggestions for identifying and correcting problems with misplaced and dangling modifiers:

1. A misplaced modifying phrase is usually some distance from the word it modifies, creating confusion about what the modified word is supposed to be.

EXAMPLES   (MODIFYING PHRASES UNDERLINED)

The man applied for a job in Chicago <u>from Toledo</u>.

The students can't hear the lecture <u>sitting in the back of the room</u>.

The house is for sale for fifty thousand dollars <u>across the street</u>.

The girl chased the elephant through the house <u>in pigtails</u>.

The young man was brought into the emergency room <u>bitten by a snake</u>.

2. To correct most misplaced modifiers, place the phrase directly after the word it modifies. Occasionally the phrase will fit more smoothly directly before the modified word.

EXAMPLES   The man <u>from Toledo</u> applied for a job in Chicago.

The students <u>sitting in the back of the room</u> can't hear the lecture.

The house <u>across the street</u> is for sale for fifty thousand dollars.

The girl <u>in pigtails</u> chased the elephant through the house.

The young man <u>bitten by a snake</u> was brought into the emergency room.

3. Dangling modifiers usually begin sentences, often start with words with *ing* and *ed* endings, and are followed by a subject they don't modify. The modifiers are "dangling" because they clearly don't modify the subject.

EXAMPLES   (DANGLING PHRASE UNDERLINED)

<u>Driving to work yesterday</u>, the road was very slippery. *(The subject,* road, *can't drive.)*

<u>Worried about her daughter's whereabouts</u>, the police were called immediately. *(The subject,* police, *weren't "worried about her daughter's whereabouts.")*

<u>Grounded for three weeks for bad grades</u>, John's sister got to use his car. *(The subject,* sister, *wasn't the one who was grounded.)*

<u>Running through the park</u>, the cool breeze felt great on our faces. *(The subject,* breeze, *can't run through the park.)*

4. To correct a dangling modifier, either (a) change the subject of the sentence so that it goes with the modifying phrase or (b) add a subordinating conjunction and subject to the modifying phrase to form a complex sentence.

EXAMPLES   Driving to work today, I noticed how slippery the road was.

or

While I was driving to work today, the road was very slippery.

Worried about her daughter's whereabouts, Gretchen called the police immediately.

or

Because Gretchen was worried about her daughter's whereabouts, the police were called immediately.

Grounded for three weeks for bad grades, John couldn't drive his car so his sister got to.

or

Because John was grounded for three weeks for bad grades, his sister got to use his car.

Running through the park, we felt the cool breeze on our faces.

or

As we were running through the park, the cool breeze felt great on our faces.

REVISION ACTIVITY 8

Each of the following sentences has a misplaced modifier. Rewrite each sentence and put the misplaced modifier in a more appropriate location. The result will be clearer, smoother sentences.

EXAMPLE   The girl showed up in a trench coat from the dorms.

REVISED   The girl from the dorms showed up in a trench coat.

1. The movie is very dull showing at the drive-in.

2. I was born in New Mexico of about one hundred families in a small town.

3. He didn't know that well how to drive a stick shift.

4. The cigarette that you finished smoking for your health is very bad.

5. He is a man used by God of many talents, for he is a pastor.

6. The girl was very wet from perspiring from Texas after the race.

7. The van was stolen from the front of the gym belonging to the school.

8. The jelly is from your knife in the peanut butter.

9. The candy bars have melted with nuts in the heat.

10. The patient has great courage in room 301.

REVISION ACTIVITY 9

Each of the following sentences begins with a dangling modifier. Rewrite the sentence to correct the problem either by changing the subject so that it goes with the modifying phrase or by adding a subordinating conjunction and subject to the dangling phrase to form a complex sentence. In each case, use the correction method that generates the smoothest, clearest sentence.

EXAMPLE	Working in the backyard all morning, my clothes got very dirty.
REVISED	While I was working in the backyard all morning, my clothes got very dirty.
EXAMPLE	Thrilled by his semester grades, everyone John knew got a phone call.
REVISED	Thrilled by his semester grades, John phoned everyone he knew.

1. Sitting on the sofa in the living room, my feet got very cold.

2. Bothered by a sore throat, Mary's doctor suggested that she stay home.

3. Angered over an unfair speeding ticket, the judge got a lecture from Ned.

4. Driving down Manning Avenue, the grape vineyards are beautiful in the spring.

5. Locked out of the house, the only way for John to enter was through a window.

6. Waiting for a taxi on G Street, four taxis drove right by me.

7. Bored by the movie on TV, the channel was changed by Gladys.

8. Trying for a school record in the high jump, the bar was raised for Marie to 5 feet 10 inches.

CORRECT USAGE

This section is for students who have problems with past tense verbs: omitting the *ed* ending or using incorrect irregular verb forms.

PAST TENSE VERBS

Not all of your writing is done in the present tense. You use *past tense* verbs when writing about an event that has already occurred, whether it happened a minute or a decade ago. The most common errors involving past tense verbs include leaving off the *ed* ending on *regular* past tense verbs and using incorrect *irregular* verb forms.

Regular Past Tense Verbs

Most verbs form their past tense by adding *ed* to the regular verb. Here are examples of regular past tense verbs:

Verb	Past Tense Form	Verb	Past Tense Form
answer	answered	instruct	instructed
ask	asked	kick	kicked
borrow	borrowed	learn	learned
climb	climbed	part	parted
count	counted	question	questioned
detail	detailed	rush	rushed
edit	edited	sail	sailed
fish	fished	scale	scaled
flood	flooded	talk	talked
head	headed	walk	walked

Regular verbs that end in certain letters offer slight variations to the basic *ed* verb ending.

1. Verbs already ending in *e*, just add the *d*.

Verb	Past Tense Form
believe	believed
create	created

Verb	Past Tense Form
hate	hated
invite	invited
love	loved
receive	received

2. Verbs ending in *y* preceded by a *consonant,* change the *y* to *i* and add *ed.*

Verb	Past Tense Form
bury	buried
carry	carried
marry	married
rely	relied
reply	replied
tarry	tarried

3. Verbs ending in *y* preceded by a *vowel,* merely add *ed.*

Verb	Past Tense Form
annoy	annoyed
betray	betrayed
delay	delayed
destroy	destroyed
relay	relayed

4. A number of short regular verbs ending in consonants preceded by vowels with a *short vowel* sound (plăn, bŭg, fĭt), double their last letter before adding *ed.*

Verb	Past Tense Form	Verb	Past Tense Form
acquit	acquitted	knit	knitted
admit	admitted	mar	marred
bat	batted	plan	planned
bug	bugged	ram	rammed
can	canned	scan	scanned
cram	crammed	slug	slugged
fit	fitted	tar	tarred

VERB ACTIVITY 10

Write the past tense form for the following regular verbs. Some verbs will add *ed*, some will change *y* to *i* and add *ed*, and some will double the final letter and add *ed*.

EXAMPLES   slice   *sliced*   cry   *cried*   plan   *planned*

1. betray
2. flood
3. cite
4. learn
5. plan
6. deny
7. marry
8. announce
9. save
10. annoy
11. time
12. dam

VERB ACTIVITY 11

The following passage is written in the present tense. Rewrite the passage changing the verbs to the past tense. Make sure to add *ed* endings to all regular past tense verbs.

EXAMPLE   Gertrude likes mustard on her rice.

PAST TENSE   Gertrude liked mustard on her rice.

Tonight the moon looks strange. Wispy clouds cover its surface, and a huge halo that looks perfectly round encircles it. Moisture drips from the air, and the moon glistens behind the veil of clouds. It appears eerie and beautiful. I watch the moon from my window and then drift to sleep. I enjoy enchanted dreams about hidden moon caves and moonmaids that lure sleepers into their caverns.

Irregular Verbs

Many verbs do not form their past tense with the regular *ed* verb ending. Instead, they form their past tense in different, *irregular* ways that involve changes within the verb instead of the addition of an ending. Although certain groups of irregular verbs form their past tense in similar ways, there are no rules to follow like the *ed* rule for regular verbs; therefore, you must memorize irregular verb forms to have them at your command.

The following is a list of frequently used irregular verbs whose forms are often confused. The verbs with similar forms are grouped as much as possible. The third column, "Past Participle," contains the irregular verb forms used with *helping verbs* such as *has, have, had, was,* and *were.* Here are examples of sentences containing the past tense and past participle verb forms:

EXAMPLES   John <u>flew</u> cross-country in a single-prop Cessna. *(past tense, action completed)*

John <u>has flown</u> cross-country many times. *(past participle + helping verb* has; *action continuing into the present)*

Lillie <u>sang</u> beautifully at the graduation ceremony. *(past tense, action completed)*

Lillie <u>has sung</u> at many graduation ceremonies. *(past participle + helping verb* has; *action continuing in present)*

Lillie <u>had sung</u> at many graduation ceremonies. *(past participle + helping verb* had; *action completed)*

Present Tense	Past Tense	Past Participle
become	became	become
come	came	come
run	ran	run
begin	began	begun
drink	drank	drunk
ring	rang	rung
sing	sang	sung
swim	swam	swum
fly	flew	flown
grow	grew	grown
know	knew	known
throw	threw	thrown
burst	burst	burst
cut	cut	cut
quit	quit	quit

Present Tense	Past Tense	Past Participle
set	set	set
choose	chose	chosen
drive	drove	driven
eat	ate	eaten
get	got	gotten
give	gave	given
rise	rose	risen
speak	spoke	spoken
take	took	taken
write	wrote	written
bring	brought	brought
build	built	built
catch	caught	caught
has	had	had
lead	led	led
sit	sat	sat
do	did	done
go	went	gone
see	saw	seen
lay	laid	laid (*to place or set something down*)
lie	lay	lain (*to recline or rest*)

VERB ACTIVITY 12

Fill in the blanks with the correct past tense and past participle forms of the irregular verbs in parentheses. Use the past participle form when a helping verb (such as has, have, was, were) comes before it.

EXAMPLES   (get) She has _gotten_ good grades on her math quizzes.

(run) George _ran_ into a brick wall.

1. (write) Ted has _____ more this semester than ever before.

2. (lead) The winding path _____ to a gazebo among the pines.

3. (drive) You have _____ me wild with your accusations.

4. (sit) Grace _____ on a stump contemplating her future.

5. (eat) Have you _____ the stuffed peppers in the cafeteria?

6. (build) Ted has _____ model planes since he was in grade school.

7. (begin) It has _____ to drizzle outside.

8. (throw) Mia _____ her back out in aerobic dance class.

9. (know) Hal has _____ some very strange people.

10. (set) Judy _____ her collection of figurines on the mantel.

11. (fly) We've _____ with six different airlines.

12. (drink) You have _____ enough coffee to last you a month.

13. (see) No one _____ or heard from Ezekiel for over two months.

14. (choose) You have _____ the most expensive brand of panty hose.

15. (come) By the time Ames had _____ home, everyone was asleep.

16. (become) You have _____ very proficient at archery.

17. (go) Mattie has _____ to collect dry firewood by the lake.

18. (bring) Grover _____ swamp mud in on his shoes.

19. (give) Reading has _____ Louise great pleasure for years.

20. (swim) Have you _____ across the lake by yourself yet?

21. (lie) Yesterday I _____ down at noon and awakened at 6:00 p.m.

22. (lay) Where have you _____ your pipe?

23. (lie) Have you ever _____ in a hammock?

24. (lay) The construction crew _____ five miles of asphalt in a day.

25. (see) Has anyone _____ my red pajamas?

VERB ACTIVITY 13

Here is more practice using irregular verbs. Write sentences using the following irregular verbs in the tenses indicated.

EXAMPLES   run (past)   Last night John ran past my house at
                                  3:00 a.m.

                eat (past participle)   You have eaten all of the cherries
                                        I was saving for the picnic.

1. fly (past)

2. burst (past)

3. choose (past)

4. fly (past participle)

5. drink (past participle)

6. write (past participle)

7. set (past)

8. rise (past)

9. take (past)

10. see (past)

11. lie (past participle)

12. swim (past participle)

13. drive (past participle)

14. become (past participle)

15. ring (past participle)

16. bring (past)

17. lead (past)

18. lay (past)

19. throw (past participle)

20. drive (past)

VERB ACTIVITY 14

Fill in your own choices of past tense and past participle verb forms to complete the following sentences. Spell correctly.

1. Freda _____ angry last night when her roommate _____ her bed.

2. The Gomez family has _____ all the way from Florida for their son's graduation.

3. It seems that we have _____ out of things to argue about.

4. It _____ raining early this morning.

5. Have you ever _____ as much cider as you _____ last night?

6. Jacqueline _____ across the lake and back in three hours.

7. That fifty-pound pumpkin was _____ with a special fertilizer.

8. Have you _____ the table for lunch yet?

9. I have _____ all along that you were a special person.

10. The balloon _____ high in the air and then _____ on a tree limb.

11. You have _____ to be very obnoxious with your Al Capone impressions.

12. Fran _____ her new car around town and _____ up boys.

13. Your father has _____, and that is the end of that!

14. Have you _____ good care of your health this semester?

15. The criminal was finally _____ to justice after years of evading the law.

16. Have you _____ all of your math homework?

17. Sammy _____ to the movies last night and _____ *Attack of the Killer Tomatoes.*

18. Have you ever _____ on a sharp tack that someone _____ on your seat?

19. You have _____ everyone with your time and patience.

20. The new Chevies aren't _____ to last like the older ones.

21. You _____ your history test easily, but you _____ your P.E. physical.

22. They _____ the missing painting and _____ it to its owner.

23. Ms. Hornsby _____ your story about little green men, but I _____.

24. Have you _____ your dear mother lately, or have you _____ her?

25. Henrietta _____ a mean saxophone at the party, and everyone _____.

26. Ito invited you to tea, but I _____.

27. Trudy has _____ twenty-three units of pottery classes and has _____ six of them.

28. The roses have _____ their flowers because you haven't _____ them.

29. Sam _____ the tree, _____ from a branch, and _____ his tongue out at a sparrow.

30. I have _____ to help you but you haven't _____, so I've_____ up hope that you'll ever become a sword swallower.

VERB ACTIVITY 15

The following passage is written in the present tense. Rewrite the passage in the past tense by adding *ed* to regular past tense verbs and by using the correct past tense and past participle forms for the irregular verbs.

EXAMPLE Clyde buys his shoes at Zody's and wears them for years.

REVISED Clyde bought his shoes at Zody's and wore them for years.

The campus goes berserk at Halloween. Boys sneak into girls' dormitories, hide in the closets, and scare them when they return from the cafeteria. Students bombard motorists' cars with water balloons, and there isn't a person asleep anywhere on campus. An army of dorm students attacks its rivals across campus. The students capture the dorm president and spray his body with green paint. They steal the dorm banner and hide it in a car trunk. Students from off campus begin a shaving cream war with on-campus students. They quit when the campus police finally intervene at 3:00 a.m. Then everyone is quiet for about a half hour, but the wildness begins again when the police leave.

SPELLING

This final section is for students who struggle with their spelling. It covers contractions and possessive words, commonly misspelled words, and homophones that cause writers problems.

POSSESSIVES

One of the most frequently omitted punctuation marks is the apostrophe that is needed in possessive words. A *possessive* word is usually followed directly by something *belonging to it*. Here are some sentences with the possessive words correctly punctuated with apostrophes. The possessive words are underlined.

EXAMPLES My <u>mother's</u> brother owns a fruit stand in the country.

<u>Today's</u> weather looks menacing with those dark clouds in the east.

I am going to <u>Celia's</u> surprise party tomorrow night.

The <u>men's</u> room at the Forum is flooded.

My three <u>brothers'</u> cars are all 1974 Plymouths.

The <u>ladies'</u> club holds its meetings at the Howbarth Tavern.

As you can see, the word directly following the possessive word belongs to it: mother's *brother*, today's *weather*, Celia's *surprise party*, men's *room*, brothers' *cars*, and ladies' *club*. Notice that sometimes the apostrophe comes before the *s* and sometimes it comes after the *s*. Here are the rules for showing possession.

1. *Singular possessive word:* Add apostrophe and *s* to the word: a boy's dog, the tree's bark, May's hair

2. *Plural possessive word:* Add the apostrophe *after* the *s:* three boys' dogs, all the trees' bark, many girls' hair

There are two exceptions to the possessive rules:

1. Plural words that form their possessive without adding s (man/men, woman/women, child/children, goose/geese) are punctuated as singular possessives ('s): men's hats, women's shoes, children's lessons, geese's feathers.

2. Possessive pronouns such as *yours, theirs, his, ours,* and *hers* do *not* require apostrophes since the form of the pronoun itself indicates possession.

POSSESSIVE ACTIVITY 16

Put apostrophes in the following possessive words to show singular and plural possessive forms.

EXAMPLES   a dog's life

the boys' club

1. the plants fragrance

2. the carpets stain

3. a soldiers story

4. many soldiers stories

5. all of the voters ballots

6. oats and barley

7. an addicts cry for help

8. six nieces uncles

9. the oceans waves

10. the mens room

11. peoples opinions

12. hamsters and rabbits

13. the moons shape

14. my parents rules

15. one grandparents hobby

POSSESSIVE ACTIVITY 17

Write your own sentences showing the possessive relationship that is given for each sentence. Follow the rules for adding *'s* or *s'*. Make sure the possessive word is followed by the thing belonging to it.

EXAMPLE	a dog belonging to Mark
REVISED	Mark's dog is a cocker spaniel.
EXAMPLE	the bones of all the dogs in the neighborhood
REVISED	All of the dogs' bones are hidden in the lot behind my house.

1. the hamster belonging to Mary

2. the snow of this morning

3. the lockers belonging to the men

4. the right to an education belonging to a student

5. the socks belonging to your grandmother

6. the station wagons belonging to six families

7. the great force of the ocean waves

8. the diagnosis of a doctor

CONTRACTIONS

A *contraction* is a word formed by combining two words and inserting an apostrophe to replace omitted letters. The most common contractions combine pronouns with verbs (I'm, he's, you've, we're) and verbs with the word *not* (isn't, wasn't, don't, won't, aren't).

Here are examples of common contractions and the word pairs from which they are formed:

Contraction	*Word Pair*	*Contraction*	*Word Pair*
I'm	I am	aren't	are not
you're	you are	wasn't	was not
he's	he is	weren't	were not
she's	she is	don't	do not
they're	they are	doesn't	does not
we're	we are	won't	will not
he'll	he will	wouldn't	would not
we'll	we will	hasn't	has not

Contraction	Word Pair	Contraction	Word Pair
they've	they have	haven't	have not
I've	I have	there's	there is
it's	it is	here's	here is
isn't	is not	who's	who is

CONTRACTION ACTIVITY 18

Write contractions for the following pairs of words. Don't forget the apostrophes.

EXAMPLE   he is <u>he's</u>

1. they are _____

2. it is _____

3. do not _____

4. does not _____

5. she is _____

6. I am _____

7. there is _____

8. they have _____

9. will not _____

10. are not _____

11. has not _____

12. you are _____

APOSTROPHE ACTIVITY 19

Put apostrophes in all of the contractions and possessive words that require them in the following sentences.

EXAMPLE   Theyre not going to the firemens ball Friday.

REVISED   They're not going to the firemen's ball Friday.

1. The chipmunks buried a years supply of nuts in the trees hollow.

2. Were supposed to be at the Smiths home for dinner, arent we?

3. The womens tennis team and the mens team were defeated in the leagues championships.

4. Havent you found your sisters new sweater or your four brothers fishing poles yet?

5. Megs response to Jacks question wasnt at all surprising to the groups leaders.

6. Cant you figure a way to curb Fredas appetite for anchovy pizza and lasagna?

7. No ones frame of mind is any better than Howies when he isnt drinking.

8. The dogs and the cats arent supposed to be in Mr. Grumbleys study.

9. The governments belief in the economys recovery isnt accepted by Willies grandfathers.

10. Youve had a difficult time with Newtons law of gravity, havent you?

COMMONLY MISSPELLED WORDS

Misspelled words account for the largest number of writing errors. Spelling errors are a nuisance to the reader, and final drafts should be free of them. Spelling is a minor problem for many writers, but it is a big problem for others. This section introduces some of the most commonly misspelled words and gives you a few basic spelling rules to follow; however, if you have serious spelling difficulties, you might seek further assistance from your instructor.

The following is the first of a number of word lists that appear throughout this section. Each list groups words that follow similar spelling rules.

Spelling List One: Words Ending in *ing*

beginning	kidding	putting	stopping
boring	letting	riding	studying
coming	living	running	swimming
dying	planning	sitting	taking
flying	playing	slipping	writing
hitting			

Words ending in *ing* are frequently misspelled. Here are the basic rules that will help you decide what to do when adding *ing* to a word.

1. *Verbs ending in e:* Drop the *e* and add *ing* (boring, coming, riding, taking).

2. *Verbs ending in y:* Keep the *y* and add *ing* (flying, playing, studying).

3. *Verbs ending in a* short vowel *followed by a single consonant:* Double the last letter and add *ing* (beginning, hitting, kidding, letting, planning, running).

4. *Verbs ending in a* long vowel *followed by a consonant:* Add *ing*, but do *not* double the final letter (dreaming, eating, sleeping, cheating). *Note:* Writers have few problems with this rule, so the words were not included in this spelling list.

SPELLING ACTIVITY 20

Following the spelling rules for adding *ing* to words, add the *ing* ending to the following words from Spelling List One:

1. come _____   5. study _____   9. ride _____   13. live _____

2. hit _____   6. run _____   10. stop _____   14. begin _____

3. play _____   7. write _____   11. bore _____   15. swim _____

4. plan _____   8. kid _____   12. put _____   16. let _____

Here is the second list of words that writers frequently misspell. Each list contains words that are similarly misspelled.

Spelling List Two: Words with *ie* and *ei*

achieve	field	neither
believe	friend	receive
deceive	grieve	relief
eight	height	review
either	neighbor	their

As you can see, each of these words contains either an *ei* or an *ie* vowel combination. Many writers misspell these words by turning the two letters around. Here are the basic rules for when to use *ie* and when to use *ei*.

1. In most words, the *i* goes before the *e* unless it follows the letter *c*. Then the *e* goes before the *i* as in *receive, deceive,* and *perceive.*

2. If the *ei* has a long a vowel sound, the *e* comes before the *i* as in *neighbor, eight,* and *freight.*

3. You need to memorize some exceptions to the *i* before *e* rule: *height, either, neither.*

SPELLING ACTIVITY 21

Write eight sentences using any two of the Spelling List Two words in each sentence. Use all fifteen words in the eight sentences. Spell the words correctly.

EXAMPLE   You can achieve more in life if you believe in yourself.

Spelling List Three: Left-Out Letters

again	opinion	stereo
always	restaurant	straight
clothes	schedule	surprise
familiar	separate	whether
February	several	which
finish	similar	while
interest	sophomore	

The words in Spelling List Three are grouped together because writers often misspell them in the same way: by leaving out a letter.

Thus, *again* is misspelled as *agin*, *February* as *Febuary*, *interest* as *intrest*, *clothes* as *cloths*, or *whether* as *wether*. The letters are often left out because of the way many people pronounce the words. Three-syllable words such as *interest*, *restaurant*, *sophomore*, and *several* are often pronounced and spelled as two-syllable words: *in-trest*, *rest-rant*, *soph-more*, and *sev-ral*. The *wh* words are frequently pronounced and spelled without the *h* sound: *wether*, *wich*, and *wile*.

Because there is no spelling rule to cover the range of List Three words, you will need to memorize them. The best tip for helping you learn them is to *pronounce* the words correctly so that you won't leave out letters by omitting syllables or sounds.

SPELLING ACTIVITY 22

Write ten sentences, including two different words from Spelling List Three in each sentence. Use the words in any order you wish, and spell them correctly. Underline the spelling words.

EXAMPLE   I <u>always</u> <u>finish</u> my English assignments five minutes before class.

Spelling List Four: Double-Letter Words

across	dinner	parallel
arrangement	embarrass	success
attitude	immediate	surround
business	impossible	terrible
different	occasion	tomorrow
difficult	occurred	

Spelling List Four contains words that are grouped together because they all contain double consonants that can cause confusion. The writer is not always certain which letters to double. Unfortunately, there is no rule similar to the rules covering words in List One and List Two to tell you which letters to double. You need to memorize the words in List Four so that you can easily visualize their correct spelling. Because these words are commonly used, you should know them well by the time you complete this course.

SPELLING ACTIVITY 23

Write nine sentences using any two of the words in Spelling List Four in each sentence. Use all seventeen words in your sentences.

EXAMPLE   Sarah made a business arrangement with her banker for a loan.

Spelling List Five: Words Ending in *ly*

actually	finally	lovely
busily	fortunately	naturally
completely	hungrily	really
easily	lively	unusually
especially	lonely	usually
extremely		

Writers who misspell *ly* words get confused about whether to drop a letter before adding the *ly* or whether to add an extra *l* to form an *lly* ending. The following simple rules should clear up the problems:

1. Add *ly* to the root word. Do *not* drop the last letter of the word (*lovely*, not *lovly*, *fortunately*, not *fortunatly*). An *lly* ending results only when the root word ends in *l* (*real/really*, *unusual/unusually*, *natural/naturally*, *actual/actually*).

2. If a root word ends in *y* change the *y* to *i* and add *ly* (*busy/busily, easy/easily, hungry/hungrily*).

SPELLING ACTIVITY 24

Add *ly* to the root words listed here, following the rules just covered for adding the *ly* ending.

EXAMPLES   clumsy *clumsily*

sane *sanely*

1. natural _____
2. live _____
3. hungry _____
4. special_____
5. busy _____
6. unusual_____
7. real _____

8. fortunate _____
9. lone _____
10. complete _____
11. actual_____
12. final _____
13. easy _____
14. love _____

SPELLING REFERENCE LIST

The following list includes more than one hundred of the most frequently misspelled words. You may use it as a convenient spelling reference when proofreading your drafts for errors. You may also want to select five to ten words per week to work on until you can spell every word on the list correctly.

accommodate	believe	disappoint
achievement	benefit	disease
acquaintance	boundary	divine
acquire	business	efficient
actual	certain	embarrass
against	chief	exaggerate
alleys	comparative	exercise
amateur	conscience	existence
amount	controversy	expense
apparent	convenience	experience
appearance	criticism	explanation
approach	dealt	extremely
argument	dependent	fascinate
attendance	describe	forty
beginner	despair	friend

government	mere	principle
grammar	naturally	privilege
guarantee	necessary	probably
height	ninety	procedure
herocs	noticeable	prominent
huge	obstacle	promise
ignorant	occasion	psychology
imaginary	occurrence	pursue
immediately	operate	really
independent	opinion	receive
intelligent	original	recommend
interest	paid	repetition
interrupt	parallel	sense
knowledge	particular	separate
laid	performance	shining
led	personal	similar
leisure	physical	studying
license	piece	success
loneliness	planned	surprise
loose	possess	tries
lose	practical	truly
luxury	preferred	villain
maintenance	prejudice	weather
marriage	preparation	whether
meant	principal	writing

HOMOPHONES

Homophones are words that sound alike but are spelled differently and have different meanings. The three homophones most commonly confused by writers are *there*, *their*, and *they're*, which we cover in the next section.

There/Their/They're

Writers frequently confuse the words *there*, *their*, and *they're*. Once you understand the use of each word, you will have little trouble distinguishing among them. However, you should always proofread your drafts for *there*, *their*, and *they're* errors because they appear occasionally in most writing.

Here is the meaning of each word:

THERE   An introductory word often preceding *is*, *are*, *was*, and *were*

<u>There</u> are five goldfish in the pond. I think <u>there</u> is room for you in the bus.

A location

Your books are over <u>there</u>. <u>There</u> are the books I've been looking for.

THEIR   Possessive pronoun (belonging to them)

<u>Their</u> car was vandalized. Joe took <u>their</u> picture.

THEY'RE   Contraction for *they are*

<u>They're</u> going to get married on Sunday. I think <u>they're</u> beautiful slides of Rome.

SPELLING ACTIVITY 25

Fill in the blanks with the correct word: *there, their,* or *they're*. Select the word or words that fit each sentence.

EXAMPLES   *They're* going to break the snail-eating record.

Their patience is waning.

There are four hummingbirds in the bird bath.

1. _____ are thousands of wheat fields in Kansas.

2. _____ webbed feet help mallards cruise across the pond.

3. _____ an unusual breed of turkey.

4. _____ is a need for voters to mail _____ ballots by June.

5. _____ coming at 9:30, but _____ will be no one home.

6. _____ new sofa will be at _____ house by morning.

7. Plant the marigolds _____, _____, and _____.

8. _____ learning algebra faster than _____ cousins did.

9. Is _____ a phone in _____ store?

10. _____ taking _____ time in _____.

SPELLING ACTIVITY 26

Write your own sentences using *there, their,* and *they're* as directed.

EXAMPLE   a sentence beginning with *their*

<u>Their</u> schedules for the fall semester are full of errors.

1. a sentence beginning with *there*

2. a sentence beginning with *their*

3. a sentence beginning with *they're*

4. *there* and *their* in the same sentence

5. *there* and *they're* in the same sentence

6. *their* and *they're* in the same sentence

7. *their, there,* and *they're* in the same sentence

8. *there* three times in the same sentence.

SPELLING ACTIVITY 27

Here is more practice using the words *there, their,* and *they're* correctly. Remember, *there* is an introductory word or shows location, *their* is a possessive pronoun (belonging to them), and *they're* is a contraction for *they are.* Fill in the correct form in each blank in the following paragraph.

EXAMPLE   *Their* shoes are new, but *they're* not bragging about it.

_____ is no doubt that Henrietta and Hank are nervous taking the test. _____ hands are shaking, and _____ frowning intently. _____ pencils are moving rapidly over the test booklet. _____ backs are hunched in effort. _____ working at a feverish clip, but _____ is a good chance they won't finish. It is a long and difficult test. _____ are one hundred multiple-choice questions and five essay questions. Finally, Henrietta and Hank stop at the bell, put _____ pencils down, and relax _____ minds. They've done _____ best, and _____ satisfied.

Confusing Duos: List One

A number of word pairs often confuse writers. They can slip erroneously into anyone's paper. The problem is not misspelling a word but using the wrong word in the wrong place. Here are some of the more commonly confused pairs with some information to help you tell them apart. (This is the first of two lists of confusing duos.)

ACCEPT   to receive (I <u>accept</u> your gift. Joy <u>accepted</u> the award.)

EXCEPT   to exclude, leave out (Everyone is going bowling <u>except</u> Millicent.)

A   comes before words beginning with a *consonant* (<u>a</u> book, <u>a</u> slug, <u>a</u> dog, <u>a</u> cat)

AN   comes before words beginning with a *vowel* or *vowel sound* (<u>an</u> apple, <u>an</u> orange, <u>an</u> answer, <u>an</u> herb)

ADVICE   what is *given* to someone (Joe gave me some very good <u>advice</u> about my major.)

ADVISE   the verb meaning to give advice (Joe <u>advised</u> me to major in computer technology.)

AND	conjunction joining words or groups of words (George is going, <u>and</u> so am I.)
AN	comes before words beginning with a *vowel* or *vowel sound* (<u>an</u> apple, <u>an</u> orange, <u>an</u> answer, <u>an</u> herb)
ARE	present tense of *to be* for plural subjects (The gifts <u>are</u> on the table.)
OUR	possessive pronoun, belonging to us (<u>Our</u> plans are uncertain. We'll go <u>our</u> separate ways.)
IT'S	contraction for *it is* (It's going to snow today. <u>It's</u> a rough exam.)
ITS	possessive pronoun (The tire lost its tread. <u>Its</u> flowers are drooping.)
KNOW	to have knowledge, to understand (I <u>know</u> the answer. He <u>knows</u> his limits.)
NO	none, negative (<u>No</u> one minds. There is <u>no</u> smoking in the library. I say "<u>no</u>.")
MINE	possessive pronoun, belonging to me (That book is <u>mine</u>. <u>Mine</u> is the red jacket.)
MIND	to behave, to oppose (The dog <u>minds</u> well. I <u>mind</u> your eating my lunch.)
PAST	time gone by (In the <u>past</u>, you have always done well. Your <u>past</u> is your business.)
PASSED	(You <u>passed</u> my inspection. His fever <u>passed</u> hours ago.)

SPELLING ACTIVITY 28

Fill in the blanks with appropriate words from the list of confusing duos.

EXAMPLE <u>No</u> one cares where we sleep tonight.

1. Mattie paid _____ way into the park last night.

2. For breakfast I'd like _____ apple, _____ omelet, _____ and _____ banana.

3. Everyone seems to be having a good time at the party _____ you.

4. If Shandra takes my _____, she'll forget about working.

5. Do you know why _____ so foggy this month?

6. We are planning to spend _____ honeymoon in Tulsa.

7. I don't _____ if you borrow my sweater tomorrow.

8. I enjoyed studying with you this morning, _____ I hope we can do it again.

9. Fenway was too tired to be good company to _____ guests.

10. Do you _____ if we take up where we left off yesterday?

11. Jack would _____ you to take _____ aspirin and _____ hot bath.

12. Your case is _____ exception to _____ rule.

Confusing Duos: List Two

Here is a second group of confusing word pairs to add to your list.

CHOOSE	present tense verb (I <u>choose</u> the present with the green bow.)
CHOSE	past tense of *choose* (Yesterday I <u>chose</u> to stay home from work.)
QUIT	not to finish, to give up (John <u>quit</u> his job with General Motors.)
QUITE	completely, wholly (Are you <u>quite</u> certain of the time? That was <u>quite</u> a show.)
QUIET	opposite of noisy (Please be <u>quiet</u> in the hospital. I would like a <u>quiet</u> moment.)
THIS	singular word that identifies or locates (<u>This</u> is a great story. <u>This</u> table is new.)
THESE	plural of *this* (<u>These</u> are the best stories I've read. <u>These</u> tables are new.)
TO	preposition of many uses (We went <u>to</u> the game. Look <u>to</u> your leader. Sheila belonged <u>to</u> the Modernes. <u>To</u> my knowledge, no one is missing.)
TOO	also, in excess (We are going to the game <u>too</u>. You have done <u>too</u> much work for one person.)
WERE	past tense form of *to be* with plural subjects (They <u>were</u> here a minute ago!)
WHERE	indicates location (<u>Where</u> are you going? Do you know <u>where</u> the dishes are?)
THROUGH	preposition of movement or passage (<u>Through</u> the years, you've grown more lovely. We glanced <u>through</u> the book.)

THREW
: past tense of *throw* (He <u>threw</u> the ball through the window. Mildred <u>threw</u> out her boyfriend.)

YOUR
: possessive pronoun, belonging to you (<u>Your</u> books are a mess.)

YOU'RE
: contraction for *you are* (<u>You're</u> the first person to call since the trial.)

THEN
: indicates time (<u>Then</u> you can go home. I did my work, and <u>then</u> I slept.)

THAN
: indicates comparison (You are smarter <u>than</u> I am. I saved more money this year <u>than</u> last.)

SPELLING ACTIVITY 29

Fill in the blanks in the following sentences with appropriate words from the list of confusing duos.

EXAMPLE   Last night you *chose* to be by yourself.

1. _____ pickles from Julio's Deli are the spiciest I've eaten.

2. _____ do you think _____ going with my anteater?

3. _____ dog was found in the neighbor's flower garden.

4. I am not _____ ready to _____ on the project.

5. _____ _____ you when we needed relief?

6. I think _____ taking _____ test too seriously.

7. Jody went _____ the races three hours _____ early.

8. I enjoy a _____ evening at home listening to_____ records.

9. I hear _____ not sure _____ tapes _____ left at school.

10. We went _____ the motions of reading our lines, but we didn't _____ have the feeling needed _____ move our audience.

11. Fred felt better _____ he had expected after the race, but _____ the exhaustion started setting in.

SPELLING ACTIVITY 30

Here is a list of all the confusing duos and trios covered in this section. Using the words correctly, write one sentence for each confusing duo and trio. Underline the words.

Examples   your/you're

You're going to the library, but your brother isn't going.

are/our

Are you going to take our advice about taking vitamin C?

1. choose/chose

2. quit/quite/quiet

3. this/these

4. through/threw

5. to/too

6. were/where

7. your/you're

8. there/their/they're

9. accept/except

10. a/an

11. an/and

12. advice/advise

13. are/our

14. it's/its

15. know/no

16. mine/mind

17. past/passed

18. then/than

Credits

Gomez, Rogelio R.
"Foul Shots," from the "About Men" column, *New York Times Magazine,* 1991. Reproduced with permission by the author.

Elizabeth Wong
"The Struggle to Be an All-American Girl," in the *Los Angeles Times,* 1994. Copyright © 1980. By permission of the author, www.elizabethwong.net.

Andrew Malcolm
"My Dad" appeared as "About Men: Dad" in the *New York Times Magazine,* February 12, 1984. Copyright © 1984 Andrew Malcolm. Reproduced with permission.

Cisneros, Sandra
"Only Daughter." Copyright © 1990 by Sandra Cisneros. First published in *Glamour,* November 1990. Reprinted by permission of Susan Bergholz Literary Services, New York. All rights reserved.

"What's The Deal with iPODS?" by Monica Early. Courtesy of Monica Early.

"Smoking in the Girls Room" by Alyssa Tiant. Courtesy of Alyssa Tiant.

"Why America Can't Compete" by Leroy Crooks. Courtesy of Leroy Crooks.

Brent Staples
"Black Men and Public Spaces," originally appeared as "Just Walk on By: A Black Man Ponders His Power to Alter Public Space," in *Ms.* magazine, 1986. Copyright © Brent Staples. Reproduced with permission of the author.

Index